FUTURE-GENERATION GOVERNMENT

Future-Generation Government

How to Legislate for the Long Term

NICHOLAS CHESTERLEY

McGill-Queen's University Press
Montreal & Kingston • London • Chicago

ISBN 978-0-2280-2475-0 (cloth)
ISBN 978-0-2280-2516-0 (ePDF)
ISBN 978-0-2280-2517-7 (ePUB)

Legal deposit second quarter 2025
Bibliothèque nationale du Québec

Printed in Canada on acid-free paper that is 100% ancient forest free (100% post-consumer recycled), processed chlorine free

Funded by the Government of Canada | Financé par le gouvernement du Canada | Canada | Canada Council for the Arts | Conseil des arts du Canada

We acknowledge the support of the Canada Council for the Arts.

Nous remercions le Conseil des arts du Canada de son soutien.

McGill-Queen's University Press in Montreal is on land which long served as a site of meeting and exchange amongst Indigenous Peoples, including the Haudenosaunee and Anishinabeg nations. In Kingston it is situated on the territory of the Haudenosaunee and Anishinaabek. We acknowledge and thank the diverse Indigenous Peoples whose footsteps have marked these territories on which peoples of the world now gather.

Library and Archives Canada Cataloguing in Publication

Title: Future-generation government : how to legislate for the long term / Nicholas Chesterley.
Names: Chesterley, Nicholas, 1988– author
Description: Includes bibliographical references and index.
Identifiers: Canadiana (print) 20240529979 | Canadiana (ebook) 20240530020 | ISBN 9780228024750 (cloth) | ISBN 9780228025177 (ePUB) | ISBN 9780228025160 (ePDF)
Subjects: LCSH: Behaviorism (Political science) | LCSH: Political psychology. | LCSH: Political planning—Decision making.
Classification: LCC JA74.5 .C34 2025 | DDC 320.01/9—dc23

This book was designed and typeset by True to Type in 10½/13 Sabon. Copyediting by Paula Sarson.

McGill-Queen's University Press
Suite 1720, 1010 Sherbrooke St West, Montreal, QC, H3A 2R7

Authorized safety representative in the EU: Mare Nostrum Group BV, Mauritskade 21D, 1091 GC Amsterdam, the Netherlands, gpsr@mare-nostrum.co.uk

For Tam, Phaedon, and Athena, with love

Contents

Acknowledgments

This book would not exist without the support of many, many people. First, an enormous thank you to my editor at McGill-Queen's University Press, Emily Andrew, who has been a champion for the book throughout and crucial in the editing process, and to the entire staff of the press, who have helped make this book a reality. Paula Sarson's copyediting and attention to detail helped catch many potential errors. Michael MacKenzie provided outstanding advice and suggestions across multiple readings and helped flesh out key aspects of the book. I have also been fortunate to benefit from the keen insights and advice of multiple people who volunteered to read drafts, including Brett Thompson, Charlie Feldman, and Darren McKee, as well as several anonymous readers who provided thoughtful comments and suggestions as part of the review process.

Excellent comments from participants in the 2022 BIG Difference BC behavioural insights conference and the 10th Annual Canadian Association of Programs in Public Administration Conference helped sharpen the arguments and analysis, refining the ideas herein. Many of the concepts also originated with my own work on individual short-termism, and I owe a debt to countless colleagues and friends for their advice on that work.

Finally, I owe more than I can ever say to my wife for being a sounding board and partner on this and countless other things. Thank you for your enthusiasm, curiosity, and partnership, and for patiently encouraging me on so many Saturday mornings while I tried to convince myself I had something worth writing down.

FUTURE-GENERATION GOVERNMENT

1

Preparing for the Dry Years

And it never failed that during the dry years the people forgot about the rich years, and during the wet years they lost all memory of the dry years.

John Steinbeck, *East of Eden*

Yuma is one of the driest, sunniest, and hottest places in the United States. It is nestled in the Sonoran Desert in southwestern Arizona, each year baking during 175 days of temperatures above 32°C and receiving a meagre 8.5 centimetres of rain. In *Star Wars: Episode VI Return of the Jedi*, Yuma was the setting for the Dune Sea, an endless expanse of sand where Jabba the Hutt left Luke Skywalker and Han Solo to be eaten by a sarlacc, a giant tentacled creature. Despite that somewhat ominous connection, Yuma is also called America's Winter Salad Bowl. Over 90 per cent of the North American winter lettuce crop and other leafy greens are grown there, along with a vast range of other thirsty crops. The secret is the Colorado River, one of the great veins of the United States. Forty million Americans rely on it for water, and the twenty-five dams that stretch across it power Las Vegas, Tucson, San Diego, Los Angeles, and Phoenix. If the Colorado River stopped running, it could force the abandonment of much of Southern California and Arizona, as well as parts of Colorado, New Mexico, Nevada, Utah, and Wyoming.[1]

The Colorado is overused, however. By the time it reaches California after passing through the Grand Canyon it once carved, the mighty river is a dirty trickle. It often runs dry before it reaches the Gulf of California and the Pacific Ocean. Major reservoirs have dropped to historic lows, and major lakes are at risk of drying up completely. For the last twenty-two years, an ongoing drought has caused the problem to steadily worsen. It may be tempting to blame climate change, but the issue precedes it. That said, rising temperatures mean droughts are likely to get longer and water levels lower.

As the rivers run dry, Americans have turned to aquifers. These massive underground reservoirs hold trillions of gallons of water. Unfortunately, they replenish slowly, if at all, so they too are starting to run out, despite local governments' efforts to manage them. Once these are gone, they may take thousands of years to refill. Cotton, hogs, corn, wheat, ethanol, alfalfa, and especially cheese and beef may all become uneconomical in a half-dozen states that are otherwise too dry for water-intensive forms of agriculture.

The fact that more water is used than the ecosystem allows for is no surprise. In the 1930s Franklin Roosevelt commissioned a committee to explore the cause of the dust bowl. The committee noted the risk of basing an expanding farm economy on a resource that was even then slowly depleting. The concept is straightforward: if you let water out of the bathtub but don't replenish it, the tub will eventually empty. Contrary to the Bible story when in response to Joseph's warning of an impending drought, Pharaoh stores up grain to prevent a famine, action in the US has been slow to come.

This is not only an American problem. About 117 million people rely on the North China Plain aquifer for water, straining the water source. India's groundwater is being consumed faster than any other country. The Arabian aquifer has been so heavily used it is now all but empty, and farms have had to be abandoned. The World Resources Institute found in 2019 that water withdrawals worldwide have more than doubled since the 1960s due to growing demand: the institute identified seventeen countries, home to a quarter of the world's population, that faced extremely high levels of baseline water stress.[2] Mexico City, the capital of Mexico, is drawing groundwater so fast that the city is literally sinking, as are some towns in the state of California.

Today almost everyone agrees there is a problem with the dwindling US water supply. Efforts are underway to reduce use. Understandably, though, no one wants to stop pumping: individual farmers and others rely on the water for their livelihoods. US states have been hesitant to change water allocations dating back to the 1800s or impose restrictions where use is currently unlimited.[3] The states that rely on the Colorado River still use too much water, as do other regions. There is a range of reasons for the predicament: any problem that spans millions of people and their livelihoods is complex. Though the problem long predates climate change or concerns about carbon emissions, the increased temperatures we now face certainly don't help.

Good regulation or oversight could help solve this problem by allocating water among users and ensuring the limited supply is not overused. Unfortunately, in many cases action has been too slow. Indeed, widespread water shortages are emblematic of a broader challenge. Whether regulating water consumption or preparing for a pandemic, our governments struggle to act on long-term problems, instead leaving them to the next government or the next generation while focusing on the present.

GOVERNMENT SHORT-TERMISM

This book seeks to understand why governments – across parties, countries, and times – frequently make decisions that benefit the present at the future's expense. Too often action on long-term problems is delayed or postponed until a crisis suddenly makes them urgent. I argue that we have systematically incentivized our governments to be short-sighted and that we suffer as a result. Governments confronted with election cycles, short-term voters, a twenty-four-hour news cycle, and the deluge of information that accompanies the modern political world are constantly encouraged to focus on the present. Consequently, they discount the future too much, undervaluing benefits to future governments and future generations. We need to change the system and introduce what I call *behaviourally informed governance* to ensure politicians and governments have an incentive to not just respond to the problems of today but also the problems of tomorrow, and manage the risks accordingly. We need governments that develop solutions not just for the next four years but for the next hundred years. Preparing for droughts in advance is far less expensive than waiting until the water is gone.

As we shall see, government short sightedness creates a range of problems for us, and especially for our descendants. If we overexploit fish stocks or other natural resources, we can permanently lose their bounty. New technologies we introduce may negatively impact our societies or environment. When we do successfully introduce initiatives with long-term benefits, such as reforms to health care or education, they can suffer from poor implementation after attention shifts or an election alters priorities. Of course, our personal decisions as well as those made by businesses, civil society, and other sectors all matter in shaping the future. But as the organization responsible for creating and enforcing the rules of our societies, as well as the largest employer and investor in most modern economies, government plays a unique role in navigating these concerns and protecting the future.

I was particularly struck by these issues during the COVID-19 pandemic. For a few years, all of us were affected by the pandemic in various ways, forced to change our behaviours and lifestyles as new waves hit or new public health measures were enacted. Yet in the twenty years before COVID-19 there were nine pandemics or close calls, from severe acute respiratory syndrome (SARS) to Ebola. Nonetheless, COVID-19 caught governments flat-footed. After the pandemic waned, government attention to the long-term issue of pandemic preparedness also fell quickly. As the former co-chairs of the Independent Panel for Pandemic Preparedness and Response noted in their 2024 report *No Time to Gamble*, despite the recent pandemic the world is neither sufficiently investing in pandemic preparedness nor is it prepared to stop a new outbreak from becoming a pandemic. The key issue identified in the report was a lack of sustained political commitment.

As I dug into the topic, it was clear this was a wider problem; it wasn't restricted to pandemics and water reservoirs. A host of long-term problems are challenging us to do better, and we and our governments are at best only inconsistently responding to them. Consider a few examples:

- Of the $100 billion spent on natural disaster aid by the international community between 1991 and 2010, 90 per cent was spent on response and reconstruction following the disaster.[4] By one estimate, each dollar spent on disaster preparedness in advance mitigates about fifteen dollars in future damage.[5]
- Fish stocks are plummeting, with over 90 per cent of them either fully exploited or overfished and total catches declining.[6] Governments continue to provide as much as $22 billion a year in subsidies to increase fishery capacity. One study of US fish stocks estimated that tightening harvest restrictions would triple the net present value of the catch compared to current regulations by allowing the stocks to recover.[7]

- Biodiversity is falling at a faster rate now than any time in human history, with current extinction rates 100 to 1,000 times higher than the baseline.[8]
- By 2040 almost 300 million people may have died from bacteria that have evolved to resist the drugs used to treat them, with economic damage of between $60 and $100 trillion. We continue to overuse antibiotics, though work has begun to address the issue.[9]
- The Intergovernmental Panel on Climate Change (IPCC) regularly releases reports about the increasing impacts of climate change, often raised as an iconic example of the need for long-term policy, the closing window to taking action, and the poor progress governments have made in addressing it.[10]
- The world is short approximately a trillion dollars a year in infrastructure investment, leading to crumbling bridges, roads, schools, and levees.[11]
- For the first time in history, there are more people age sixty-five and older than there are children under five. The ongoing and dramatic aging of world populations holds tremendous implications for disease, family structure, pension plans, labour supply, and economies.
- There is increasing anxiety over what are sometimes called existential threats, from nuclear weapons and asteroids to pandemics and artificial intelligence (AI), and not just among tech billionaires. One estimate of the risk of an event occurring that would destroy humanity in the next one hundred years is as high as one in six.[12]

Many other issues could also make the list, from the decline in democracy worldwide to government debt, underinvestment in education, and concerns over falling rates of innovation in our economies. Some of these are long-term problems that may not receive sufficient attention until a crisis emerges. Others are creating problems today but require long-term, sustained attention to address, of a kind that does not always align well with elections or news cycles.

The stakes are only getting higher. As the scale of impact from human decisions increases so do the potential consequences of not thinking beyond the present. Our scope for affecting our future, both positively and negatively, has never been greater, and the problems we face are increasingly long term. In many cases, such as geoengineering to prevent climate change or the development of AI, our future impacts are uncertain, especially in the very long term; we may be unsure of both the likelihood and extent of the harm we could cause. Given the potential scale and irreversibility of the damage we could do, some level of prudence and risk management seems wise. At the same time, being too risk averse and focusing insufficiently on innovation and the potential for significant, long-term gains is also problematic. Unfortunately, the long-term nature of our problems sits in tension with the short-term nature of our governments.

Doom is not inevitable, however. Our governments successfully plan for the future some of the time. Governments invest effort, money, and time into preparing for future problems or delivering programs that require long-term effort or attention. But there is room to improve.

As a behavioural economist, I turned to research on behaviour change and incentives to understand how we can do better. It is easy to criticize governments for short-termism, but politicians respond to the incentives and systems they are given. If we want politicians to act for the long term, we need to design our societies so that they give politicians incentives to do so. Much has been written about how governments should nudge their citizens to make better choices: encourage them to get more exercise, save more for retirement, and eat healthier foods by changing the structure of the choices they make. This book considers nudging in the opposite direction: what should incentives and nudges look like to motivate long-term thinking by governments and decision-makers?

This is not a question of right versus left. Liberal readers may be worried about climate change and low investment in education, while conservative readers may be concerned about the long-term impact of government deficits or the decline of the family. Both should worry that our governments seem largely unable to look beyond the present and effectively plan for the future. Right or left, it is in everyone's interests to have thoughtful governments that work to anticipate problems before they arrive instead of putting off action until minor problems become crises.

Fortunately, many people before me have thought about how to help individuals plan for the future, and though intertemporal decisions by governments have been relatively understudied, there is thoughtful work by political scientists and others looking at the actions of governments and what is sometimes called democratic myopia.[13] While political scientists often identify cognitive biases as a factor in government short-termism, using behavioural science to develop solutions is relatively less common. In this book I look at what research from the behavioural sciences can teach us about how we can encourage our governments to do better. Four major strategies can help: measure the right outcomes, make long-term planning the easy option, encourage our governments to make commitments, and adopt an agile approach that allows for experimentation and learning. Leaders and governments today can make changes that help nudge future leaders and governments to be less short-termist, or even nudge themselves if they stay in power.

I frequently use Canadian examples, as that is the jurisdiction where I have the most personal experience, but this is not an issue specific to Canada; we will also see examples from the US, the UK, Europe, and elsewhere. How we design our governments and what we demand from them weakens or strengthens their incentives to prepare for the future. On behalf of our children and our children's children, it is essential we get them to do better.

* * *

Humanity's relationship to long-term planning changed with the introduction of agriculture. Planting crops, unlike nomadically hunting and gathering, made preparing for the future critical to ensure there were seeds to plant and crops to grow. Concerns over drought and crop yield persist, though on a different scale from early humanity. Today, however, we are confronted with an increasing list of problems that require long-term thinking to mitigate, from resource depletion to natural disasters, inequality to job automation, antibiotic resistance to aging populations.

What our long-term challenges have in common is that they reflect a decision about how important the future is relative to the present. As individuals we struggle to make sacrifices to improve our future, whether that is skipping dessert or saving more money for retirement. Economists and psychologists have found we are *present biased*: we care too much about the present and not enough about the future. Making this worse is our modern, instant-gratification world, with entertainment on demand, same-day shipping, and credit cards. When tomorrow does come, we often regret not doing enough, but by then it is often too late.

It should be no surprise that since we struggle to prepare for the future as individuals, so do our governments. As consumers, we demand what we want as quickly as possible; as voters, it means the policies we support tend to be Band-Aids rather than permanent solutions. It is much easier to ignore future environmental and economic problems than to take the painful steps to resolve them today, especially if the consequences fall on generations not yet born. As a result, we vote for policies and leaders that are themselves short-term, and politicians focus on the immediate issues voters tell them they care about. If voters are frustrated with traffic and demand more roads, politicians will seek to build them, even if building more roads rarely helps reduce congestion in the long term.[14] Voters also may not trust governments to deliver on long-term promises, making them prioritize short-term gains.

Short-term voters aren't the only reason governments don't plan for the future, and not all short-termism is wrong. As we shall see, there are valid reasons to prioritize the needs of today, not least uncertainty about what the future will look like. The problem is not that governments discount the future at all; it is that governments discount the future too much. To put it technically, they discount the future more than the socially optimal discount rate. They too are present biased and focus excessively on short-term issues without solving long-term ones. Politicians have little incentive to pay attention to the future, and not just because voters may not push them to do so. In democracies, the government of the day knows it needs to focus on winning the next election. Long-term benefits won't help if the party is no longer in power. The modern, hyperactive world makes short-termism worse by focusing attention on the present to the exclusion of long-term considerations. Ever faster technology developments and news cycles, paired with poor measurement of the future implications of current decisions and loud stakeholders for present problems, demand the attention of governments, distracting them from even their best-laid plans. Governments can and do plan for the future or take costly actions in the present to benefit future generations, but they are biased toward the present on average, meaning they undervalue long-term benefits and projects unless the future benefits are particularly significant or tangible (for example, due to a recent natural disaster).

Often, this present bias appears in the form of inaction. Many of the challenges we as a society need to solve are common property problems or some form of public good. Clean water and air, healthy fish stocks, and natural disaster readiness are all shared resources, so people have an incentive to overuse or underinvest in them, leaving the costs to others. Solving these issues is not easy and often requires national and international co-operation. Unfortunately, such challenges are intensified by the fact that government short-termism reduces the incentive to fix them.

The problem is frequently that although a certain policy would provide significant, diffuse benefits to the future, enacting it would impose costs on a specific group today. Investing money to improve retirement benefits for future generations deprives the current one of resources for their own use, for example. Policies that apply to all groups in the present can already be challenging for governments, since there is typically strong opposition from the negatively affected group but not strong support from the more dispersed beneficiaries. Think of building a new transit system, where a small interest group is deeply affected because they will have to move or face disruption, while a much larger group of commuters is moderately benefited. These sorts of decisions are even more challenging when the benefits are in the future and the beneficiaries of a policy do not exist yet. The unborn beneficiaries have no voice to argue for the policies and no votes to support them with, whereas the living opposition can be loud. Addressing the issue will annoy stakeholders who currently use the resource, and future generations who will benefit are not around to make their case. By the time the resource is exhausted or the advantages felt, a new government may be in place. The longer the time horizon over which the consequences of a decision will be felt, the greater the incentive to ignore the decision.

In the present, the government can sometimes redistribute resources from those who benefit from a policy to those who lose out to try to satisfy everyone, but redistributing resources from an unborn generation to compensate the present one can be difficult or impossible. If it is not possible to compensate the losers from a policy, should government proceed anyway? This gets to the heart of a society's values, and whether government should be concerned with the greatest good for the greatest number, protection of the vulnerable, or some combination of the two.

In the face of election cycles, fickle voters, and constant pressure on governments to respond immediately to short-term crises, it can feel like we are doomed to short-term thinking from our leaders. I've been told that democratic governments will always be focused on the short-term, since no government that must be re-elected every four years cares much for the future beyond that term. Some scholars have even suggested that we must compromise our democratic principles or adopt autocracy in order to overcome long-term challenges.[15]

Nonsense. Democracy is not somehow broken beyond repair. Governments have successfully planned for the long term in the past, and they will do so again. As we shall see in the following chapters, there have been many successes, both in the past and today. The recent US and international efforts to measure natural capital – the value of our forests, wetlands, and natural ecosystems – and not just GDP is a step in the right direction. Finland's parliament has had a standing Committee for the Future since 1993, which has helped sustain government attention on the future there. Norway's trillion-dollar sovereign wealth fund has taken what could have been easy come, easy go oil income and turned it into long-term wealth, in contrast to many others countries which have little to show for a resource boom. In 2015 Wales passed the Well-being of Future Generations Act and established a Commissioner of Future Generations to push long-term thinking. The Spaceguard program, tasked to NASA in 1998 by the US Congress in response to concerns about asteroid impacts and now an international effort, has tracked over 90 per cent of large asteroids and 98 per cent of extinction-threatening asteroids, a major step forward in terms of avoiding that long-term threat. All these examples represent significant successes and advances in preparing for our collective future.

Leadership, too, can play an important role; short-term voters may increase the pressure on leaders to act the same, but long-term leaders can also influence voter preferences. The result can be a positive or negative feedback cycle, as voters select for short-term leaders and become increasingly short-term as a result, or future-oriented leaders help build voter support for long-term decisions and give themselves more space to act. Changes that support the efforts of those in power to consider the long term, as we shall explore in this book, can help kick-start that virtuous cycle, encouraging leaders to further govern for the future. There have been and still are many successful leaders who have solved long-term issues. And there will be more. Indeed, humanity's record is impressive in fighting poverty, hunger, and illness; increasing access to education and clean drinking water; upholding the rule of law; and building strong institutions. The present bias of governments, in other words, is a problem but it is not an inevitable catastrophe. Governments do invest in long-term projects, such as mitigating disasters, reducing government debt, or fighting climate change, just not as much as they should.

Getting governments on track requires an increase in the incentives for them to operate for the long term. The key is to identify strategies that can help governments do so, which may require structural changes to how our governments work that will give them the necessary space to ensure that our children and our children's children have what they need to lead meaningful lives. There are clear, concrete strategies we can adopt to do better and focus on what's important. How we construct the world around us shapes how we plan for the future. If we shape our institutions and our societies correctly, we can make ourselves more likely to care about the future and better able to plan for it. We may not eliminate short-termism entirely, but we can limit and control it.

PLANNING FOR THE LONG TERM

This book presents four strategies governments and voters can use to help our leaders plan for the long term. Some are fairly easy, such as demanding governments measure not just GDP but also the long-term health and wealth of a country. Others are relatively difficult, such as encouraging voters to reward governments that take an evidence-based and thoughtful approach to policy-making that includes testing ideas and building an evidence base before rushing in to passing laws. All the strategies are about changing how governments do business, encouraging our leaders not just to put out fires but also to develop policies that are fireproof.

The strategies I propose draw inspiration from the lessons of behavioural science about individual behaviour. Someone looking to resist present bias and save more for retirement, for example, can draw up a budget, set up default or opt-out savings plans, pre-commit to thriftiness by carrying a credit card with a low limit, and explore new ways of saving money. Governments can try similar strategies. This analogy between individual and group has limits though: governments are organizations, often organizations of organizations, and groups of people face different dynamics and biases than individuals, including the politics and power involved in group decision-making.[16] Still, studying how individuals can better plan for the future can help us understand how we can support our governments do the same. Ultimately, decisions by governments are still made by individuals, whether that individual is a president, parliamentarian, or bureaucrat, and as more power has been centralized in individual leaders, that individual's present bias can increasingly affect the system as a whole.

To be clear, I am not suggesting that with a few minor tweaks government can suddenly focus on the future and solve our long-term challenges. There are, however, concrete steps government can take to do better. Insights from behavioural science can help us contemplate how to shape our governments and institutions so that those leaders can resist their own and others' short-termism. Though not a focus of this book, the strategies can also apply in a business context, where observers have raised concerns about increasing short-termism on the part of CEOs and senior managers as a result of the tyranny of quarterly reporting cycles.[17]

Chapters 2–4 set out the problem: as individuals and as governments, we are biased toward the present. Chapters 2 and 3 consider how individuals behave when it comes to planning for the future. Chapter 4 turns to the incentives governments face and why they are also short-termist. By understanding the incentives of governments, we can better understand what needs to change to ensure the future is attended to.

Chapters 5–8 consider how we can do better. Drawing on insight about human biases such as salience, availability, taking the easy option, confirmation bias, and overconfidence in predicting the future, I set out four broad strategies that could encourage governments to plan for the long term. Measuring the right things to make the impact on the future obvious, making long-term thinking easier for governments, making commitments that necessitate thinking long-term, and adopting an iterative approach that allows for experimentation and learning can all reduce procrastination and improve how well our societies prepare for the future.

Some of these strategies are designed to increase voters' and politicians' attention to the future, improving how we measure our impact on the future and increasing the salience of long-term decisions. This also helps voters hold their governments accountable for their planning, or lack thereof, for the future. As behavioural science has shown, a remarkable range of behaviour can be changed by making things more or less salient, even if the fundamental incentives do not change. When our neglect of the future is due to inattention from voters or distraction from governments, these strategies can be powerful. In some cases, however, governments may intentionally prioritize the present to improve their electoral fortunes or due to polarization of issues. There, strategies such as commitments – binding governments to pay attention to the future, even if they might prefer otherwise – may be more effective. Alternatively, an iterative, experimental approach can be particularly powerful when governments are not sure what the future impact of a decision will be or how likely those impacts are. In that case, taking a step-by-step approach that allows for learning at each stage means policy-makers can pivot and adapt as necessary as the future unfolds. Ultimately, a combination of all strategies is probably best, depending on the issue and context.

In chapters 9 and 10 I consider two case studies that demonstrate how these strategies could be used to support long-term thinking by governments. Climate change and infrastructure investment are both areas in which governments have struggled to prepare for the future, and more can be done.

Finally, chapter 11 examines some of the limitations on the strategies explored here. Behavioural science can suggest strategies to improve the forward-thinking nature of our institutions and leaders, but it is by no means a panacea. Nudges have limits, and even if we can successfully confront and mitigate the short-term pressures on our governments, cognitive biases are not the whole story. The complex organizational dynamics of government – different stakeholder groups and factions with their own agendas both within and across generations and who may resist changes to the status quo – means the dynamics of politics and power are crucial to implementing reforms and solving long-term challenges. Cultural, technological, and economic barriers may all exist, and short-termism is often entangled with other biases and challenges, both for governments and for individuals. Behaviourally informed strategies may also sit in tension with other values, such as letting future governments and voters make their own decisions or the value of public debate on an issue. As a behavioural scientist myself I focus on lessons from individual behaviour, but insights from political scientists, philosophers, and scholars of public administration and other disciplines are also needed. My goal is to provide a complementary set of tools from behavioural science to encourage our leaders to counter short-termism and prioritize the future.

If you have just one takeaway from this book, I would suggest a theme that underlies almost everything discussed within: the need to experiment with new forms of governance and decision-making in order to adapt our systems and societies to the modern world. Some of the strategies we explore may resonate while others may not, or they may seem impractical or infeasible for your context. That's okay. Perhaps the most important lesson is that improving and reforming our sometimes-creaky systems, drawing on insights and wisdom from a wide range of disciplines, can shift our focus to what matters most and solve or at least mitigate the wicked, complex problems we face, while avoiding compromise on key values like democracy. Behaviourally informed governance can be applied to design institutions to counter many biases beyond those related to short-termism, and there are many other possible innovations in how we govern and organize ourselves that are worthy of consideration. None of us have a monopoly on what works, and testing and trying new things, even when they don't work, is the only way to figure out what does, especially in the long term.

* * *

In 2022, as the pandemic ebbed, I became a father for the first time. Having a child made me wonder about what his life will be like. Born in 2022, he will likely live until the twenty-second century. Perhaps by then, when he turns seventy-eight, medicine will be so advanced that he will still be in excellent health, keen to take advantage of the world around him. What kind of world am I leaving him? Am I doing what I can to leave behind a world at least as good as the one I entered when I was born? Am I satisfied with a one-in-six chance that an existential risk will destroy him and all humanity in the next hundred years?

None of the strategies discussed in this book are perfect: a determined demagogue can overthrow institutions that took generations to build. Nonetheless, these strategies can push politicians to think beyond today and help citizens hold them accountable. Astute readers will point out that whatever incentives governments as a whole face, there is also a complex ecosystem of incentives facing any single politician: their hopes for the future and their children, their career ambitions, and their mood on any given day. All true. In this book I largely focus on the system as a whole, not because individual actors aren't important but because when one looks across time and political parties, it is clear that short-termism is not exclusive to any given individual. Instead, it arises again and again in different parties, countries, and times.

Certainly, it is not the case that governments never plan for the future. It is a feature of government that failures are shouted from the rooftops, while successes rarely get any media coverage. Many government departments and public officials are thoughtful and forward-looking and have successfully prepared for a wide range of crises and problems. Nevertheless, there is room for improvement. From changing demographics to infrastructure and education, government debt to water management, the modern world faces an increasing number of long-term challenges, and we need governments equipped to deal with them. To do so, we need to be thoughtful about the decisions we take and the institutions we build.

Action on long-term issues is possible, including on the water shortages mentioned in this chapter's opening. Australia's irrigation systems were built around 1900 by the same Canadian brothers who built some of California's first irrigation systems. Unlike in the US, however, Australia's recent decade-long drought prompted serious action.[18] The water allocation system was reformed and billions were invested, increasing efficiency and conservation. Water use dropped significantly, and Australia is better positioned to tackle future droughts. This book sets out a case for encouraging governments to act before the drought is so bad that people are dying of thirst. Governments can act on these issues, and it is up to us to demand they do.

PART ONE

The Problem

2

Why Are We Short-Termist?

We tend to act like the doomsday clock has a snooze button.

Batman, *Justice League* (Zack Snyder, dir., 2017)

Before we talk about governments, it may be helpful to first consider ourselves as individuals. We, too, procrastinate urgent tasks, ignore long-term problems, give in to short-term temptations, and struggle to plan for the future. Understanding why we behave this way can help us discern why governments struggle with the same things. Indeed, many of the challenges governments confront have parallels to those individuals contend with. This chapter explores human short-termism, also known as present bias. Underpinned by evolution, we are psychologically built to be biased toward focusing on the present and neglecting the future. Worse yet, the modern world acts as a stimulant to present-biased thinking, focusing our attention on the here and now to the exclusion of later.

It is no surprise that individuals succumb to short-term temptations. We may set an alarm for 7:00 a.m. the night before, but when the alarm goes off, we tend to hit the snooze button and roll over. We may plan to do our taxes over the weekend but come Sunday night find we've not started them. Sometimes it feels like we would rather find anything else to do rather than start the projects we decided were urgent only a few days beforehand. This reflects a broader psychological truth: we care more about "now" than "later."[1] Asked to choose between $1,000 now and $1,000 in a year, almost everyone prefers the money now. In order to get someone to wait you have to offer them more money to compensate: $1,050, maybe, or $1,100. We're biased in favour of things that happen immediately: pleasure is sweeter and pain sharper when they happen right now. As psychologist George Ainslie notes in his book *Picoeconomics* (the *pico* refers to the small scale of economics within the human self), this means we give in to temptation immediately while attempting to delay things we don't like for as long as possible.[2] We want that kick of pleasure in the present, not the jolt of pain. As a result, when we sit down to file our taxes (or organize our retirement savings, do our homework, or prepare to go to the gym), which feels unpleasant today but will make us happy later, we get distracted by cat videos on YouTube, which are hilarious now, even if we later regret not doing those other things. The more unpleasant the task or the less benefit it will provide, the more we may be incentivized to delay.

There is an evolutionary justification for this.[3] If you are a hunter-gatherer on the savannah and you see a lion, you run. If you stop to worry about whether you will have enough food in a year – much less the long-term impacts of stress and hypertension on your health – you'll likely get eaten. In an unstable environment with limited resources, constant threats, and high uncertainty, planning for the future is wasteful; the now is where clear and present dangers must be navigated. Evolution understandably selected for short-termism, with human preferences evolving accordingly.

As we explore further in the next chapter, some of our short-termism also relates to our aversion to risk and loss. Economists often differentiate between risk and uncertainty, sometimes called Knightian uncertainty after the economist Frank Knight. *Risk* is a measurable chance something might go wrong, like a 50 per cent chance of flipping heads on a coin, while *uncertainty* refers to the unknown probability of different outcomes. There is some level of uncertainty in almost everything, outside of controlled environments such as a laboratory or a casino, but some things are more uncertain than others. The future, especially the distant future, is both risky and uncertain: we don't know what will happen, and we are not sure how likely different possibilities are. People are typically risk averse and prefer less uncertainty, and they also worry more about losses than they are excited about gains.[4] When it comes to the future, this can compound with present bias by making us overly likely to avoid risks, even if they have the potential for long-term innovation and transformative wins. For a single individual, it may make sense to avoid taking on too much risk. As a society, taking risks is how we innovate and improve.

For early humans, the scale of impact on the future was also much less. Lower population densities and limited technology meant the potential to affect the environment or world at large was limited; actions today could only affect the future so much. Nomadic lifestyles meant it was relatively easy to move around and find new food sources. Inhabitants could anticipate that the lives of their successors would be similar or identical to their own. What mattered was the here and now.

The problem is that this short-term bias no longer matches our modern, long-term environment. Not getting eaten by a wild animal is no longer our primary concern. As humans turned to agriculture, the need arose to plan for next year's harvest. Today, climate change, resource overuse, the national debt, and the emergence of new technologies can have problematic impacts decades, even centuries, in the future and require long-term planning to solve. There's no harm in taking a break or choosing the easy road from time to time. The problem is not that we discount the future; it is that we overly discount it.

To be clear, it is not my claim that people (or governments) are short-termist or myopic all the time. People act for the future in their personal and professional lives in all sorts of ways at all sorts of times. In many respects, the world is richer, cleaner, and safer than it was generations ago. Situational factors, such as our external environment and social and cultural influences, as well as dispositional factors, such as our personality, mood, and beliefs, can all affect the decision we make at any particular time. My claim, and the finding of considerable research, is simply that on average we are present biased, a bit too likely to discount future benefits or ignore future costs.

Our present bias can be more damaging when it comes to benefits that serve only our children, or generations after them. This raises questions of intergenerational equity – in effect, how we should be dividing up resources between different generations, including those not yet born. We may intuitively believe that future generations should have the same opportunities as we have had, but in practice we frequently disregard them in legal or political discussions. Our interest in the future diminishes as it gets further away. In other words, if we struggle to care about our own retirement, it can be harder still to care about the retirement of our great-great-grandchildren, or the health of their environment or wealth of their economy. Even the question of allocation between current generations is challenging, such as how many resources should go to older people as opposed to the youth, though it underlies many modern debates over elder care, youth unemployment, student debt, health care, pensions, and other topics.[5]

TIME INCONSISTENCY

We value the present over the future. But what makes this particularly unfortunate is that when the future arrives, we often change our minds or regret our past decisions. In one experiment, subjects were asked to select a movie from a provided list to watch the next week. Given the choice, a majority of students chose a "highbrow" film (e.g., *Schindler's List*) over a "lowbrow" film (e.g., *Mrs. Doubtfire*). When they returned to the lab a week later and were told they could change their selection and then watch it immediately, however, the subjects were much more likely to choose one of the fun, lowbrow movies.[6] The same pattern emerges in food. Studies find that a majority of people will choose fruit over chocolate if they will receive it in a week, but that a majority prefer chocolate if they are to receive it immediately.[7] Similarly, we buy fruit at the grocery store to eat later but chocolate to eat immediately, which is why it's chocolate, not fruit, next to the checkout counters.

People are allowed to change their minds. What makes this interesting is that it only goes in one direction: people choose the hard, good-for-you options for their future, but when the moment arrives they regret that decision and prefer to maximize their enjoyment. Almost no one plans to do the easy, fun stuff in advance but at the last minute chooses the healthy, character-building option. In other words, our decisions are *time inconsistent*: they change over time. We pick the healthy options for tomorrow, but when tomorrow comes we switch.

What this means is that we – and our governments – are both likely to neglect the future and regret it when that future arrives. What troubles economists and psychologists though is the inconsistency. Why do we choose one thing today and then change our minds when tomorrow arrives? If you know you are going to choose *Mrs. Doubtfire* in a week's time, why pick *Schindler's List* now? In other words, why are we surprised when we procrastinate? The explanation draws on a model that has been used in a wide range of contexts to describe human behaviour, from the Buddha's introduction of the elephant and the rider to more modern research on the brain and how it functions.

MULTIPLE SELVES

When we think about ourselves, such as our preferences or experiences, a specific part of our brain lights up – the ventromedial prefrontal cortex. This part of the brain is involved in self-control and the inhibition of emotional responses, as well as risk and fear. Since many of us think about ourselves quite frequently, this region in the brain lights up fairly often. What is interesting, however, is that it lights up less when we contemplate our decisions in the future than it does for our decisions in the present. The more patient we are, the more the prefrontal cortex lights up for future decisions, and the more impatient, the less it lights up.[8] We really do see our future selves as different people, and the greater the difference we see, the more impatient we are. What's the point in rewarding our next selves?

Interestingly, the prefrontal cortex is believed to be one of the last parts of the brain to evolve, and it is larger in humans than in most other animals. This planning, future-looking part of us is an integral part of what makes us human. The prefrontal cortex sits in contrast, however, to what is sometimes unfairly called the "lizard" brain: the limbic system, insular cortex, and some other parts. This responds to immediate stimulus directly and lights up at the prospect of immediate rewards. If you're hunting and gathering on the African savannah, the lizard brain is key: if you see a lion, run. If you're working on Wall Street, in contrast, your lizard brain's first reaction to a market crash might be to sell, but your prefrontal cortex can remind you the market is still fundamentally strong and that this might actually be a good time to buy.

This visualization of the brain in two parts is a vast oversimplification, of course: our brains are complex, and the two systems are closely linked. That said, it provides a good starting point, and behavioural scientists have extended it as a way of modelling and understanding behaviour. We can think of people facing a conflict between their present and future selves, represented by those two parts of their brain. Behavioural scientists think of this as *multiple selves*, a topic I explored in my own research on how public policy can help people better plan for the long term in areas such as retirement saving, energy-efficient technology adoption, and dieting.[9]

The idea of multiple selves says that we can think of our present self and future self as two different people. As a result, we don't treat them the same; we like good things to happen to our present self, who we identify with directly, and we care less about the future self. Like a dysfunctional colleague, the present self constantly delegates work to future selves rather than doing it in the present.

The problem of present bias is therefore literally a problem of "self"-control. This explains an observation by economist Thomas Schelling, who won the 2005 Nobel Memorial Prize for Economic Sciences for, among other things, his work preventing nuclear war by understanding game theory and the strategy of conflict. As a boy, Schelling saw a movie about Admiral Byrd's trip to Antarctica, and learned that as a child Byrd used to go outdoors in short sleeves to toughen himself against the cold. Emulating his hero, Schelling would resolve each night to go to bed with one blanket too few. That decision was made before he fell asleep; he would then wake up in the middle of the night too cold to sleep and curse the boy who made the initial decision. By the next bedtime though, it was the warm boy again, dreaming of Antarctica, who set aside a blanket.[10] His 9:00 p.m. self liked the idea, while his 2:00 a.m. self was a lot less happy about it.

When we are reminded that future us is still us, we are much more likely to save for the future. When researchers digitally age people to show what they will look like decades hence, those people more than double how much money they allocate to their retirement account compared to people who haven't been shown what they will look like when they are older.[11] Your future self is suddenly tangible, someone you can clearly identify with your current self.

Earlier, we saw that decisions are time inconsistent. We choose *Schindler's List* and fruit a week in advance, but when the day arrives, we prefer *Mrs. Doubtfire* and chocolate. We tell ourselves that we should do our taxes the following weekend, but somehow when that weekend rolls around we find something – anything! – else to do. The theory of multiple selves helps us explain this behaviour. The present self likes the idea of healthy eating and watching highbrow films but delegates the task to the future self while indulging in sweets and lowbrow movies. All of us are in a permanent business partnership, not with another person, but with ourselves. The past us, the present us, and the future us all have different desires and expectations, but only the present self gets to make decisions. Thus, our decisions change over time.

Unfortunately, our choices today play a significant role in what we get tomorrow. If I choose to eat sugar today and assign the task to my future self of going to the gym and starting a diet somehow, when that self takes charge, he never feels the same way, and leaves the task to *his* future self. Ultimately, I never do get around to working out and dieting, and my future selves are left with an increasingly unhealthy inheritance. The existence of multiple selves can therefore explain why we so often regret our failures to prepare for the future. There is some justification for caring more about the present than the future, but we take our disregard for the interests of our future self too far and become present biased.

As we shall see, the theory of multiple selves provides a helpful parallel to how governments work. As different parties win elections and take power, the "self" in charge changes. Of course, the parallel is imperfect: as individuals we still usually care for our future selves to some extent, whereas governments may actively dislike future governments from other parties. In countries where an election can happen at any time, there is also an element of unpredictability that does not apply to individuals, and governments can act in the short-term to actively preserve their power and win elections in a way that does not apply to individuals. Nevertheless, the change in self over time creates challenges for individual long-term thinking and self-control that can provide insights for the challenges faced by governments. The same strategies we use for self-control and better long-term decision-making can help with government long-term planning.

Many other factors can affect how much we discount the future. It may be complicated to decide how much to discount the future, for example, and that complexity may encourage us to adopt simpler heuristics (simple rules and mental shortcuts) instead.[12] Though this pattern of valuing the present more than the future is true on average, it also varies widely by person. Factors such as genetics, age, gender, education level, income, marital status, intelligence, and a range of others all correlate with how much someone discounts the future, though it can be difficult to tell which way the causation runs.[13]

That is not the end of the story, however. Our present bias is made worse by the modern world and the constant pressure of social media and other distractions, which often seem custom-built to keep us focused us on the present.

ENVIRONMENT MATTERS

As we saw above, early humans likely evolved to be present biased based on their need to focus on the short term. But more recent humans also lived in a very different world than we do now. Hundreds of years ago, humanity lived in a fairly stable world. Most people could expect to live and die in the same place. They, their parents, and their children would all likely eat the same food, practice the same religion, live in the same house, and potentially serve the same royal or imperial family. If they were religious, they may have seen themselves as part of an eternal process.

In Europe, a tangible sign of that conviction is the soaring cathedrals built by medieval stonemasons as tributes to their faith. Building them could take generations, with builders dying before the structures were complete. Notre-Dame de Paris took approximately a century to build (the first time; after burning down in 2019 reconstruction was considerably faster), and Cologne Cathedral took six hundred years. Perhaps the most long-term building project underway today, the whimsical yet monumental Sagrada Família in Spain, stems from the same sentiment. It was designed by the deeply religious architect Antoni Gaudí in the 1880s and is still not complete more than one hundred years later. When pressed, Gaudí noted that his client, God, was not in a hurry. Most of our modern buildings, however, are not built with an eternal client in mind.

Starting with the Enlightenment, the idea of progress eclipsed much of this stability. If humanity was not stuck in a constant cycle or fixed state but rather on a steady upward track toward perfection, then constant change could and should be expected. The future would be very different from the present, inspiring everything from revolutions and scientific advancement to, later, a whole genre of TV shows such as *The Jetsons*, which speculated about what humanity's future might look like. If humanity would be very different in the years to come though, it also meant there was much less value in preparing for that future. Who could know what future generations might want or believe?

The present feels even less stable. Technology changes at a stunning pace. The decline in religion and increase in social and geographic mobility contribute to a feeling of instability, reducing the connection people feel to any one place or cause as well as their connections to one another. The present is also marked by a massive surge in information: the rise in information technology, including social media, has allowed for a huge increase in the quantity of information produced and disseminated. The gulf between Generation Y and Generation Z can feel enormous, far wider than that separating generations a few centuries ago.

Culture also affects how we treat the future, probably for many different reasons. Research has found that people from Western cultures are on average much more present biased than those from Eastern ones, with neuroimaging actually showing differences in how the brain responds to present or future rewards.[14] Just showing people iconic pictures from America can make them more impatient and less willing to wait for a package to be delivered.[15] Religious people discount the future less than those who are not religiously inclined.[16]

Given how widely different cultures vary, it can be challenging to identify what specific factors matter, especially since a lot of research has traditionally used university students as subjects, who may not be representative of their broader cultures. That said, countries with higher GDP and lower growth rates tend to have people who are more patient, as do those with a higher emphasis on punctuality and working speed as well as those with cultural attitudes that value the long term and accept uncertainty.[17] These factors may reflect an underlying cultural emphasis on future rewards and patience over immediate rewards. Major events such as conflicts or a natural disaster may also affect how much we care about the future, with increased instability or trauma causing people to focus more on the short term.[18] Some research has even suggested that how languages are constructed, particularly whether a language grammatically emphasizes the distinction between present and future, can make people more or less short-termist.[19] Of course, there can also be wide variation within cultures, and genetics almost certainly plays a role.

In other words, the environment we are in, culture included, affects the decisions we take. It is our *choice architecture*, to use the term from behavioural science. Surprisingly, this is a relatively new insight for economists, who have often argued that people respond to incentives and act in their own best interest. Early economists such as Adam Smith or John Maynard Keynes might have accepted that people make mistakes or are not always perfectly rational, but later generations of economists started to assume that people were rational, so if they were discounting the future then it must be rational for them to do so. As a result, the famous perfectly rational *Homo economicus* was born, capable of instantly solving complex mathematical equations and predicting the future and always knowing what is best for economicus' long-term interests.

Perfect rationality makes changing behaviour with policy easy: subsidize it or tax not doing it. In a world of perfect rationality, the best way to affect behaviour is to change the costs or benefits of doing it. Unfortunately, this doesn't always work in the real world. We might believe this is how consumers should behave, and there is value in having a model of optimal behaviour. But as a model of actual behaviour, whether we are considering lottery winners who go bankrupt in a year or our own planning for our future, it seems suspect. To improve it, economists turned to psychology and the relatively new field of behavioural economics.

Consider the case of retirement savings. The traditional economic policy to increase retirement savings is subsidies; pay people to save. Canada has registered retirement savings plans and tax-free savings accounts to help subsidize and encourage retirement saving, for example, while in the US over $100 billion a year is spent on subsidies for savings accounts such as the 401k. Harvard professor Raj Chetty, a brilliant economist and recipient of a MacArthur genius grant, asked the very reasonable question of whether this approach worked. Chetty and his co-authors found that subsidies for saving are about 1 per cent effective: *for every hundred dollars the government spends, people save about a dollar more of their own money.*[20] The effect is minuscule, despite the size of the incentives. It would be easier for the government to give people the money when they retire!

Fortunately, Chetty also has a solution. He points out that policies that raise retirement contributions if individuals take no action – having employers automatically contribute to retirement accounts, for example, even if employees can easily opt out – are significantly more effective than financial incentives. The context in which we take decisions can be as or more important than what is at stake.

This is exactly what we see in practice. Yale professor of finance James Choi and his co-authors find in studying 401(k) retirement savings plans that if participation is left to employee choice, participation rates are around 30–40 per cent after six months at a firm. In contrast, if employees are automatically enrolled at a default savings rate, participation in the plan is about 85 per cent, even though the options available are identical in each case.[21] Such is the power of defaults and changing the choice architecture.

The lesson is that small things, like whether we are automatically signed up to save for retirement or not, can make a big difference to what we decide, even if the financial incentives don't change. Opting in to a retirement savings plan is not a big effort, but it does create a transaction cost that can discourage us from doing it, despite whether the eventual payoff – a well-funded retirement – may be worth it. An explanation was introduced by Daniel Kahneman, as discussed in his magisterial text on the psychology of decision-making, *Thinking, Fast and Slow*.[22] System 1, he suggests, is our knee-jerk, intuitive system. If I ask you for the capital of France, you can't avoid thinking of Paris; it isn't a conscious choice. When you first learned to parallel park, however, you almost certainly had to stop and think about it. That's System 2, the slow, methodical system. Neither is better than the other, and each has its uses. System 2 is more likely to find us the best solution, but does so at the cost of time and energy that we might prefer to devote to other things. System 2 is affected by incentives. If I offer you $100, you may slow down and triple-check your mirrors as you parallel park. System 1 is less so. Knowing there is $100 at stake doesn't affect whether you think of Paris when I ask for the capital of France.

System 1 is, however, deeply affected by the environment. It uses heuristics to guide behaviour that depends on the presence or absence of environmental cues instead of analysis. Most of the time, these cues are reliable, which is why we evolved to use them, but sometimes they can mislead us. Our intuitive response can depend on our mood, a recent conversation we've had, the pictures on the walls, or a million other small details that System 2 would ignore. If we want to change behaviour, incentives for System 2 are one answer, but another is changing which cues are present. By changing the choice architecture – the context of the decision – we can affect what choice System 1 makes.

These small variations can make a big difference to how people behave, and not just for retirement. The Nobel Prize–winning economist Richard Thaler and the Holberg Prize–winning legal scholar Cass Sunstein, authors of the book *Nudge*, point out that putting vegetables at eye level in a school cafeteria increases vegetable consumption, even if the chips and candy are only a few shelves down, because System 1 prioritizes what it sees first.[23]

If you've ever emptied the house of snacks when you went on a diet, bought an alarm clock that rolls away from you when you try to hit snooze, or used smaller dinner plates in order to encourage yourself to eat smaller portions, you've shown awareness of our tendency to choose differently based on context and exploited it to improve your behaviour. One of my favourite examples is spendthrifts who freeze their credit cards in a block of ice to ensure they have a cooling-off period before they can make any purchases (microwaving it would destroy the card's magnetic strip). Like Odysseus having his sailors plug their ears with wax to avoid the alluring song of the Sirens in Greek mythology, you anticipate temptation and shape your environment to avoid giving in.

In effect, when you make these changes you are introducing a small cost – in time, money, or energy – into your decision, one that must be paid immediately. Still hungry? You need to get up to refill your small plate. Want to go shopping? You have to wait a few hours for your credit card to thaw before you can use it. Want to sleep in? Get up and catch your alarm clock first. These small costs work for the same reason we have problems in the first place: we are biased toward immediate rewards and punishments. Since we tend to overweight costs today relative to the future, even small costs in our environment today can have a magnified impact in changing our behaviour. Often this is a bad thing: our desire to avoid a short-term cost means we lose out in the long-term. Sometimes, though, we can harness that bias for good. When we introduce short-term costs like getting a new plate or thawing a credit card, we discourage ourselves from overeating or overspending. The small short-term cost has a big effect on our behaviour.

What does all this have to do with planning for the future? The modern world has been shaped for us in ways that make it harder, not easier, to plan for the future. Modern advertising and social media are designed to appeal to our present self and exploit our biases. Online services are designed to minimize the effort it takes to just stay online, click on the next link, or watch the next autoplay video. In other words, they take advantage of our System 1 automatic processing, cueing us to focus on an endless stream of tweets, Facebook messages, text messages, emails, BuzzFeed articles, and other distractions. Nicholas Carr, in his book *The Shallows: What the Internet Is Doing to Our Brains*, worries that the modern world is literally remapping our brains to make concentration and deep thinking more difficult.[24] Whether at home or at work, we are constantly interrupted and connected, with our time for deep, long-term work ever more limited. Partly as a result, too often the default in the modern world is short-term reactivity not long-term thinking.

Another take on the same problem is presented by Alvin and Heidi Toffler in the 1970s book *Future Shock*. The Tofflers argue that our increased technological and social rate of change leaves people suffering from stress and disorientation.[25] Modern society, they argue, with its rapid industrial changes compels workers to constantly change employers and update their skills and expertise and also makes other elements more transitory, such as relationships and homes. The Tofflers popularized the term *information overload* to describe the difficulty people have understanding an issue or taking decisions when they are confronted with excessive information. Researchers have since confirmed the concept in a range of other contexts. When presented with an overflow of information or options, people can freeze, delaying or avoiding taking decisions.

The modern world is tailor-made to make this worse with its high rate and volume of information production alongside almost costless duplication and dissemination of information on the internet. This can also contribute to the risks of fake news or the distribution of disinformation, since voters in a state of information overload may struggle to assess the quality or reliability of information they receive. As Nate Silver, the popular statistician and founder of the political prediction website FiveThirtyEight, has observed, the volume of information in the world is increasing exponentially but relatively little of the information is useful: the signal-to-noise ratio is getting worse, not better.[26]

There are also benefits, of course. In Ancient Greece, Socrates worried that the introduction of writing would make people forgetful and give them only the illusion of wisdom. The introduction of the printing press in the fifteenth century evoked similar concerns that the ready availability of books would lead to intellectual laziness. These concerns dramatically underestimated the benefits of writing and the accessibility of books. Similarly, the modern access to information and technology is a significant blessing, and most of us would not choose to return to a pre-smartphone past.

Still, all of us have experienced feeling overwhelmed by the modern world. With infinite information at our fingertips, how can we tell what matters or plan for the long term? And, how can we find the time to pay attention to it with Netflix, Instagram, X, and other applications clamouring for our attention? As the modern world has become more complex, we are increasingly forced to rely on instinctive decisions and heuristics. Or we may simply delay or defer our decisions due to information overload. Either way, we end up not dealing with the long-term problems that confront us.

Fortunately, by artfully changing our environment – individually and as a society – we can help ourselves plan for the future. Of course, we can't prepare for everything, but we can try to give the future the attention it deserves while still enjoying ourselves today. The same is true of governments: changing their choice architecture and the methods by which they make decisions can help alter how much they prioritize the future, giving us the ability to nudge them in better directions. First, though, we turn to a more fundamental question: should we care about the future at all?

3

How Much Should We Care About the Future?

In every deliberation, we must consider the impact on the seventh generation.

Seventh Generation Principle, often attributed to the Haudenosaunee (Iroquois) Confederacy

Chapter 2 explores the evolutionary and psychological foundations of individual present bias and how our modern environment makes that problem worse. But should we care about future generations at all? Conversely, should we care about them just as much as we care about those of today? Answering these questions is essential to making appropriate trade-offs between now and later. Policy-makers regularly make these sorts of decisions: do we invest in making roads safer today or building levees for tomorrow's floods? Such decisions implicitly require us to decide how much we care about tomorrow compared to today.

Unfortunately, economists, philosophers, and others are divided on whether and how much we should care about the future. The key point of debate is over what is called *social discount rates*: how much should we discount the future – that is, value it less – compared to the present? One of the original developers of discount rates in economics argued that using discount rates was ethically indefensible, but as we shall see, modern economists generally agree that discounting the future, at least a little bit, is probably reasonable.[1]

PLANTING THE CAROB TREE

Some early economists saw our attachment to the present as a failure of some kind. Arthur Cecil Pigou, the British economist and University of Cambridge professor, wrote in 1921 that it could be a failure of imagination, since "our telescopic faculty is defective, and that we, therefore, see future pleasures, as it were, on a diminished scale ... it implies that people distribute their resources between the present, the near future, and the remote future on the basis of a wholly irrational preference."[2] Pigou has often been overshadowed by John Maynard Keynes, but he was also the originator of Pigouvian taxes, such as a carbon tax.

The argument that we should care about the future as much as we do the present is not unique to economists. Exhortations to care about the future are common across many cultures and eras, often arguing that each generation stewards the Earth for future generations. Confucius observed that "a man who does not think and plan long ahead will find trouble at his door," while the Great Law of Peace of the Haudenosaunee Confederacy, effectively their constitution, urged their peoples to "have always in view not only the present but also the coming generations, even those whose faces are yet beneath the surface of the ground – the unborn of the future Nation."[3] The Bible remarks that good people leave an inheritance for their children's children.

A traditional Jewish story tells of a man planting a carob tree, which would take seventy years to bear fruit. When asked if he thought he would live another seventy years, the man replied that he ate the fruit from the trees planted by his forebears, and he planted this tree for his children. Islam, Buddhism, Hinduism, and other faiths express similar sentiments. Modern environmentalists no longer use religious language, but many of them would agree with the sentiment that we have a moral obligation to care for the world not only for our benefit but also for that of future generations. Even devout capitalists worry about a focus on short-term returns by CEOs and investors, though not necessarily for moral reasons. Ultimately, how much one cares about the future is more a personal, ethical decision than anything. Nonetheless, there are a few ways to think about why we might care: self-interest, the moral imperative for stewardship and justice, and biology.

The case based on self-interest is straightforward: if my home is in danger of flooding, I will bear the costs if I don't invest in flood insurance or reinforce my basement. Similarly, if governments don't adequately prepare for hurricanes or other natural disasters, then we risk greater losses down the road. In this case, the argument for caring about the future is clear: only in truly desperate times do we risk sacrificing our future to preserve our present. Farmers plant seeds even when they are hungry, because they know by harvest they will need those crops.

This argument is limited, however. Governments' actions often affect people not yet born at a price paid by current generations. Stopping the current drop in biodiversity may mean curbing some of our current habitat-destroying behaviours, but much of the benefit will flow to our children's children and generations beyond that. Self-interest does not reliably guide us on how to think about future generations.

A second perspective on why we should care about the future is stewardship. Many of the benefits we enjoy today are because past generations invested for the future. As noted, when stonemasons in the Middle Ages built cathedrals, they often didn't live to see their designs realized, but we still enjoy those cathedrals. Having been given the world by our predecessors, the argument goes, we have a responsibility to pass it on in turn. It may not be identical to what we have been given but remains in a condition such that our successors have the same opportunities and options we did. We hear the same notion in everyday contexts: when someone does us a favour, we talk about paying it forward or returning the favour. The golden rule, do unto others as you would have them do unto you, represents a concrete expression of stewardship. In one interpretation, stewardship implies that future generations have rights of their own, even if they are not yet born. As members of a sort of trans-generational community with those future people, we have a moral obligation to respect those rights and pass on a world that provides opportunities similar to our own.[4]

The scale of impact we have on the natural world can make the imperative for stewardship still more compelling. Early societies could pollute, of course: there is a riverbed in Jordan that was polluted by early copper working around seven thousand years ago.[5] Generally, lower population densities and limited technology meant that early cultures were simply not able to affect future generations to the extent we are today. They were also typically more connected to the land: in ancient Greek, Roman, and Hebrew societies, for example, farmers were expected to give first fruits, the first agricultural produce of the harvest, as a religious offering in thanks for the harvest. It is a rare shopper in Walmart who thanks the land when they buy a head of lettuce.

Just because we can have an effect on the natural world doesn't mean we will, and many people devote their lives to trying to protect the environment. The scale of modern technology, however, means there is significantly more uncertainty over the possible impacts of our decisions than in the past. The complex modern world means not only is there a chance we may damage human health or the environment through our decisions, but we may be unsure how likely that damage is – true Knightian uncertainty. We also often face an asymmetrical set of possible consequences; at best we manage to preserve or slightly improve the environment, but at worst we could destroy it utterly. We only have to destroy the natural world once for it – and us – to be gone forever, and we could well do so by accident through a new technological or societal innovation. The risks can be highly visible, such as that of a nuclear winter, but also more subtle, such as the gradual buildup of chemicals from pesticides and industrial processes in our environment that have a long-term impact on human health.

The precautionary principle, the idea that when there is uncertainty we should be cautious and avoid harm, can be over-applied: sometimes the possible benefits justify taking risks, in the same way treating cancer with chemotherapy does damage to the human body in the hopes it will lead to a net improvement. Taking on some risk today can be the correct decision for the long term, if it leads to an important long-term discovery or improvement. Requiring the proponent of an activity to always bear the burden of proof that it is safe, as stronger formulations of the precautionary principle require, can also accidentally rule out almost all action, since it may be difficult to absolutely prove safety. As Cass Sunstein has argued, if the principle is applied evenly to both the risks of action and inaction, it can lead to paralyzing gridlock, with both acting and not acting deemed unacceptable due to potential risks.[6]

The asymmetric nature of the risks technology can create in the long term and the potential for extreme costs arising from the level of technology we have today does suggest, however, that prudence is appropriate for us to be good stewards. Managing risks on behalf of future generations is part of good stewardship, requiring careful thought about what risks might emerge and how much uncertainty there is. Failing to do so could have harmful, possibly catastrophic, consequences for our descendants.

A different way to think about intergenerational equity is in the context of justice. One of the best-known arguments for this was advanced by the philosopher John Rawls, who argues for justice as fairness in his seminal work *A Theory of Justice*. He clarifies this in two principles: that each person should have an equal right to the maximum possible set of basic liberties, as long as those liberties don't infringe on others, and social and economic inequalities should be arranged so that they benefit the least advantaged most and do not make it harder for the poor or less powerful to reach positions of power, such as political office.[7] Rawls suggests that to identify what is just, we should consider what we would choose for society if we knew nothing about the talents, social class, wealth, ethnicity, or other factors that we would be born with. Since we are unable to choose based on self-interest, we are forced to choose to the benefit of society.

Rawls's two principles follow from this idea, which he calls the veil of ignorance. If we didn't know who we would be born as, we would want everyone to have as much liberty as possible. If a specific group in society is severely disadvantaged, whether for reasons of race, gender, religion, or otherwise, a decision-maker behind the veil of ignorance would likely choose to help those individuals, to minimize the risk of being born to a disadvantaged group. If we are forced to consider life as a slave, it becomes much harder to justify slavery. Indeed, an expanding circle of sympathy – based on society's increasing ability across history to take the perspectives of others through literacy, mobility, and mass media – is likely one of the drivers of the decline in violence in modern societies.[8]

The veil of ignorance is typically used to discuss inequalities in the present. It applies equally well, however, to intergenerational justice. If we do not know to which generation we will be born, then it is clear we should structure society to preserve some level of justice between generations, rather than allowing one generation's manner of existence to harm a later one. As a result, Rawls argued for the principle of "just savings": saving sufficient money or assets so that future generations could also be well off.

Another way to look at the same problem is to say that to be ethical, a decision must give equal weight to the interests of everyone affected by it. The modern take on this principle is found in discussions of "nothing for us without us," in other words policy decisions should not be made without engaging those affected by them. Of course, future generations cannot literally be included in a decision if they are not yet born, but in taking a decision, we can consider the consequences to them and ask ourselves what decision is best if we give equal weight to them and ourselves. A modern take on this question is the recent philosophical case for long-termism. As Will MacAskill, a philosopher at the University of Oxford, has argued, long-termism suggests that distance in time should be thought of like distance in space: if we believe we should donate to charity to help those who live thousands of miles away, then we should do the same for those living thousands of years away.[9]

A final way to think about intergenerational equity is based on biology. At the extreme, some evolutionary biologists have argued that biology can serve as the basis of morality. American biologist and Harvard professor Edward O. Wilson suggested that a fundamental tenet of morality is to support the survival of a large and diverse gene pool over generations.[10] Clearly, if we accept that, it provides a strong argument for caring about the welfare of future generations. Even if we do not accept a moral imperative to support the flourishing of future generations, biology can still provide some insight into how and why we might care about the future. The theory of natural selection says that behaviours or traits that help genes propagate will be more likely to do so. In a population, individuals with those traits will become more common, and over time crowd out those without the traits. What traits are selected for will depend on context and environment. In this sense, it serves almost as an extension of the self-interest argument.

We may not be alive in the future, but our children or their children might be, as might the children of our siblings, and we share their genes. Evolution doesn't just mean we selfishly maximize our own survival; it includes those related to us. As biologist J.S. Haldane dryly remarked, he would gladly give up his life for two brothers or eight cousins: we share half of our genetic material with siblings and an eighth with our cousins.[11] So if we are looking to maximize the long-term success of our genes, leaving the world a shattered husk for our children is probably not a good idea.

Of course, in the real world we don't see people exclusively helping their own relations; instead, people behave altruistically, often helping others they have never met. The same impulse that prompts us to donate to emergency relief in a country we have never been to may entice us to help generations we will not live to see. Biologists have suggested various motivations for this sentiment, such as signalling virtue and evolutionary fitness on the part of the giver, increasing appeal to potential mates. Similarly, giving to future generations may be a good method of signalling our quality or values, encouraging others to co-operate with us in the present.

HOW MUCH TO VALUE THE FUTURE

In sum, there are sound ethical reasons for us to care about future generations. Economists, however, generally agree that it makes sense for society to value the future at least a little less than the present. As we have seen, this reflects how we actually behave: we treat future benefits as less important than present ones. We procrastinate, we delay, and we prioritize tasks and decisions that affect the present over those that affect the future. And there are good reasons to do so, to some extent. Those reasons are typically captured in three different arguments for discounting the future. The future is uncertain, it might be richer, and there is an opportunity cost to forgoing benefits now.

Uncertainty provides a clear justification for discounting future generations. If we lower our standard of living today in order to save more for the retirement of future generations, what happens if that money is wasted by a future government or stolen by criminals, technology changes to extend lifespans and make pensions unnecessary, or most dramatically a solar event of some kind means the end of the world? We have pressing needs today that are guaranteed, such as buying food or paying for housing. That means spending a dollar today gives us guaranteed return, while saving it might not. It makes sense to demand a relatively high rate of return for things that aren't immediate, because if we have to wait for them, they become uncertain. As John Maynard Keynes pointed out in 1923, in the long run we are all dead.[12] If we don't worry about the future, there will be more to go around today.

A very tangible application of this occurred in Columbia professor Walter Mischel's famous marshmallow test, in which he left children alone in a room with sugary snacks, having told them they would get a reward if they didn't eat them, and then measured how well they could resist temptation. The children who were best able to resist temptation – which they did through a variety of cute strategies, such as singing to themselves, sitting on their hands, or in one particularly impressive case, taking a nap – grew up to earn more and generally be more successful in life. Further research has cast doubt on how much the study measures willpower as opposed to just being a proxy for socio-economic background: kids from wealthier families both resist temptation better and earn more as adults, but that doesn't mean resisting temptation causes higher earnings. Interestingly, however, a minor change to the experiment can dramatically change the results. If kids are first given a reason to believe the experimenter is untrustworthy (i.e., the experimenter promises to give them something and then reneges), almost no child will resist eating the snack in the second round.[13]

In other words, the experiment does not just measure willpower; it also measures trust in institutions and the system as well as factors like optimism, which are probably greater for kids in higher socio-economic groups. The more confident you are about the future, the more willing you are to risk waiting for a reward, which helps both in laboratory experiments and likely in life, at least in stable countries. In countries with unstable governments, or for populations where government has been a menace or source of discrimination and unfairness rather than a help, long-term thinking may be unhelpful. Uncertainty cuts both ways, and our actions may increase or reduce risks in the future, rendering decision-making under uncertainty particularly difficult. Either way, the unpredictability around what the future holds provides a reason not to overinvest in preparing for it.

The second reason we might care more about the present than the future is that for much of recent history, the future has proven to be richer than the present. If we're worried about inequality, particularly intergenerational inequality, then we might think it's not fair to take money from the poor (the present) and give it to the rich (the future). The future might have better technology than us, which means it will be easier to solve problems; investing in a technology that may never be used because a better one is invented in the future is wasteful. The Victorians worried about the large amounts of horse manure littering the streets in the late 1800s and whether it would eventually block horse-powered transport altogether, only for engines to make the problem irrelevant.

That isn't an unreasonable argument, but it is awkward. Sometimes the future is poorer than the present: ignoring climate change because we think our grandchildren will solve it is only sensible if they can actually do so, and it's impossible to know if that's true. On average humanity has experienced progress throughout history, but there have been downs as well as ups, and it would be wrong to store up trouble for the future if it were to turn out they are worse off. The cost of fixing something can also increase over time: even if our children are richer than we are, repairing a highway, for instance, will be more expensive the longer we wait. In the extreme case – existential risks such as nuclear war that could destroy humanity – this argument clearly does not hold. If humanity will not exist in the future as a consequence of our present decisions, they cannot be richer than we are.

A third reason used to explain discount rates is the value of time. If you have a choice between having money today and having money tomorrow, there is an inherent advantage in having it today; you can use it for other things, which may bring their own benefits over time. If governments spend a million dollars on flood protection and only reap the benefits in five years, then they don't have the million available to spend today on anti-poverty programs or building roads. The opportunity to do something else with the money is lost. Having a million dollars in five years is worse than having a million dollars today because that leaves five years of missed opportunities to spend it and make a difference (or make money on the stock market, the standard economics example). So, the argument goes, it makes sense to discount the future relative to the present. This insight is what underlies much of investment theory, which involves deciding whether to invest in projects over time. As Tyler Cowen and Derek Parfit have pointed out, however, this argument can be misleading. Some benefits, such as enjoying nature, cannot be simply invested for a return, and it may be better to capture any impacts of the value of time in direct terms rather than as a justification for discounting the future.[14]

As a result of all these considerations, there is wide acceptance among economists that it is correct to discount the future to some extent, though how much is highly contested. The 2006 report *The Economics of Climate Change: The Stern Review*, for example, used a low discount rate of almost zero and argued for urgent, radical action to address climate change.[15] When the same study was repeated with a discount rate of around 3 per cent, the urgency largely disappeared, though some action was still justified.[16]

Scholarly estimates of the appropriate social discount rate – that is, how much society should discount the future – vary widely. As the *Stern Review* shows, a difference of even a few percentage points can make a significant difference to what policies are justified. The US Office of Management and Budget recently proposed setting its standard social discount rate for assessing policy impacts to 1.7 per cent, down from 7 per cent in the 1990s.[17] The UK uses 3.5 per cent and France 4.5 per cent.[18] The value chosen does not just affect future generations. A higher social discount rate also implies we should spend more on the young as opposed to the elderly in the present, for example.[19]

The research is mixed on estimating discount rates partly because individuals vary.[20] Many factors can affect someone's discount rate, and different people facing different choices can understandably discount the future different amounts. Psychologists frequently use the five-factor model – openness to experience, conscientiousness, extraversion, agreeableness, and neuroticism – as a way to study personality, and research has found that high neuroticism and low conscientiousness are related to short-termism.[21] Age, race, sex, number of dependants, test scores, time spent in nature, and even living in a culture where past inhabitants had more productive crops have also been shown to affect an individual's discount rates, among many other factors, and this remains an important area of research.[22]

Discount rates also may not be particularly helpful in the context of the distant future, especially given how uncertain we are over what that future may hold. Even a fairly small discount rate will mean at some point the value placed on the welfare of the distant future is close to zero, which seems morally tenuous. Just because they are our children ten times removed does not necessarily mean we do not value their standard of living. On the other hand, a very low or zero discount rate implies we should be saving a very large amount of our current wealth for the benefit of the future. In effect, because of how many people may live in the future, a low discount rate suggests current generations should live in poverty to benefit later ones, which also seems unreasonable. If we use the discount rates from the *Stern Review*, for example, by one calculation we should be saving about 97.5 per cent of our current economy's output for the benefit of future generations.[23]

More recent research has suggested solving some of these problems by introducing social discount rates that decline over time, so that costs and benefits are discounted more in the near future than in the distant future.[24] This can rather elegantly be explained by people's uncertainty about the future of the economy, which increases the more distant in time the forecast is. Intuitively, increased uncertainty about the distant future encourages people to be more prudent and thus discount the future less. A declining rate helps resolve the tension between believing the future matters and not wanting to sacrifice quality of life entirely in the present by allowing for both to be true, and it can have significant policy implications since it weights costs in the distant future more heavily. When considering nuclear power, for example, using a declining rate makes the future costs of decommissioning a plant and dealing with nuclear waste more significant, potentially reducing its appeal relative to a flat discount rate.[25]

Ultimately, the point is that valuing the present more than the future is not inherently incorrect, and people will inevitably vary in how much they choose to do so. Putting off tasks that may end up unnecessary or may change is a reasonable strategy. If you do your taxes too soon, you'll have to redo them when you get your final pay slips. Governments that focus too much on the future and not enough on the present may be unduly harming their citizens. If that was all there was to our bias toward the present, then humans would be in good shape.

As we have seen, that is not the whole story. Sometimes our evolved tendency to delay tasks can be harmful, not helpful. When we miss deadlines to address future problems, we aren't just pragmatically delaying tasks until we have more information. We, and our governments, are present biased to our collective cost. It is that problem this book aims to address.

ETHICS FOR THE FUTURE

The future is potentially vast. The average mammalian species lasts one million years. As Oxford University researcher Max Roser points out, about 117 billion humans have been born since the beginning of humankind 200,000 years ago. In the next 800,000 years, another 100 trillion people are projected to be born and die.[26] Everyone who has ever lived, everyone you have ever met, read about, studied in history, or seen on TikTok, is only 0.1 per cent of the total number of humans that will exist. When we think about the future, we are thinking about a nearly inconceivable number of potential people. Even if we don't believe they are quite as important as the people of today, their sheer number means we should be careful about ignoring them or doing irreversible harm. That is especially true given our built-in bias toward the present.

Reflecting on these questions, the United Nations Secretary-General's report *Intergenerational Solidarity and the Needs of Future Generations* draws several conclusions from the ethical framework around intergenerational justice:

- A priority should be minimizing harm to future generations and doing that which benefits both present and future generations, for example avoiding irreversible impacts to ecosystems.
- Policies that work to the advantage of both present and future generations should be favoured.
- Where risks to future generations are clear and consequential, present generations should be prepared to forego some benefits.
- Education must play a critical role in transmitting scientific and other knowledge to future generations. Actions could include enhancing civic education and leadership training to strengthen concern for intergenerational justice.
- Long-term scientific research and development are important to develop alternatives to depleted resources, use resources efficiently, and manage long-term threats.[27]

People ultimately vary in why they care about the future – you may find some of the above arguments more compelling than others. Most people would agree that we should care about the future at least somewhat. In our everyday lives, however, moments that require planning for the far future are relatively uncommon. Retirement planning is still for the benefit of our future selves, not unborn generations, though we struggle to do it anyway. Governments, in contrast, frequently make decisions with impacts that will ripple through the generations. How they make those decisions, and how much they value the future in doing so, can have transformative impacts on future generations, both good and bad. It is to government decision-making we turn next.

4

Why Are Governments Short-Sighted?

Governing for the future is both important and difficult. Important because it means getting to grips with the long-term issues that will shape the lives of future generations; difficult because it rubs up against the short-termism that is inherent in the politics of the electoral cycle.

UK House of Commons Public Administration Select Committee, "Governing the Future"

During World War II, the US was desperate to develop the nuclear bomb ahead of Germany and maintain a technological advantage. To do so, they needed to produce plutonium, and lots of it. They would produce that plutonium at a site in Hanford, Washington, due to its proximity to the Columbia River and its distance from people, given the concern over an accidental explosion. The plutonium manufactured there would be used in the first nuclear bomb ever detonated. Over the following forty years, the site would produce two-thirds of the plutonium in the US nuclear arsenal.

As Michael Lewis points out in his book *The Fifth Risk*, the Hanford site is now also a catastrophe of a cleanup job.[1] When it was shut down at the end of the Cold War, decades of radioactive manufacturing had led to dumping 120 million gallons of high-level waste and 444 billion gallons of contaminated liquid into the ground. Left at the site are 177 storage tanks, each roughly the size of a four-storey apartment, holding among other things 56 million gallons of high-level waste. The site represents approximately 60 per cent of the high-level waste managed by the US Department of Energy. High-level waste is sufficiently dangerous to kill you in a few seconds of exposure. The rest of the waste would take longer.

Given the urgency of World War II, one can understand that the American government felt a need to focus on the short term in establishing the site. Beating Germany to the bomb was the priority, rather than ensuring proper safety and waste disposal measures. In the years since though there is far less of an excuse for mismanagement. Over the years, Hanford's residents experienced higher than usual rates of miscarriage, cancer, and genetic disorders, which were largely ignored. Sixty-seven of the 177 tanks have failed in some way, leading to leaks that pollute the groundwater and waste that slowly drifts toward the Columbia River. In one particularly depressing incident in 2017, a tunnel that was built in the 1950s to hold low-level waste collapsed. In response, workers dumped truckloads of dirt into the hole, leading to truckloads of radioactive dirt that also needed to be disposed of, while the original collapse still needed fixing.

A clean-up would be hugely expensive. The Department of Energy spends approximately 10 per cent of its annual budget on Hanford already and has not been making much progress. An original plan developed in 1988 called for the clean-up to be finished in thirty years, by 2008. In 2008 it was decided 2040 was more realistic. A 2012 study by the US General Accounting Office pointed out there remained a number of serious unresolved technical and managerial problems, suggesting it will likely be longer yet. Hanford and the failure so far to effectively address the environmental hazards it poses illustrate a number of the challenges in addressing long-term problems, as we explore below.

* * *

We've seen that humans don't just discount the future but also struggle with a problem of multiple selves, which can make us focus on the present and not enough on the future. Our modern environment can exacerbate this tendency, fixing our attention on short-term crises rather than long-term problems. What does all this have to do with governments? Governments are made up of individuals, who are themselves subject to present bias. Our leaders and legislators take policy decisions and are influenced by many of the same factors that we are as individuals: the more uncertainty there is over how necessary a decision is and the lower the immediate reward or the higher the cost to a politician for taking it, the greater the tendency for a politician to delay taking action on it.

In addition, how governments are structured can often mean they face challenges that look remarkably similar to present-biased individuals. The present self – that is, the government in power at the time – has only a limited identification with future governments because it may not be re-elected. A government may act to benefit its members or minimize the risk of losing power, even if that imposes costs on future governments or society. The result is the same conflict between selves as at a personal level, with the present government manoeuvring around the future one. Governments also face a modern environment that can constantly draw their attention to short-term crises rather than long-term goals, much like individuals.

This does not mean that individuals or governments never take actions that benefit the future at a cost to the present. Present bias is just that, a bias. On average, the bias suggests that both individuals and governments undervalue long-term benefits and overly focus on the present. But some actions will have such significant rewards in the future, or such a clear motivation in the present (for example, immediately after a natural disaster), that action happens anyway. If we imagine a government trying to allocate funds across various projects, some short-term and some long-term, the long-term projects still get some investment. But because governments are present biased, they spend less on the future than they should. Governments can and do act for the long term, just not as much as would be optimal.

The analogy with individual behaviour has limits. Even if decisions are ultimately made by a single president or prime minister who is subject to individual biases, governments are institutions and do not always behave in the same way as individuals. Collective decision-making can be better or worse than individual decision-making, and groups of people can be subject to different biases and behaviours. Organizations can harness this difference, bringing together the wisdom of diverse groups and improving outcomes, but there are also risks. Groups may be more likely to amplify errors in individual judgment, succumb to peer pressure, experience polarization, and appeal to the least common denominator, among other dynamics.[2]

At the level of individual politicians, leaders are likely to be more interested in public policy issues than an average citizen and have access to teams of people to do research and provide advice, which can also impact their decisions.[3] That said, a number of scholars have remarked on the increasing centralization of power in the hands of a few individuals in many jurisdictions, such as a prime minister and their close advisers, a trend related to what is sometimes called the presidentialization of politics.[4] Since individual leaders are themselves subject to present bias, the more that decisions are taken by a single person or small number of leaders, the more that their own present bias may influence those decisions.

In addition to group biases, group decisions will depend on the allocation of power across different stakeholders and factions. If a policy has long-run benefits overall, a powerful or well-organized group that prefers a more short-termist approach might still successfully block it. In policy decisions without a temporal element, a government can potentially redistribute some benefits from winners to losers to convince the losers to support the policy anyway. Redistributing resources away from people who are not yet born to people living today may be difficult, if not impossible, making it harder to apply redistribution to compensate groups for their losses and convince them to support long-term policies.

Once a group decision is taken, the collective may still not be unanimous. For individuals, the same person is both making the decision and carrying it out. In contrast, supporters of a decision within a group may need a way to encourage or coerce those who disagree to comply, or to ensure participation from those who are not motivated to take action personally to solve a collective action problem. To address climate change, for example, society needs to find ways to motivate or require action from individual members to reduce emissions, even if they do not wish to do so. This diversity within a group applies to both present generations and future ones. When a generational tension exists, not everyone within a single generation will agree or be universally opposed to the interests of another generation. Some groups in the present will win and some will lose, and the same is true for those in the future. In most cases there will be distributional impacts, with winners and losers in both generations and a need to weigh the relative benefits and costs for each group in order to make decisions.

Thus, making and carrying out a decision in a group requires navigating the power and disagreement within the group. If a nudge successfully gives a leader space to address long-term issues and motivates them to do so, that is a step forward, but the hard work of engaging political opponents, forging consensus, and encouraging action remains, unlike in the individual case. Theories of cognition that explain individual behaviour in terms of multiple selves can only go so far in capturing these group dynamics. A nudge may help increase the number of people within a collective who support long-term action and make it easier for leaders to prioritize the future, but challenges persist that do not have a close analogy with the individual case.

Governments also typically have much more scale for impact than individuals. Decisions that a government takes may ripple through the next century or more, unlike most decisions we take as individuals. The sweeping mandate of modern governments and their enormous potential impact on the future make long-term thinking more important and can make it more difficult by ramping up the uncertainty over how decisions will play out and what the conditions will be in the very long term.

Though the analogy between governments and individuals has limits, it can also be useful. The comparison can help us identify factors that may press governments to be short-termist and explore possible solutions. Our exploration of individual behaviour suggests three pressures that may bias governments toward the short term:

- Democratic election cycles mean that governments may not be in power by the time the future arrives, and policies they enact may be reversed if the new government disagrees with them. The present government has little incentive to incur a cost today in exchange for benefits that will appear under the next government.
- Voters themselves are present biased and reward governments that behave in the same way, or they do not trust governments to deliver long-term promises and therefore do not bother to push for them. This challenge is heightened by the fact that the people who benefit most from long-term policies are not yet born and are typically unrepresented in policy discussions, while present generations bear the cost of action today and make up the current electorate.

  Importantly, leaders also affect and are affected by voter preferences, creating risks and opportunities. Long-termist leaders can help shift public opinion to be more future looking, while short-term public opinion can influence leaders to be the same, resulting in the possibility of positive or negative cycles of reinforcement as the two groups affect each other.
- The hyper-paced modern world, with its twenty-four-hour news cycles and modern political news coverage, can trigger a scarcity

> mindset that focuses leaders on putting out urgent fires and addressing short-term crises, distracting them from longer-term initiatives. The same features of the modern world that focus individuals on the present encourage governments to follow suit.

All these factors are exacerbated by the reality that the future is uncertain. Governments may be unsure whether a problem will still exist or be as challenging in the future; whether a proposed policy or action will solve the problem; and whether, if they choose to take action, future governments will stay the course or instead cancel or adjust a program. Even a highly future-oriented government may not bother taking action if they believe a future government will reverse course, making their efforts pointless. A government already worried about its electoral fortunes, or under pressure from voters or the media to focus on the present, may choose to ignore what are ultimately uncertain costs or benefits in the future. As we have seen, choosing to discount the future more due to uncertainty is not wrong. The problem is that the combination of uncertainty with election cycles, voter present bias, and the modern world can lead to too much discounting and a failure to invest sufficiently in the future.

All three pressures – election cycles, present-biased voters, and modern distractions – play a role in discouraging government action in the case of the Hanford cleanup. First, every government has an incentive to make it the next government's problem. The biggest risk is if the waste reaches the Columbia River, in which case the cleanup costs could suddenly dramatically escalate. Such an accident is unlikely to occur under any given government, and the cost of preventing it would reduce what a government has available to spend. Consequently, every government has an incentive to do as their predecessors did: delay. Any one government can console itself with the improbability that the effects will be felt during their mandate. Moreover, if one did increase funding for the Department of Energy to address the risk, it might well be reversed by a subsequent government, making the effort useless.

Second, there is relatively little demand from voters for change. Voters also often focus on immediate crises, and although Hanford may be a crisis, it is a slow-moving one. Children who might be affected by a leak into the Columbia River are not yet born or politically active, nor are the generations after them who might also be at risk. As Lewis points out, even the Hanford residents themselves have an incentive not to scrutinize the problem too closely: they rely on the $3 billion spent every year on maintaining the site for their livelihoods.[5] Voters may also not trust government promises to address the issue, discouraging them from bothering to push for change.

Finally, long-term potential crises like the Hanford site do not attract the scale and scope of media attention that immediate crises do, reducing the pressure on the national government to pay attention. Of course, if a leak into the Columbia occurs coverage will be widespread, but by then the problem will be much harder to address. At that point, there will be considerable pressure on the government to take action, and it will be blamed for not acting sooner. The pressure and blame come after the crisis, not before.

The best indication of the impact of incentives for short-term thinking may be that, as Lewis points out, the Department of Energy has never conducted a comprehensive study of the risks at Hanford. No one has ever really wanted to know the extent of the risk, lest it be harder to ignore. Voters could start calling for better cleanup, or at least a mitigation of the risks. No government has had an incentive to tackle that problem; far easier to leave it for the next generation, or at least the next government. There is plenty of uncertainty when it comes to the Hanford site. Perhaps it won't leak or a new technology could facilitate cleanup. Spending too much on it might crowd out other legitimate priorities. Nonetheless, it is difficult to escape the view that more long-term thinking could be helpful.

The three pressures can also apply in other contexts. Let's examine them in more depth.

SHORT-TERM ELECTION CYCLES

An election cycle can minimize the incentive for democratic governments to act for the long term. A typical electoral term is only a few years, and after that political rivals may be in power. Each election may bring a new party or parties into office, sometimes with diametrically opposed ideologies and preferences. Fundamentally, this creates an incentive for governments to ignore the long term: paying a short-term political price for long-term benefits holds little appeal for a government that expects to lose an election as a result of the short-term costs, while the benefits will flow to their rivals. Implementing wise economic policies may help the economy in five years, but if it involves short-term pain for the economy today, governments may hesitate: taking action for the long-term will get their rivals elected and give them the credit, while acting for the short-term will promote their own re-election but perhaps create problems in the next mandate.

At a very simple level, this can mean governments take decisions to maximize their chance of winning elections without worrying about the long-term consequences. A classic example is increasing government handouts to key electoral areas, which provides short-term benefits to the recipients. In the long term though it can fuel unsustainable government deficits or require the reallocation of funds from more significant priorities, potentially overheating the economy, creating an economic bubble and leading to a sort of political business cycle with booms before elections and busts afterwards.[6] Since such handouts can also increase the chance of re-election, however, governments may still have an incentive to increase spending shortly before people vote.

This is, in fact, exactly what we see. Research on eighty-five developed and developing countries has found that government deficits increase in election years by almost 1 per cent of GDP, with a larger effect in developing economies than in developed ones.[7] The election effect is often cited as an explanation for last-minute government handouts before elections in developing countries, such as the introduction of generous welfare systems or large cash subsidies. More recent work has found similar though more subtle effects in established democracies: Katsimi and Sarantides find that Organisation for Economic Co-operation and Development (OECD) countries typically shift spending toward current expenditures and reduce long-term investment in advance of elections and are more likely to reduce taxes.[8] Instead of increasing spending in absolute terms before an election, which voters might object to, developed governments instead shift their spending toward more short-term, high-visibility projects such as road construction.

The scale of the political budget cycle, and how it varies across countries and elections, is contested. In part, this reflects the fact that there are many ways this can be done: it is easy to observe (and criticize) a brand-new spending program that happens to occur in districts a government is fearful of losing in the next election but harder to track reallocations of money between several different priorities, delays in planned spending cuts, or simply temporary reductions in enforcement of certain unpopular measures. Ultimately, it is clear that governments have a strong incentive to spend money in advance of an election in order to increase their electoral support, even to the long-term detriment of the economy. Eventually, this pattern breaks down, often due to a crisis of some sort, and governments are forced to take action by reducing spending or increasing taxes. The election cycle means the current government may not be in power by the time the crisis happens, so it can avoid responsibility. Unfortunately, solving a crisis is usually more costly than avoiding one.

The size of the election effect varies. Not all elections are competitive: an election with a weak or incompetent opposition, where the incumbent is highly favoured to win, puts little pressure on the incumbent to sway voters or avoid imposing short-term costs on them, making short-termism less likely. Alan M. Jacobs at the University of British Columbia, in his book *Governing for the Long Term*, points to the German introduction of the first old age pension in the world as an example.[9] Otto von Bismarck and his government in Germany had a commanding majority and widespread support when the pension was introduced, and although the policy risked losing some support in the short term due to the cost of mandatory pension contributions, this was unlikely to make them lose the next election. On the other hand, Bismarck was concerned about future increases in support for the socialist opposition party if people endured poverty in retirement. Introducing the policy thus cost them little politically in the short term and had potential electoral benefits in the future by reducing support for the opposition once benefits started to be paid out.

The election effect can also lead to more complex dynamics. When the UK first established its old age pension plan, government officials who tended to focus more on the long term than their elected counterparts were vociferously opposed to establishing a fund to pay for future pensions because they expected that future elected leaders would spend it on other things.[10] These public servants behaved similarly to what is called a *sophisticate* in behavioural science research: anticipating a future failure in willpower, they argued against saving in the present. If a government believes the next one will cancel its program or spend what it has saved, then there is no point in saving in the first place. Worrying about the electoral cycle, whether by voters or officials, can lead to doubt and cynicism which discourage action today and can intensify short-termism.

This problem of a lack of incentives for a government to tackle the long term is exacerbated by individual incentives within a government. In many democracies, politicians and ministers are highly mobile: they are frequently moved between departments after only a short time at a helm and are also at risk of losing their seat or having their party lose office in an election.[11] By the time a long-term issue emerges to be accountable for, they have frequently been replaced. In the UK, for example, Rory Stewart promised in August 2018 to resign as prisons minister if he did not succeed in reducing the level of drugs and violence in UK prisons by August 2019. Helpfully, he provided a list of ten jails on which his performance could be judged.

A year later, he had been promoted to a different department; had run for leadership of the Conservatives; and Boris Johnson, who had won the leadership, had assigned the prisons file to a third minister in three months. The prisons hadn't improved, but given Stewart didn't stay at the department, it's difficult to argue that he should be accountable. Much the same happened with Michael Gove's reform prisons initiative, set up when Gove was justice secretary but halted when he left in 2016. Stakeholders who seek to build relationships with a minister are constantly restarting from the beginning, and ministers are regularly being dropped into an emergency with no context or experience on the file. The change in ministers means two steps forward are followed by two steps backwards, and the next person appointed has still less space and time to address the problem. The same pattern often holds true for senior bureaucrats.[12] Having ministers around the cabinet table who have experience in a range of portfolios can be helpful in providing advice and expertise, but the cost is high in terms of long-term focus and relationships.

Thus, even if the same party remains in power, individual ministers and politicians have an incentive to focus on the here and now: regardless of the next election, their careers will be determined by the next year or two, and any long-term consequences of bad decisions will likely emerge after they have changed departments or roles. Pleasing the president or prime minister, impressing the media, responding to questions from peers all matter today: the fact that a project introduced by a minister will fail in a few years will likely not affect their career by then. Of course, politicians may still care about the future and want to do their best for the next generation, but it is challenging to maintain that focus when their career and personal incentives very much depend on the here and now.

* * *

The electoral cycle has another consequence: even if a country remains relatively stable, leaders change over time. This is more common in democracies, of course, but dictatorships also see regime change as leaders die or are overthrown. This can lead to inconsistency over time as different leaders take different positions or choose different directions for their country. In some cases, this can be a strength, as leaders correct errors of the past; in others it can prevent a consistent approach to solving problems. Above we saw that having transitions between governments reduces their incentive to plan, since they likely won't be in power by then anyway. It also creates a more practical problem: every time the government changes, planning can be thrown into chaos as a new head of government takes over, and some long-term decisions that have been taken may be intentionally reversed or simply not implemented.

The US is particularly prone to poor transitions between governments, in part because of the complexity of their system. When you think of presidential appointees, you likely think of the cabinet and top White House staff, perhaps thirty or forty people. That is a lot when you consider the significance of choosing people who will make billion- or trillion-dollar decisions, but it's manageable in the roughly seventy days between the election and inauguration.

The reality is much more complicated. Every time the party in power in the US changes, approximately four thousand positions must be filled, over one thousand of which require confirmation by the Senate. Many positions are never filled.[13] The new government must also prepare budget requests, write a State of the Union address, and then, as a sideline, actually start delivering on their campaign promises. They must do this despite often having little familiarity with the work of the various departments and agencies involved and being overwhelmed by the vast flood of information coming their way. By the time the new government fully grasps the challenges it faces, the next election has quite possibly already begun.

Some transitions are better than others. The Bush-Obama presidential transition in 2008 is often highlighted as particularly successful. To its credit, the Bush White House had prioritized a good transition, attempting to leave the incoming Obama administration as much information as they could to ensure a smooth transfer of power. Before the election had happened, and as Obama and Bush criticized each other during the 2008 campaign, senior officials from the Bush administration were meeting with members of both the

Republican and Democratic presidential candidate teams to start the planning process.[14]

Even that relatively successful transition experienced problems. Senate appointments still took months or more. In the 2009 financial crisis, there were many spots left unfilled at the Treasury. The Secretary of the Treasury Timothy Geithner was surrounded by empty desks, hardly conducive to planning a thoughtful response to a major crisis. And some balls were dropped. The Bush administration had invested considerable work in trying to improve government hiring processes, which can be depressingly slow. Hiring speed is hardly a partisan issue: Republicans and Democrats do not fight over the subject in election campaigns. Nevertheless, the Obama administration started all over again when they came into power, rather than learning from what had come before or building on it. Of course, that's nothing compared to the 2016 Trump transition, in which Trump fired his entire transition team on the day he was elected. Many departments never received new appointees, and some had their senior people pack up and leave without any sense of when new leaders might arrive.[15]

Once new leaders are appointed, governments may choose to reverse decisions of their predecessors as part of their campaign strategy. The situation is close to the ancient Greek historian Herodotus's (flawed) description of Persian customs: to make an important decision, they would discuss it while drunk, and then the following day have the same discussion while sober. If they took a decision sober, he reported, they would then schedule a time to reconsider it while drunk. Not an optimal design for consistent planning.

Long-term plans naturally take a long time to implement, and changes in leadership, goals, or the party in power can impede successful implementation. Sometimes, these changes reflect differences in opinion or direction: other times, new governments overturn the plans of their forebears not because they disagree but simply because they are distracted by their own priorities or because rejecting them delivers political or ideological rewards. As countries have become more polarized in recent years, this factor becomes increasingly problematic: there is little incentive for governments to implement long-term policies if they know their successors will immediately reverse them upon election.

As the above example of the Trump transition suggests, this effect is particularly strong when political outsiders win elections. Insiders, typically parties with a history of being in power, are less likely to shake up established ways of doing things. Outsiders, by contrast, may be more likely to overturn standard practices, reject norms, or confront existing institutions such as legislatures, creating more uncertainty for parties currently in power who find it difficult to anticipate their successors' actions.[16] Changing how things are done can be valuable when the status quo is dysfunctional, but the resulting instability further reduces the incentive for incumbent governments to plan long term. If there is a broader trend toward the election of outsider parties that seek dramatic changes to the system, it will likely further reduce the incentive for governments to plan beyond the end of their mandate. That said, it may bring benefits if voters are electing outsiders due to the failings of insiders.

Planning is still worthwhile, of course. If long-term plans are disrupted, planning can still have short-term benefits, compelling project teams to think through possible obstacles and issues, getting everyone on the same page, and helping inform program design, even if the actual plan changes over time. Good planning can also anticipate disruption and help design programs and policies that can weather the uncertainty elections introduce. Many projects continue across multiple governments, especially when the matter is less polarized. But election cycles can introduce chaos in the system, increasing the uncertainty planners face and disrupting long-term plans. In some cases, governments may decide it is not worth starting a long-term project or initiative if the election cycle creates too much uncertainty. Long-term programs, which require sustained attention and care to deliver, may wither.

One remedy sometimes proposed to mediate the impacts of election cycles is to move to a system with more centralized power and fewer democratic checks and balances. Supporters argue that fewer changes in government and leaders with more centralized power and less exposure to electoral pressures could increase the space leaders have for long-term planning. A monarch need not worry about election cycles or present-biased voters and can implement long-term policies by fiat even if there is opposition.

This has worked in some places. Lee Kuan Yew in Singapore, for example, is often recognized as one of the most successful politicians of his time. When he took power in 1959, Singapore was a poor country with no natural resources and a real per capita GDP of less than US$5,000. When he retired in 2011 Singapore was one of the wealthiest countries in the world, with a real per capita GDP of around $50,000 and a reputation for clean, incorruptible government (though not democracy) and orderly and prosperous living. Lee Kuan Yew didn't shy from this narrative, titling his memoir *From Third World to First: The Singapore Story: 1965–2000*.[17]

Lee Kuan Yew's success was in part due to long-term thinking: he invested heavily in education and anti-corruption, both policies which tend to have short-term costs but long-term payoffs. He was also an authoritarian, however: he was quick to use legislation to crush opposition and limit inflammatory speech, and Singapore has harsh penalties for law-breaking and a system that discourages strong opposition. It is possible that Lee Kuan Yew's ability to enact long-term policies was increased by the centralization of power under his party, and Singapore remains effectively a one-party state (though the popularity of his party has fallen somewhat in recent elections).

China is another example of a country with centralized control and power that has seen rapid economic growth, moving hundreds of millions of its citizens out of poverty and rapidly becoming a global power. Some observers have argued that its success in investing in long-term projects, such as smart cities and solar energy technology, is not despite its authoritarian approach but rather would not have been possible without it.[18] If only more countries were less democratic, the argument goes, they could focus on the long term and ignore the short-term pressures of an electorate, boosting economic growth, supporting innovation, fighting climate change, and otherwise leading to wiser and more thoughtful governance. Some scholars have gone further and rejected democracy entirely when it comes to future thinking. Jørgen Randers, professor of climate change strategy at the Norwegian School of Management, for example, has suggested that he does not "believe it will be possible to convince people to forgo potential consumption growth … [S]uccess in limiting consumption will require an element of benevolent authoritarianism."[19]

In my view, however, reducing democracy typically does not help support long-term thinking. Indeed, there are very few examples of dictatorships that fare better than the world's democracies in making long-term decisions, whether protecting the environment or keeping stable, clean, and trustworthy governments, with Singapore as a notable exception.[20] There are three reasons for this. First, dictators can themselves be short-termist, especially when it comes to their own power and avoiding being overthrown. The lack of checks and balances means they can inflict serious harm on their country in pursuit of their short-term goals. Even supposedly well-intentioned dictators frequently succumb to the temptation to do anything to preserve their own power, often with the justification that what is good for them is good for the country. Surrounded by obedient supporters, keeping a long-term perspective is not easy.

Second, dictatorships may seem to have a mania for planning cycles, as seen in the Soviet and to some extent Chinese governments, but they are not necessarily responsive to the wishes of the population or reacting to changes in preferences.[21] Almost by definition, dictatorships are not as good at gathering or responding to signals on the ground as democracies, which are designed to respond to the populace. This allows for more focused planning cycles but can also lead to catastrophe when plans are followed despite their clear failure, as exemplified in Soviet farming reforms. More recently, the Chinese response to the pandemic was initially extremely effective but struggled to keep up with changing conditions and the evolving pandemic, perhaps partly due to the limitations of the dictatorship model. As scholars have pointed out, modern societies are extremely complex, and dictatorships with centralized power are typically not well suited to understand and respond to the needs of the future.[22] Inclusive, deliberative-democratic processes are much better placed to judge what societies should collectively do because they are designed to help weigh the legitimate but conflicting concerns of the population.

Finally, recommending philosopher kings also tends to ignore the possibility of vagabond princes. Succession is a real challenge for dictatorships and other governments that invest significant power in a single individual or office. Absent checks and balances, one poor leader, which is almost inevitable at some point, can destroy what generations of good leaders have built. Investing ultimate power in a single person may address the challenges of electoral cycles, but it does so at a high long-term cost: the ability to check dictatorial power. A classic example of this cycle is from ancient Rome. Emperor Marcus Aurelius is perhaps best known either for his work of Stoic philosophy *Meditations*, a book still popular today for its reflections on self-mastery and Stoicism, or his representation in the movie *Gladiator*. Aurelius was the last of what are sometimes called the five good emperors; Rome flourished under Nerva, Hadrian, Antonius Pius,

Lucius Verus, and Marcus Aurelius. Edward Gibbon, one of the preeminent eighteenth-century historians, went so far as to argue it was the period of the world "during which the condition of the human race was most happy and prosperous."[23] One assumes slaves and other disadvantaged groups would not have agreed, but the period ended when Commodus, Marcus Aurelius's son, took over. With absolute power invested in the emperor, it took only a decade for him to usher in a period of megalomania, assassination, and chaos, culminating in the assassination of Commodus himself and a civil war in which five different men claimed the title emperor in the space of a single year. Burning libraries is easier than building them.

As Dani Rodrik, a Harvard economist who focuses on economic growth and development, has pointed out, for every Lee Kuan Yew there are many more terrible leaders under whom at best economic growth is poor and at worst the economy and people's lives are utterly ruined. Over the long term, democracies grow more predictably than authoritarian states, have more stability in economic performance, handle negative economic shocks better, and pay higher wages.[24] Even if a country currently has good leaders, investing absolute power in them or removing the checks and balances of democracy tends to lead to problems eventually. Curbing democracy is not a solution to short-termism: checks and balances are themselves an important part of long-term success.

SHORT-TERM VOTERS

Election cycles help drive government behaviour, but their impacts are worsened by the second factor influencing government planning: the preferences of voters themselves. Even absent the election effect, governments may not feel they will be rewarded for planning for the long term. Research has found, for example, that voters will reward a party for delivering disaster relief after a natural disaster occurs but not for investing in disaster preparedness spending.[25]

This stems from four related dynamics. First, voters have legitimate immediate needs, and those facing urgent problems are frequently also the most motivated to vote, write politicians, and attend political demonstrations. Second, voters are themselves present biased and care more about immediate problems than long-term gains. Third, for long-term issues, the people most impacted may not be born yet. And finally, and in some cases perhaps most importantly, voters may not trust governments to deliver what they promise. Even if voters are passionate about long-term policies, they may not bother to support them if they are doubtful that leaders will deliver them, whether due to cynicism about government incentives or skepticism about their competence. For all these reasons, voters may reward governments that also prioritize the present over the future, pressuring them to be short-termist.

The challenge of legitimate immediate needs crowding out attention to more long-term issues gets at the heart of the fact that governing is a matter of trade-offs, prioritizing one problem over another. By definition, this means some issues get more attention than others. If short-term priorities have the most vocal adherents, then they will also receive the most attention. That means immediate problems, such as the loss of jobs for fishing communities, can often outweigh long-term problems, such as the overexploitation of fish stocks. Of course, solving short-term problems is important, and this is not to diminish the importance of addressing immediate needs. Unfortunately, since preventing overfishing in the first place is typically much cheaper than trying to generate jobs in fishing communities and establish stability when the fish are gone, this short-term focus can be self-defeating for the country, even if it is good electoral politics. Too many communities have collapsed when the fish stocks did, as in the twentieth-century collapse of the Atlantic Canada cod fishery and subsequent bankrupting and disappearance of entire communities along the coast.

A second factor is that present-biased voters and other stakeholders (such as lobby groups) underrate policies that will help them in the future and overrate those that help them today. They are also reluctant to experience certain costs today for uncertain benefits in the long term. Importantly, this does not suggest that voters do not care at all about the future. As we have seen, research on present bias suggests they may care more about the present than they should, but the future still matters to them.

Present bias can affect which policies voters support and which parties they vote for. In work I did with Paolo Roberti at the Free University of Bozen-Bolzano, for example, we found that impatient voters are more likely to support governments that offered short-term rewards but long-term costs, a common feature of populist governments. In effect, these governments offer easy solutions to complex problems that are appealing in the short term but costly in the long run.[26] This tendency can be particularly bad because once populist governments are elected, they have an incentive to capture institutions to ensure their re-election. Without that capture, they face losing an election in the long term based on the costs of their policies. A populist government in power might seek to limit the independence of journalists, for example, or influence the Supreme Court and independent election body to ensure they win the next election. The more short-termist that voters are, the more likely that parties are to attempt this sort of corrupt behaviour.

In other words, voters' short-sightedness can lead to not only individual policies being short term but also a long-term corruption of institutions as populist governments struggle to stay in power over time. Short-sightedness can change the incentives for the government as a whole and trap voters in a scenario where, once the populists are elected, they make it increasingly hard to get rid of them. As Roberti and I find, countries with more short-termist citizens are more likely to elect populist governments providing short-term solutions. Voters in South American countries appear to have more short-term preferences, for example, which may be related to the climate and geography as well as the degree of development in that region, among other factors.[27] This may contribute to the success of populist governments there.

The rise of algorithms and social media threatens to heighten this short-term bias by voters. Algorithms trained on a given data set replicate the biases of that data set. If as humans we behave in short-term ways, then unless we are careful our algorithms will do the same. Research suggests, for example, that if Facebook algorithms are trained on data from people's use of the newsfeed, which people tend to click on fairly mindlessly and with significant bias, the result is very different than if those algorithms are trained on the people someone knows, which is based on who you decide to friend and is less of an automatic decision.[28] Once trained, however, these algorithms can then drive further behaviours, creating a reinforcing cycle of automatic decisions leading to algorithms that encourage more automatic behaviour, which then informs future algorithms. If that automatic behaviour is short-termist, as we can expect it to be based on human biases, then we may be creating a problem.

A third factor is that for the very long term a constituency may not exist yet. When governments are mulling over projects that will help our children or our children's children, that group may not be of voting age or even born. Future generations cannot raise issues, vote, or campaign on their own behalf, and this reality has two effects. First, they cannot contribute to or influence policy discussions and debate due to their lack of voice, so their potential interests and points of view are neglected in policy discussions. Second, democratic governments must respond to the issues voters care about or risk getting voted out of office, so naturally they focus on the issues that matter to voters today, not future voters. Both effects mean that in policy discussions and decisions, issues with implications for future generations who lack voices and votes are neglected or ignored. Since the unborn also can't buy or boycott products, their potential preferences are ignored by markets, compounding the problem.

This creates what is in some ways a tragedy of the commons. Voters benefit today by acting in a short-term manner, such as by overexploiting natural resources or using chemicals that will affect the health of future generations, and the costs are borne by future generations. Though voters may still want a good future, they are incentivized to be overly short-termist because they do not bear the full cost of their decisions, the future does.

A final dynamic underpinning pressure from voters for governments to be short-termist is uncertainty about whether governments will deliver what they promise. Politicians may renege on promises, a new government could take power and cancel a program, or other events could emerge which cause program failure or cancellation. Research finds that voter uncertainty can be the single biggest driver of voter short-termism, and reassuring voters about how likely delivery of a long-term policy is can help increase support for the policy.[29] The more complicated a policy or the further into the future its expected benefits, the more citizens may doubt its success, and if they are not sure the policy will succeed, then why bother pushing for it in the first place?

This can create a vicious cycle. If voters do not prioritize long-term issues, then governments do not take action on them, further fostering distrust and cynicism that make voters prioritize long-term issues even less. The decline of trust in government in many countries means this issue is likely to be an increasing challenge. As pressure increases on leaders to focus on the short-term, governments may increasingly struggle to deliver results in the long term, and trust may fall further. Efforts to increase public trust, though valuable, are often difficult and slow to succeed: trust takes time to build, and a citizen that already distrusts government will likely be skeptical of efforts to change that view from the government itself. Worse yet, governments who face low public trust may get caught in a trap where they find it hard to build public support for long-term policies that could improve public trust.[30] On the other hand, stable, well-functioning democracies with policies that have cross-party support can also benefit from the opposite dynamic, leveraging the trust their citizens have in government to create more space for long-term decisions.

* * *

The influence of short-term voters speaks to a tension between two different models of government. In one model, politicians are seen as delegates of those who elected them; they are meant to represent the views of their constituencies and not exercise any judgment or preferences of their own. The alternative is a trustee model in which politicians are chosen to act on behalf of their constituents but are trusted to use their own judgment and discretion to that end. Edmund Burke, a supporter of the second model, argued that "your representative owes you, not his industry only, but his judgement; and he betrays, instead of serving you, if he sacrifices it to your own opinion."[31]

If governments defer to the wishes of voters who demand short-term policies, they are following the delegate model of representation. Modern communications have given the public the ability to closely track their elected representatives, and increased transparency helps ensure governments are accountable to and engaged with citizens. This is generally good. Past politicians had tremendous scope for corruption in part due to the inability of their constituents to exercise oversight. In some cases, though, it can increase pressure on politicians to bow to public pressure for short-term solutions. If voters expect a politician to defer to their preferences at all times and they do not, then supporters will understandably be frustrated. That said, it is not enough to say that because voters are short-termist, they will always push their elected representatives to be the same: politicians retain considerable scope to vote differently than their constituents' preferences. Research suggests that in the US, legislators' votes align with the wishes of voters around 65 per cent of the time – frequently, but hardly every time.[32]

This deviation from the wishes of voters may be for good or for ill. In some cases, this may be politicians exercising their judgment about what is best, but in others it may reflect pressure from potential campaign donors and special interest groups. Unsurprisingly, research has found that the wishes of affluent groups in the US are far more powerful in predicting policy outcomes than the wishes of low- or middle-income Americans, though the wishes of lower-income groups are more influential shortly before elections, especially federal ones.[33] Voters may simply not have the time or interest to follow decisions facing Parliament or Congress, or they may feel less strongly about some issues and be prepared to grant political leaders more space to act on their own. In those situations, politicians must exercise their own judgment. Indeed, part of the role of leaders can be to change the views of voters. Influence goes both ways; though short-term voters may pressure leaders to be more short-termist, long-term leaders can also help change voter preferences.

Leaders are not all-powerful. One estimate is that around 20 per cent of voters align their votes to their favourite leader, while more than 30 per cent have a greater preference for their favourite party.[34] The impact of leadership also varies based on the issue, the country, and the leader involved, with highly polarized elections or less effective leaders reducing the potential impact. Leadership can be critical, however. The ability to move even a small percentage of voters on an issue can be essential to the success or failure of a policy. This effect also means that leaders are not just at the mercy of short-term voters; instead, long-term leaders can help encourage voters to be the same. Indeed, in the best case a virtuous feedback cycle is possible; structural changes that help leaders focus more on the long term can help them shift voter preferences to reflect the same, which in turn helps leaders be even more so. The opposite is also possible: as voters become more short-termist, they may start to select more short-term leaders, which further affects the electorate.

One example of the role of leadership is the recent highly unpopular changes to the French pension plan introduced by the French president Emmanuel Macron, including moving the state pension age from sixty-two to sixty-four. Agree or disagree with the changes, Macron's reforms are a clear case of leadership against the wishes of a large segment of the population, following, as it did, months of riots and protests. Macron and others have argued the reforms are essential to prevent a long-term collapse of the French pension plan, after decades of trying to solve the problem. At the time of writing, the long-term fate of those changes and whether they will survive a change in government is still unknown, but for them to succeed, Macron likely needs voters to gradually accept them. If the current level of opposition continues, the next president may well reverse the changes and be forced to explore other options to try to stabilize the pension plan. Either way, Macron's personal brand and leadership have certainly affected the discussion, with opponents drawing on existing criticisms of Macron as out of touch and elitist.

Though Macron's changes are an example of long-termist policy, in an unfortunate twist that compounds the incentive for governments to be short-termist, politicians too are subject to present bias. As a result, politicians may often underrate future plaudits for introducing beneficial long-term policies and overrate criticism they may get in the present for any costs associated with them. Politicians do have some space to act for the long term, even if voters focus on the present. But that space is limited. Politicians can survive voting against the wishes of their constituents from time to time, but they cannot do so on every issue, as exemplified by the damage that pensions reform has done to Macron's popularity. It is unreasonable to expect politicians to constantly act against their electoral interests, and if they did, they would rapidly be out of a job with more pliant politicians replacing them. The shorter term their constituents, the more pressure they may experience, pushing them to support short-term solutions or neglect long-term problems.

SHORT-TERM WORLD

As we have seen, election cycles and voters can both increase the pressure on politicians to act short term. A third factor echoes one of the pressures on individuals: the hyperactive modern world can distract governments from the long term and focus their attention on the present. If anything, the pressures are stronger on governments. Rapid technological change and constant flows of new information mean governments are required to react, not act, and are continuously flooded with a deluge of information.

In the 1930s and '40s then president Franklin D. Roosevelt delivered his fireside chats, a series of radio addresses on the Great Depression and World War II that were instrumental in quelling rumours and explaining his policies to the 60 million Americans listening (about half the total population at the time). He gave about thirty of these addresses over the twelve years of his presidency. When encouraged to do them more frequently, he responded:

> The one thing I dread is that my talks should be so frequent as to lose their effectiveness ... Every time I talk over the air it means four or five days of long, overtime work in the preparation of what I say. Actually, I cannot afford to take this time away from more vital things.[35]

Roosevelt's ability to think through and deliver the chats, a crucial part of his leadership with significant long-term benefits, came in part from how much time he could dedicate to preparing them. It is almost impossible to imagine a modern leader dedicating four or five days to a single topic or speech, much less doing so repeatedly. Instead, modern politicians, who address the public daily, speak less well than Roosevelt and spend less time focused on important long-term issues. A politician sending hourly tweets or one giving daily pandemic briefings has only so much time to spend on long-term decisions and also has less time to think through the content and its long-term implications.

Public administration scholar Donald Savoie notes that the lives of political leaders in the past were relatively leisurely, with the limited role of government both reducing the scope of issues to contend with and making it easier for leaders to keep up with the existing files.[36] In the early 1900s Woodrow Wilson reputedly worked only three to four hours per day, and Calvin Coolidge slept eleven hours per day. The schedules of today's elected officials and bureaucrats, in contrast, can be punishing. It is easy to forget the enormous scale that modern governments operate at. They are comparable to the largest of multinational corporations, employing hundreds of thousands of people, collecting and spending billions or trillions of dollars, and with responsibilities across the country and in many other countries. Even when governments identify a few key priorities, the everyday business of sending out benefit cheques, helping people find jobs, and collecting taxes must go on.

A politician may well wake up in the morning determined to do something about climate change or government debt, but on any given day they may face constituents who have lost their passports; a petition put forward by a group of voters on a subject the politician knows nothing about; and a request from their president or prime minister to appear on a news show later that day to speak for the party on a story that has emerged in the past twenty-four hours. This issue is not limited to elected officials. Consider this extract from Roderick Rhodes's lovely "Everyday Life in a Ministry," an ethnographic research project looking at the lives of permanent secretaries, the most senior unelected officials in the British government (equivalent to deputy ministers in Canada, departmental secretaries in Australia, and chief executives in New Zealand):

> First, the permanent secretary's schedule is hectic. His life is a continuous series of meetings, planned and unplanned. The pace is fast and unrelenting. In all three private offices, the private office told me the permanent secretary wanted to avoid back-to-back meetings, and in every office the permanent secretary had them most days of most weeks. Thus, at 4:00 p.m., the permanent secretary arrives at his fifth meeting that day and cannot remember why he is there. He confesses to his lapse of memory, asks a junior colleague "to get him up to speed," then takes over the meeting after a few minutes when he remembers ... Thinking time, writing time, reading time: all were at a premium.[37]

Permanent secretaries and deputy ministers are at the mercy of their calendars, and their calendars are largely filled with short-term updates and day-to-day issues. Crises frequently emerge, and when they do strategy comes second to crisis response, with everything else on hold until the crisis is resolved. If ministers do not ask for strategy and long-term thinking from their officials, it is difficult for officials to dedicate time to providing it. The same is true elsewhere. Alexander Evans, a career diplomat who has also held posts at Yale, Harvard, and the Library of Congress, cites interviews with senior officials in the Bush and Obama administrations, and "each found urgent operational work trumped long-range thinking. Operational work was visible, and guaranteed time with the president and senior cabinet officials. Strategic work was less visible unless tied to a specific operational challenge."[38]

The need for politicians to respond to short-term urgencies is not new. Harold Macmillan, UK prime minister from 1957 to 1963, supposedly complained that the worst part of being prime minister was: "Events, my dear boy, events." But past politicians had fewer demands on their time and faced significantly less pressure to respond to events in real time, in contrast to today's twenty-four-hour news cycle as well as the rate of change of underlying events and the speed at which reactions spread across social media. Tony Blair, the former prime minister of Britain, complained that when he campaigned in the 1990s, he handled one issue per day; by 2005, it was three, with the first two already forgotten by the evening interview.[39] Yet, the news cycles Macmillan and Blair faced look primitive compared to a world of Facebook, X, and fake news. A modern leader might have to respond to questions on dozens of different topics over the course of a day, and in some cases send dozens of tweets. Many governments seem unable to get beyond responding to short-term events, and like individuals, the number of short-term distractions requiring attention is higher than ever.

Attending to short-term crises is not wrong, of course. Some events require the full attention of a government and prioritizing them over the long-term may be correct. No government spent 2008, the peak of a financial crisis, or 2020, in the jaws of COVID-19, worrying about long-term issues. The problem is that when a government devotes itself to a short-term issue, long-term issues may languish or grow steadily worse. When that short-term issue is a major crisis, as in the two examples above, this is understandable. However, the focus of the day is often caught up with strings of smaller, more political events: corruption scandals, public relations disasters, or news from abroad that consumes attention and focus.

The sheer scale of incoming information and news for a modern politician can be hard to fathom. Sorting information is often more of a challenge than finding it.[40] New ideas and technologies emerge quickly and spread faster. Carl Benedikt Frey and Michael Osborne, two economists best known for estimating that nearly half of US jobs could be automated in the next twenty years, point out that telephones took seventy-five years to reach 50 million users; Facebook took three and a half years; and *Angry Birds*, the digital game, took thirty-five days to reach the same number.[41] Every *minute* in 2023, the world watched forty-three years of streaming content, did 6.3 million Google searches, sent 41.6 million WhatsApp messages and 241 million emails, and liked 4 million Facebook posts, producing a total of about 100 megabytes of data per person per minute or the equivalent of hundreds or thousands of pages of text.[42] This speed is not just limited to technology either. New fashion trends, cultural practices, viral videos, and other phenomena can spread like wildfire across social media.

Unfortunately for our leaders, they are often expected to have opinions on and responses to all these events and trends before they have had a chance to reflect. Worse yet, a single ill-considered reaction or comment can itself become a meme or social media event, consuming yet more bandwidth and time and generating more short-term pressure. No politician wants to go viral for saying something that makes them look unprepared or ignorant.

Even within their own bailiwick, individual politicians are expected to have thoughtful and informed opinions about new bills or legislation moments after they are released, despite the fact that bills may run to hundreds of pages. Electorates and a twenty-four-hour news cycle demand instant opinions and action in response to an endless stream of new events. There is little time for sober reflection or analysis and little ability to maintain focus on the long term.

The recent surge in attention toward the power and potential of AI is just one example of both the pace of technological change and the pressure it creates for politicians to respond. Prophets of AI warn of the potential for world-ending consequences if the right policy decisions are not made, while the technology continues to evolve and change in real time. Politicians are under significant pressure to respond, often without having had the time to understand or use the technology themselves. There is also a constant stream of related news to which they have to react; new AI firms being created, new technological applications or risks emerging, new AI researchers making public statements or calling on governments to do something. None of these things are necessarily bad, but a politician could be forgiven for feeling overwhelmed. A politician in the fifteenth century hoping to fully understand the printing press and assess its long-term consequences could have taken decades to assess the risks, while one worried about the privacy implications of AI today must respond to daily updates.

The modern twenty-four-hour media can make this incoming pressure more acute. The media is an ever-present threat lurking in the background, and ministers and bureaucrats live in a "media goldfish bowl that can take any problem and turn it into a crisis."[43] Twenty years ago, this was sometimes referred to as the CNN effect: the ability of the media to affect how governments prioritize issues by focusing immediate or ongoing coverage onto a topic. Sometimes, this is good:

it can raise the profile of issues that politicians might otherwise prefer to ignore. Today though the media often ends up going from short-term crisis to short-term crisis, focusing governments on an issue just long enough to create some soundbites, then moving to the next issue.

The twenty-four-hour news cycle means that there is always some sort of story going on that requires a response, but in order to fill twenty-four hours of news there is a continuous need for the next story. Media outlets have realized that the public tires of hearing about the same thing, no matter how important; however, always presenting something new means constantly looking for new comments or responses from politicians and governments. As Howard Rosenberg and Charles S. Feldman, both former journalists, relate in their book *No Time to Think*, the key factor in the modern news cycle is speed: getting it right is replaced by getting it first.[44] The result, they point out, can be mistakes as well as a public that loses faith in traditional media. Being ready to answer questions from the media can be a full-time job for a politician: thinking about the long term rapidly becomes impossible. This pace can be frustrating for journalists as well. One respected Canadian journalist points out that a few decades ago, there were no web editions or blogs, or a Sunday version of some papers, so they could attend a political event on the weekend, contemplate the impact, and write a thoughtful story in time for the Monday deadline.[45] Today, that seems like an unimaginable luxury.

It can be tempting to blame the media for short-termism and accelerating an already short news cycle. In truth, twenty-four-hour news coverage is the result, not the cause, of many of these trends. In a hyper-accelerated world, the rapid rate of change means it is natural for citizens to demand fresh news on an ongoing basis, and the media responds to that demand. In a world where new apps are released daily and technology is continuously updated, it is understandable that citizens feel pressure to stay up to date. In meeting this need, the media also reinforces the trend, leading to a still greater sense of acceleration.

The rapid news cycle has benefits: the public gets access to news quickly, and the media plays an invaluable role in society supporting transparency and accountability. The problem is that even when the information is correct, the deluge of information means that readers don't have time to absorb or assess it. The recent rise in concerns over fake news points to a readership that does not have time to evaluate the reliability of what they read, instead sharing information without pause. It also means politicians must be up to date on every possible issue whenever they speak to the media.

* * *

What impact does this torrent of information have on governments and leaders? First, it may focus government attention on short-term issues directly. The impact of media attention can be particularly problematic because of what are called *attention cascades*. In effect, as people start to pay attention to an issue, other people assume the issue must be important and start paying attention themselves, further accelerating the cascade.[46] This can focus attention on the short term, since the media often does not prioritize stories based on long-term importance.

In one study of five thousand natural disasters, for example, gradual disasters such as famines and droughts required thousands of times more deaths than sudden and highly visible crises such as volcanoes and earthquakes to draw the same amount of media attention.[47] Disasters that had more news coverage received a larger response from authorities, but it is not clear why some types of death should be prioritized by authorities over others.[48] Politicians that rely on headlines as a way of identifying what to focus on are over-focused on highly visible, short-term issues, and under-focused on slow-burn, long-term issues, at least until the long-term issue sparks a crisis itself. In other words, they are short-sighted.

Even a government that is elected hoping to address long-term issues may find they are swept up in a current of events and short-term urgencies that prevents them from doing so. The modern world has increased the pressure on politicians to react and respond in the now, making it harder for them not to get caught up in the constant day-to-day churn of events that require responses or spin. In the clamour around the short-term, governments can struggle to identify or prioritize long-term issues.

The volume of information and the need to react immediately also affect the psychological state of decision-makers. Work by Sendhil Mullainathan and Eldar Shafir, professors at the University of Chicago and Princeton University respectively, has highlighted how the experience of scarcity can make it difficult for people in poverty to plan for the future or think beyond the needs of the immediate moment.[49] Politicians and senior bureaucrats may not be low income, but they are desperately short of time, and this can lead to a scarcity mindset, narrowing attention and even reducing IQ. Scarcity focuses us on the immediate problem, creating a sort of tunnel vision that means we neglect other concerns. Unfortunately, the more we expect politicians to respond to the constant stream of crises and other events, the more a scarcity mindset can manifest, leading to increasing neglect of the long term. Just as income scarcity can drive decisions that solve a short-term problem but create a long-term one, such as borrowing from a payday lender, so too politicians may be tempted to take the short-term fix to whatever problem confronts them, even if it creates a long-term issue.

As Mullainathan and Shafir point out, policy-makers can be quick to judge the poor as irrational or unmotivated to do better, when they should be asking whether there are situational factors leading to specific behaviours. The same holds true for politicians: if our modern world forces them into a cycle of scarcity, then we need to find ways to help them manage or avoid that cycle and the short-sighted tunnel vision it can create. Payday borrowing and short-term political action can represent a response to scarcity, a need to put out fires, rather than a lack of awareness or sophistication.

Businesses face the same problems. CEOs may not be selected through regular elections, but they face tremendous pressure to respond to the now, from quarterly earnings reports, regular investor calls, and other channels. Twenty-four-hour news cycles mean businesses must constantly respond to events, derailing long-term planning or prioritization and creating a scarcity mindset. Unfortunately, this can often cripple their future. A 2017 study argued that based on five criteria – investing relatively little, cutting costs to boost margins, initiating lots of buy-backs, booking sales before customers pay, and hitting quarterly profit forecasts – 73 per cent of firms are focused on the short term.[50] The remaining, relatively long-term-focused 27 per cent of firms performed better than their peers in terms of revenue growth, investment rates, stock price growth, and number of jobs created.

Though it is still emerging, AI may also increase the distractions facing policy-makers. AI provides a way to promptly produce endless custom, unique letters about a topic that can be sent to politicians or used to provide input on a given policy. What does it mean to run a consultation and ask the public for input if 10 million letters are received in response, with 99 per cent of them written by an AI controlled by a single individual or group? The rise in deepfakes and other fake but realistic AI-generated content ultimately means more noise that can drown out important long-term issues. Of course, AI may also provide tools for politicians to identify and negate distractions. Time will tell whether AI ends up a help or a hindrance. But in the short run the development of the technology is likely to complicate rather than simplify things as society struggles to adapt to AI's new capabilities.

In summary, the deluge of events and information in the modern world can both focus attention on short-term crises and provoke politicians into a state of scarcity, narrowing their focus and ability to plan for the long term. In the same way that such interruptions can preclude deep work by individuals, they can do the same for politicians, who are forced to respond to the day-to-day rather than ensure they are tackling the key issues. In a world where a Twitterstorm can provoke a scandal or provoke resignations in hours, governments do not have the luxury of taking time to reflect and plan. We live in a very different world than that of Roosevelt's fireside chats, where the president of the United States could take four or five days to prepare a single, high-impact speech.

The modern world is marked, perhaps above all, by the speed at which information flows. Our governments do not have the option of turning off or tuning out. Instead, they must find ways to stream out the unimportant or non-essential so that they can prioritize the important, or they will find themselves drowned in minutiae, struggling to respond to every crisis before ending their time in office and realizing they have not yet achieved anything of note.

OTHER FACTORS IN GOVERNMENT SHORT-SIGHTEDNESS

Behavioural science helps highlight how all three factors discussed above can pressure governments to be present biased, similar to their impact on individuals. Of course, this is not the whole story. Governments are complex organizations, and a wide range of cultural, institutional, and other arrangements can affect how they take decisions and the reforms they might adopt, independent of any behavioural element and regardless of whether there is a temporal element to the decision or not.[51] These arrangements can also limit or exacerbate the impact of the election cycles, short-term voters, and attention scarcity explored above. The breadth in variation between governments and countries makes it impossible to capture all factors that might apply, but this section explores a few other features of interest.

We have already seen one example of how the selection process for leaders can impact short-termism: elections. Democracies are perhaps particularly vulnerable to some of the modern pressures that lead to short-termism given their reliance on voter support. The less a leader relies on voter support to stay in power, the less they need to grapple with elections, short-term voter preferences, or the twenty-four-hour news cycle.[52] Although as we saw earlier dictatorships can have their own problems related to the lack of checks and balances, poor information flow, and leadership succession.

A related issue is the question of term limits and how long leaders can stay in office. In the US, for example, no person can be elected to the office of president more than twice, while in Canada prime ministers can serve as long as they keep winning elections. Intuitively, we might expect that term limits increase the potential for long-term thinking, because in their second term a leader has a reduced incentive to care about electoral results since they cannot run anyway. Evidence for this, however, is mixed. Some research suggests that term limits can reduce long-term policy effectiveness by reducing the incentive for politicians to maintain their reputation in their final term.[53] In simple terms, if a leader does not need to win another election, in their second term they may choose to focus on long-term issues, but they may equally focus on other projects or simply work less hard. Other research has found that term limits may reduce the time legislators dedicate to securing spending for special interests and focus more on other concerns, which may be good for long-term policy-making.[54] Term limits may also increase instability by leading to more frequent changes in leadership, disrupting long-term initiatives, and reducing the expertise at the top.[55] The impact of term limits on long-term thinking is therefore somewhat mixed and likely dependent on different factors or circumstances. Of course, there are other reasons for term limits, such as reducing the concentration of political power in a limited set of actors and reducing the barriers to entry for new leaders.

Countries also vary in which government roles are elected, including members of cabinet as well as upper houses such as a senate. In Canada the unelected Senate explicitly seeks to provide what is often called a sober second thought on laws introduced by the House of Commons. Senators are appointed based on regional representation and once appointed their terms last until they are age seventy-five. Their roles are intended to provide a check on the decisions of the House of Commons and ensure that regional interests are captured in discussions, while still generally deferring to the elected House of Commons. As one senator has written, though the Senate has significant constitutional powers, success requires "a practice of voluntary self-restraint and reasonable deference to the elected House of Commons."[56]

The Senate is thus weaker in Canada than in the US, where it is an elected body. However, by forcing the government to re-explain its thinking and defend key decisions, as well as by proposing amendments to laws, the Senate helps provoke reflection and public discussion. And since senators do not need to win elections or generally defend themselves to the media and public, they are sheltered from some of the short-term pressures discussed above. Senators' long terms, lasting until they are age seventy-five, also mean they often have institutional memory that a recently elected government may lack. Though long-term considerations are not explicitly included in its mandate, by its nature the Senate provides an opportunity for the long term to be considered.

Though it has been criticized for being undemocratic, and thus potentially less responsive to the needs of the population, the Canadian Senate can help bring a sober, longer-term perspective.[57] As I discuss later, however, there is room to further improve the Senate's focus on the future. The Senate could set up a dedicated committee focused on the long term, for example, or formally include the long term as part of their assessment of bills. Its mandate to consider the impact of legislation on the various regions of Canada could naturally extend to considering the impact of legislation on future generations. And if constitutional changes were made its membership could be revised to include representatives of the future.

Another factor that can affect long-term thinking in government is how much power is centralized with the leader. Donald Savoie has described Canada and the UK as "court governments" where power lies almost entirely with the prime minister and a few senior advisers.[58] The priorities of the prime minister can be delivered quickly and effectively, while issues that do not matter to them get bogged down in process and delay. In contrast, the Australian prime minister must negotiate with an independently elected Senate, while an American president must navigate an often-difficult Congress. This centralization of power may be helpful if the president or prime minister is actively focused on the long term; however, as a key political figure and one of the busiest people in the country, the leader is often particularly subject to the short-term pressures described above. The more power is centralized in a single or small set of individuals, the more individual present bias may affect decisions across the government. In addition, an understandable scarcity mindset may set in if one person is trying to make decisions on everything, further increasing focus on the present.

In the US, the direct election of the president personalizes American politics and increases the emphasis on the president as the symbol of the elected party. This emphasis on the party leader is increasingly visible in other jurisdictions, in a trend referred to as the presidentialization of politics.[59] Presidentialization further increases the power and impact of individual leaders and the role of leadership in influencing the national dialogue and priorities, whether through Rooseveltian fireside chats or Trumpian tweets. As the Roosevelt and Trump examples illustrate, this centralization of power can magnify the impact of an individual leader, which can be positive or negative.

Different institutional designs can also affect the demands on leaders' time, adding to the short-term pressures or carving out space for long-term thinking. The US system, for example, places enormous emphasis on fundraising. In preparation for the 2022 mid-term elections, research suggests US members of Congress spent about thirty hours per week fundraising from call centres, almost an additional full-time job on top of their actual responsibilities.[60] Quite apart from any biases to the political process this might induce, one imagines that members of Congress find their minds turning constantly to the short term when so much of their time is consumed with daily funding targets rather than legislation or policy-making. The future is easily lost in the shuffle of these short-term priorities (and derailed by special interest groups who make campaign contributions and may also be short-termist or seeking to defend the status quo).

Finally, the division of powers can also matter. In the US the strong division of powers comes with a large number of checks and balances and what are called veto points, opportunities for organized groups to block policies they oppose. Given long-term policies are often difficult to enact because they impose short-term costs on at least some groups (if there were no costs, they would be uncontroversial), the increased number of veto points can reduce governments' ability to invest for the long term by increasing the opportunities for smaller subgroups to veto a decision. As Alan M. Jacobs notes, how much this limits long-term policy-making can depend on how vetoes and political influence are distributed across groups, how confident a government is about winning the next election, and the power of the government to push through the various checks and balances (e.g., because of a large majority).[61]

* * *

The above factors largely relate to the selection and power of elected officials. However, the functions and role of unelected officials and bureaucrats can be as important in how short-termism is encouraged or passed through the system. In theory, the unelected officials who make up bureaucracies and support elected leaders can help with the long term because they are not subject to election cycles and so are more (though not entirely) sheltered from the media and the need to respond to the day-to-day. The fact that bureaucrats typically continue in their role across multiple elections positions them to develop long-term relationships with stakeholders and deeper subject matter expertise. By offering a continuous perspective on policy issues that is more insulated from short-term political pressures, the bureaucracy can stay focused on the future, even when elected leaders focus on the short term. Joseph Heath, professor at University of Toronto's Munk School of Global Affairs and Public Policy, notes in his excellent study of the role of the civil service that unelected officials are frequently delegated considerably more power than the common conception of the state as a single hierarchy with all major decisions taken by the political head would suggest.[62] This is particularly true of Westminster systems such as Australia, Canada, or the UK, which tend to have a largely permanent class of officials with considerable expertise.

In practice, though, bureaucracies, whether Westminster or not, often struggle with short-termism. Advising a minister who is focused on the short-term inevitably pressures bureaucrats to do the same. Bureaucrats may prioritize urgent over long-term issues, whether due to a shortage of resources, the pressure of day-to-day crises, or a lack of demand from elected officials, and can also be overly focused on individual transactions and micromanaging specific files when a crisis flares up.[63] Scholars have expressed concern about the capacity of public services to provide strategic, long-term advice.[64] Public services can be a significant force for long-term thinking; however, for what is in many ways a permanent institution, they can still be deeply affected by short-termism in the system.

Part of what determines this short-termism is the relationship between the bureaucracy in a department and their minister, both informal and formal. The relationship was famously lampooned in *Yes Minister*, the hit British TV series that featured Sir Humphrey Appleby, the senior public servant in a department, constantly outwitting his neophyte minister. Appleby's deep experience and networks across the government meant that he almost always got his way over his minister, despite his minister's best efforts. In practice, there is more truth in this than bureaucrats would like to admit and less than politicians fear. Bureaucrats do have influence on policy decisions, but ultimately ministers call the shots, especially on priority or high-level decisions.

The relationship can be mediated by other groups. In many countries, ministers employ partisan-political appointees who are not elected but are also not members of the bureaucracy and work directly for the minister. These offices can play a range of roles, including overseeing communications, advising, and managing issues and stakeholders, many of which originally lay with the bureaucracy but in recent decades have moved to these partisan appointees. Arising partly as a result of the vast increase in work and demands on ministers but also as a way to check bureaucratic power, in many jurisdictions these appointees now provide a distinct source of advice focused on political considerations.[65] This division of labour between the office and the bureaucracy can be helpful, providing a source of political advice and perspective for the minister. However, if the office is focused on political or short-term issues management, then this may encourage the minister to focus on the same.

The existence of dedicated units within the bureaucracy to focus on the long term may help advance long-term thinking by sheltering the work from more short-term pressures, but they often have their own limitations. In Canada, for example, Policy Horizons is an organization dedicated to foresight and taking a future-oriented mindset. Unfortunately, it is divorced from the decision process in the Canadian government. Although it does interesting work, many public servants have never heard of the organization, and its impact on policy decisions is unclear.[66] The independence of Policy Horizons helps protect it from short-term pressures, but there is an inevitable trade-off in terms of influence and impact. Another model is the UK Prime Minister's Delivery Unit, which was set up to keep focus on implementing key long-term priorities even while the government was distracted and is discussed further later on. Other advisory services, such as think tanks, consultants, and lobbyists, may bring fresh ideas into the policy process, but can also be more subject to short-term pressures from stakeholder groups or the media, passing their short-termism to the government.

Short-termist or not, bureaucracies also have their own limitations. It is the bureaucracy that is stereotyped as full of employees of the Department of Motor Vehicles: infamously slow, obsessed with process, and unresponsive to user needs. Politicians may be more subject to short-term pressures, but trying to excessively insulate the bureaucracy from political pressures, as is sometimes suggested, can limit democratic legitimacy and risk government becoming overly disconnected or detached from the needs of society.[67]

* * *

As the preceding discussion illustrates, the range of factors that can pressure a government to be short-termist is broad. Governments are large, complex organizations, varying widely between and within countries. Drawing on work by Jonathan Boston and Alan M. Jacobs, both scholars who have written on government short-termism, a broader list of key considerations and institutions that can affect government short-termism could include:[68]

- basic constitutional arrangements (e.g., a federal or unitary state, presidential or parliamentary leadership, representative or direct democracy, and other checks and balances);
- number and design of legislative institutions (e.g., whether there are two legislative bodies, and whether they are elected);
- design of electoral systems, including election frequency and voting rules;
- rules on political finance, especially campaign finance;

- nature of the party system, the number of parties, and negotiations between them;
- design and staffing of the bureaucracy, including appointment process for senior staff and length of tenure;
- budgetary process and how funding is allocated across priorities;
- level of delegation of decision rights on issues to non-elected officials;
- existence, or lack thereof, of future-focused institutions;
- nature of interest groups, their political strength, and how much they may push for one policy over another;
- electoral safety, strength of opposition parties, and how concerned a government is with popular support;
- nature of policies or problems under consideration (e.g., who will benefit from a policy in the future, ability to defer costs or bring forward some benefits, and complexity of benefits to explain);
- level of uncertainty around the impact of a long-term issue, or how successful a proposed response will be;
- sufficient institutional capacity to develop and implement long-term policies;
- preferences, goals, cognitive disposition, and causal beliefs of leaders and their ability to sway voters;
- political culture and dominant values, including polarization;
- analytical frameworks used for developing policy advice; and
- strength of short-termist pressures in business and the not-for-profit sector.

All these factors can affect the pressure on governments to be short-termist. Though it can be tempting to assume that democratic political leaders are driven solely by a desire to maximize their chance of winning elections, in practice a range of factors influence their behaviour, including their own preferences, other political institutions, and their choices in the face of uncertainty.[69] Decision-makers do try to assess the costs and benefits of any proposal, for the country as a whole and for particular groups, and this can include future generations. The pressures to focus on the present, however, can make it difficult.

There may also be other biases at play. Governments are subject to behavioural biases of many kinds. In the Behavioural Insights Team report *Behavioural Government*, they observe that how governments notice issues, how they deliberate on them, and then how they execute their decisions can all be subject to a variety of biases, from confirmation and optimism bias to the illusion of control.[70] These biases may not specifically relate to short-termism, but in some contexts they can still focus the government on short-term priorities.

Ultimately, governments take decisions in a complicated, frequently chaotic environment with a wide range of players and interest groups. They may face considerable uncertainty about the impact of their decisions or policies, or considerable pressure from voters and lobby groups to act in a certain way. The modern media and focus on the present combined with the volume of information and scarcity of time for leaders to think and reflect all heighten short-termism. Helping our leaders carve out more time to think long-term and increasing the incentives for them to do so are priorities for resisting short-termism, as we shall explore in the rest of this book.

How do we encourage governments to be more long-termist? Weighted against the increasingly strong incentives for governments to be short-termist, the key is to create incentives for them to focus on the future. Governments may be structured to be short-termist and biased toward the present, but there are other biases we can leverage to nudge them in the other direction by introducing more behaviourally informed governance.

Faced with multiple reasons to focus on the short term and prioritize urgent tasks, our democratic systems need to create incentives for governments to think beyond tomorrow and keep the future at the forefront of their policy agendas. Four major strategies, informed by strategies individuals use, can help: measure the right outcomes to take advantage of salience and availability bias, make long-term planning the easy option to take advantage of the human bias to do what is easy, commit governments to specific decisions by creating costs to deviate, and take an agile approach that allows for experimentation and learning instead of seeking to predict the future. In effect, today's governments can implement changes that help nudge the governments and leaders of tomorrow to focus more on the future. It is to those that we turn next, starting with ancient Venice and the birth of gross domestic product (GDP).

PART TWO

Solutions

5

Measure What Matters

> Gross National Product counts air pollution and cigarette advertising, and ambulances to clear our highways of carnage. It counts special locks for our doors and the jails for the people who break them. It counts the destruction of the redwood and the loss of our natural wonder in chaotic sprawl. It counts napalm and counts nuclear warheads and armored cars for the police to fight the riots in our cities. It counts Whitman's rifle and Speck's knife, and the television programs which glorify violence in order to sell toys to our children.
>
> Yet the gross national product does not allow for the health of our children, the quality of their education or the joy of their play. It does not include the beauty of our poetry or the strength of our marriages, the intelligence of our public debate or the integrity of our public officials. It measures neither our wit nor our courage, neither our wisdom nor our learning, neither our compassion nor our devotion to our country, it measures everything in short, except that which makes life worthwhile.
>
> Robert F. Kennedy, "Remarks at the University of Kansas, 18 March 1968"

Venice in the sixteenth century was the second-largest city in Europe and one of the richest in the world, despite some recent reverses against the Ottomans. Thanks to the Venetian Arsenal, Venice also did an excellent job measuring and building its long-term wealth. The Arsenal was a complex of shipyards and armories representing one of the earliest large-scale industrial sites in history and dedicated to the construction and maintenance of the Venetian fleet. Covering 45 hectares (15 per cent of Venice), its sixteen thousand employees included Galileo, who worked as a consultant to address problems faced by shipbuilders, and made it a respectably sized medieval town all on its own. As much as 10 per cent of the Venetian government's annual revenues were spent on maintaining the site.[1]

The Arsenal was a hive of activity. Different areas were devoted to producing various parts of ships or other maritime supplies, including munitions, rope, and rigging. Up to one hundred ships could be held in different stages of production and maintenance. Using a canal, the Arsenal also had a moving assembly line: galleys floated down the canal and were brought to the appropriate workers, a technique that would not become popular elsewhere until the Industrial Revolution. Hundreds of years before Henry Ford, the Arsenal could build a ship in an assembly-line process in less than a day. Constructing a similar vessel in the rest of Europe could take months. The entire Venetian fleet – over three thousand ships at its peak – was in a constant cycle of maintenance at the Arsenal, with shipwrights repairing damage and preventing the salty Mediterranean from eating away at the vessels.

The Arsenal gave Venice the power to control the Mediterranean, making the city one of the richest and strongest powers in Europe. Its merchant vessels and warships dominated Mediterranean commerce and advanced Venice's interests, supporting the palaces and art that still attract tourists today. Importantly for us, the Arsenal also reflects a focus on measuring what matters.

Venice didn't just keep track of how many ships they had or how many new ships they produced in a year: they also carefully maintained and upgraded their existing ships. Their fleet, more than anything else, was their national wealth, and they measured and maintained it carefully. Today, maritime fleets are less central to national wealth, but infrastructure like roads or broadband, the natural environment, the health of the population, the quality of national institutions, and a range of other factors make our countries good or bad places to live. Unfortunately, the most commonly used measure of government performance often neglects these factors, focusing instead on gross domestic product (GDP).

MAKING THE FUTURE SALIENT

GDP tracks how much a country has produced in a year. It measures the flow of income, similar to your annual salary, instead of the stock of wealth, comparable to net worth. The focus on GDP distorts government incentives, encouraging them to focus on short-term increases to national income and neglecting long-term increases to national wealth. This chapter focuses on the unfortunate reality that governments, the media, and public discussions of government performance often track and consider national income, but spend less time measuring national wealth. We focus on GDP but not on what I call GDW, *gross domestic wealth*.

As we see in chapter 4, one reason governments don't care much about the future is simple: voters don't hold them to account for it, and by the time problems arise an election has happened and the government has changed. One reason is that governments and citizens frequently have little idea what impact their decisions are having on the future because governments do not measure it. Without measures, governments cannot be held to account for their decisions. What's more, research on human biases suggests that what we choose to measure can have a significant impact on behaviour.[2] If we measure learning through standardized exams, teachers may focus on what will be tested; if we measure the number of calls taken in a call centre, employees may cut calls short or be less helpful. What is measured matters, though what matters may not be easily measured.

The effect can be subtle. For example, including the cost of a tax in the posted price reduces how much people buy.[3] Either way they pay the tax in the end, but in the US the tax is added at checkout, while in the UK it is included in the sticker price, and that discourages people from buying as much in the UK. Most people could use their phone to make the calculation, but they don't. We simply accept the information we're given and base our decision on it, without considering other factors. This is the salience bias: we focus on information that is obvious or easily accessible and neglect information that is less prominent.[4] Measuring or tracking something can make it more salient, affecting our decisions. For instance, measuring information about energy use can help reduce household energy consumption, about spending can encourage saving, and about calories can affect dietary decisions.[5] Indeed, one of the few things that correlates with losing weight is weighing yourself every day.[6]

A second human bias can come into play. The availability bias is based on the observation that we assume what we can easily remember is more important than things we struggle to recall. For example, when asked if there are more words in the English language that have *k* as the first or the third letter, most people believe there are more in the first category. Daniel Kahneman, the Nobel Prize–winning behavioural scientist, suggested with his co-author Amos Tversky this is because it is much easier to remember words that begin with *k*. In fact there are three times as many words with *k* in the third position as in the first.[7] Similarly, seeing news stories about airline accidents or lightning strikes can make people believe these are more common than less featured topics such as car accidents, even though the latter are vastly more common. If we don't measure an issue, government employees or politicians may well neglect or forget about it, reducing its perceived importance.

The impact of what is measured can be significant. The former Facebook employee Frances Haugen, in her whistleblower testimony to Congress, suggested that Facebook's choice of metrics meant it prioritized number of users and social interactions over decreasing misinformation or hate speech. Bonuses were tied to maximizing social interactions. In that environment, she argued, it didn't matter that social interactions might be encouraging problematic content or putting users at risk, because the only yardstick that counted was increasing social interactions. Facebook executives were making short-term decisions that increased growth and users but also made it a more toxic platform.

What organizations choose to measure affects what their employees value and do. That said, measurement isn't everything. Measures themselves may be flawed or limited, and not everything can be easily measured. More abstract concepts such as creativity or the meaning derived from serving your community may not be as easy to measure as profit or number of widgets produced, but that doesn't mean they are less valuable. Economists can measure the statistical value of a human life by assessing how much people would be willing to pay to avoid the risk of injury or death, and doing so is essential in making policy decisions such as how much to invest in road safety, but people often find the idea of putting a dollar value on a life uncomfortable and intuitively disagree with the values that result.[8] Just measuring something may also be inadequate if the information is not salient or presented in a behaviourally compelling way, as we see in the next chapter.

The bottom line is that measuring our long-term impact on the future is a foundational element of fighting government short-termism, letting us harness the human bias toward what is measured to encourage long-term thinking. Our first tool in improving how much attention governments pay to the future is therefore straightforward: measure how we're doing. Without measurement, it's a lot easier to ignore problems and harder to track progress or assess whether we need to change strategies.

Unfortunately, discussions of government performance too often focus on a single measure of short-term revenue not long-term wealth. GDP is often used as the ultimate measure of national success by governments, the media, and the public. But GDP only measures the flow of income in a given year; it tracks how much is produced, not the stock of how much wealth is owned in total. Using up natural resources, physical assets, and human capital can all increase GDP in the short term. Why not loot the future or destroy the natural environment to build pyramids? Environmental harm isn't included in GDP, whereas the salaries paid to pyramid-builders increase GDP.

The fact that governments and public discussions usually focus on GDP means governments and voters have little idea how decisions impact the wealth of their country. This distorts government behaviour, focusing attention on maximizing short-term income while neglecting long-term wealth-building. If voters were perfectly rational, this wouldn't matter. We'd collect the information we need, and if we didn't need it, we wouldn't collect it. In practice though the focus on GDP matters. A report for the French government by economics Nobel Prize winners Joseph Stiglitz and Amartya Sen along with economist Jean-Paul Fitoussi points out, "What we measure affects what we do; and if our measurements are flawed, decisions may be distorted … [W]e often draw inferences about what are good policies by looking at what policies have promoted economic growth; but if our metrics of performance are flawed, so too may be the inferences that we draw."[9]

In the context of planning for the future, the implication is that if we can measure the future consequences of our decisions and make them more salient, then we will pay more attention to them. There are many ways to do this. Perhaps the simplest is to have a balance sheet that measures our national assets and liabilities. Are we saving for the future, or are we borrowing against it?

THE BIRTH OF ACCOUNTING

The roots of GDP, and accounting itself, lie with exactly that idea. They also happen to lie with the Republic of Venice, in the work of

Friar Luca Bartolomeo de Pacioli, a mathematician and collaborator with Leonardo da Vinci. Born in 1446 in Tuscany, he moved to Venice around 1464, where he worked as a tutor to the children of a merchant and on his own education. More importantly for GDP, he is also known as the father of accounting. Good accounting is at the core of tracking national wealth and is also an ancestor of modern GDP.

In 1494 Pacioli published *Summa de arithmetica, geometria, proportioni et proportionalita* (*Summary of Arithmetic, Geometry, Proportions, and Proportionality*) in Italian rather than the more traditional Latin, which would have limited its accessibility. It is the first known description of double-entry accounting, which would rapidly become one of the fundamental tools of business. It also, incidentally, introduced the rule of seventy-two, which helps calculate the returns of compound interest. Two per cent interest means your bank account will double every thirty-six years (seventy-two divided by two). Double-entry accounting is a method of tracking what you own and what you owe, as well as how that is changing. In a balance sheet, everything you own goes in a credit column (*credit* comes from the word for loan or trust in Latin; today credits are usually called assets). Everything you owe goes in a debit column ("what is owed" in Latin, today called liabilities).

Double-entry bookkeeping has had a formative influence on many areas of history. For the first time, merchants could easily track how much they were worth. It allowed bookkeepers to avoid errors and made auditing easier: since the two sides must balance, if they don't add up, then something is wrong. Pacioli himself advised that people should not go to bed until debits equalled credits. Double-entry gave merchants a straightforward way to track the progress of their businesses, and auditing made it easy for them to ensure their employees were honest. In Renaissance Europe it had moral and religious connotations: God's responsibility for judging sins and souls was conceptualized in similar terms. Keeping your books well wasn't only financial probity but also a near holy act echoing God himself.[10]

A more economic benefit came with the arrival of joint-stock companies, in which outside investors could buy stock in a firm, much like stock markets today. If you plan to own but not be involved in managing a firm you need a reliable way to check its operations. Double-entry bookkeeping made such audits easier and paved the way for the establishment of stock markets and the modern financial world. Fundamental to modern finance is the ability to track and understand the profitability of investments: without accounting, much of modern business and finance would be impossible.

The double-entry approach also limited the power of monarchs. Kings and rulers had a tendency to borrow money and then never pay it back. If checking accounts was just a matter of adding up recorded credits and debits, then the middle class could expect to be able to check the books of at least minor officials, if not the king. Much like a modern investor demanding to see the books of a firm, commoners as well as other officials could demand to see a mayor's books, helping hold local officials to account.

Double-entry could also be a tool of royal power. Henry VII, one of the richest kings in Europe, used it to keep track of his subjects and extract as much tax revenue from them as possible. Wealthy subjects were required to post a bond against their behaviour, forfeited if they misbehaved and carefully tracked in the king's accounting books. Henry personally audited his treasurer's books, his spidery initials signing every page and in some cases every line.[11]

MODERN GDP

In short, double-entry bookkeeping was a leap forward in transparency, whether you were a stockholder, a citizen, or even a king. One might assume, therefore, that double-entry bookkeeping, with its focus on assets and liabilities, has become only more popular in modern times. That is true in business. Firms are required to keep books that meet international accounting standards, including balance sheets as well as income statements. Balance sheets show what they own or owe at a given moment in time. Income statements show how much money they have made or lost over a period of time.

Governments have shown less enthusiasm for measuring their stock of assets. Most governments release income statements in the form of budgets, but national balance sheets, which would track the total assets held by a country, are often left to gather dust or are not created at all. The difference is that wealth and assets are stocks, not flows, though they may provide economic services of some kind. A tree bears fruit which can be sold and counted in GDP, for example, but the value of the tree itself is not included. Measuring income but not wealth leaves a gap because some services may have value but are not well captured by GDP (e.g., benefits to human health or happiness) and because some wealth may not provide yearly benefits, such as minerals in the ground. The focus on income can also lead to perverse incentives: over-fertilizing a fruit tree might temporarily increase fruit production but harm the tree in the long-term.

The reason for this limitation is in the origins of GDP. As Diane Coyle explains in her book *GDP: A Brief but Affectionate History*, the government of Franklin D. Roosevelt responded to the Great Depression by asking for more statistics: if they were to do better, they needed a way to know how they were doing.[12] Simon Kuznets, who would win the Nobel Memorial Prize in Economic Sciences for his work on the subject, rose to the challenge and invented GDP. Before Kuznets, the American government had used highly inaccurate numbers such as share price indices and total freight car loadings to estimate economic activity. GDP was a significant improvement and would be further developed by economists in other countries, such as James Meade and Richard Stone in the UK (both of whom would eventually get the Nobel in Economic Sciences, Meade for trade theory and Stone for his GDP work directly).

GDP is a measure of economic activity. There are a few ways to calculate it, all of which are in theory equivalent: we can add up all the spending in the country over the year, all the production, or all the incomes, including both physical production and services. These are supposed to be equivalent because when you spend money, it buys something that was produced, and becomes someone else's income. Typically, economists will consider all three and try to make sure they are as close as possible. When economists say that the GDP has increased by 3 per cent in a given year, it means that the country is producing 3 per cent more stuff, earning 3 per cent more money, or spending 3 per cent more than last year.

GDP can be challenging to measure well. Technical decisions about how it is calculated can make a significant difference, and data can be difficult to collect. On 6 April 2014, for example, Nigeria's GDP doubled, catapulting them to the status of largest economy in Africa, due to technical adjustments of how GDP was calculated. The economy itself had not changed, but 2013's estimate was half of what it should have been. And the calculation is getting more complex in the modern economy: the UN's guidance on how to calculate GDP has ballooned to 722 pages, from fewer than 50 when it was first published in 1953.

Although GDP provides a useful measure of something important – how much the economy produces – there are also some fundamental issues. Kuznets himself had some concerns about GDP. His report to the US Congress in 1937 was quite clear on its limitations:

> The valuable capacity of the human mind to simplify a complex situation in a compact characterization becomes dangerous when not controlled in terms of definitely stated criteria. With quantitative measurements especially, the definiteness of the result suggests, often misleadingly, a precision and simplicity in the outlines of the object measured. Measurements of national income are subject to this type of illusion and resulting abuse, especially since they deal with matters that are the center of conflict of opposing social groups where the effectiveness of an argument is often contingent upon oversimplification.[13]

More recently, GDP has come under fire for several different reasons. At a basic level, it fails to include several sectors we might think create value. An obvious one is household work: hiring a cleaner instead of cleaning your house yourself increases GDP because you don't pay yourself. If you marry your cleaner and stop paying them a wage, GDP falls even if they keep cleaning the house.

Another common criticism is that material well-being may not be the same as happiness, and what we should really care about is the happiness of our population. Bhutan, for example, tracks a national happiness index (while remaining poor and authoritarian, which may not be a good sign). Unfortunately, these are hard to measure and tend to correlate with GDP, making them difficult to use well – if whenever happiness is high, GDP is high, then it's not clear what we're learning from using happiness instead. Though there is significant variation, this is roughly what we see: countries with a high GDP also score well on national measures of well-being.[14] This doesn't mean that GDP is the same as happiness. Rather, our current methods of determining whether people are happy, such as surveys, are imprecise, making what they tell us difficult to use well. Well-being, not GDP, seems like a perfectly reasonable goal for policy, indeed probably a better one – the challenge is doing it in a meaningful way. This is an important and ongoing area of work.

When we consider the long term, the key failure of GDP is its status as an income statement not a balance sheet. In the same way that if all you look at in a business is the income statement, you may not realize they are selling essential factories or machines to temporarily boost revenues, governments are able to sell or overexploit assets in order to boost GDP, even if they make the country poorer in the future. In other words, if everyone suddenly moved to a different country, so that the population was zero, then GDP in the original country would be zero – no economic activity. There would still be roads, bridges, airports, and natural resources in the country though, and if people moved back they wouldn't have to start from scratch. GDP misses the actual assets and liabilities of a country.

As individuals and businesses, we would never consider adopting this narrow a measurement. If you only measured your income and not your savings, you would probably have an unpleasant surprise when you got to retirement. If businesses only tracked their profits and ignored their balance sheets, they would inevitably start selling off assets to boost profits while damaging long-term earnings (though this sometimes happens anyway given the short-term focus of the stock market). In a particularly egregious example, wars and natural disasters can be good for GDP: when buildings and other assets are destroyed, countries increase spending to replace them, which shows up as an increase in GDP. It is nonsense, however, to claim that a country would be wealthier. If a hurricane hits New Orleans and destroys buildings, GDP might actually increase because people have to rebuild what was destroyed. Yet New Orleans would clearly be worse off: they are merely rebuilding what was lost.

When GDP was developed, in a time of depression and subsequent war, production was the bottom line: politicians wanted to know how many tanks they could produce. Today, as we wrestle with problems from global-warming to education, the balance sheet is significantly more important. Without using a balance sheet, governments don't provide an estimate of where they are at a moment in time; they tell their citizens only how much money they are making and spending. For that reason, it's extremely challenging to tell how governments are doing with regard to long-term wealth-building. A measure of gross domestic wealth, in contrast, could help inform government policy and decisions based on their impact on the long-term wealth of the country and help citizens hold them to account for it.

OUT OF SIGHT, OUT OF MIND

So what do we miss about the long term without a national balance sheet? Four big gaps emerge. First, and perhaps most obvious, are our physical assets: infrastructure such as roads, bridges, buildings, and machinery. GDP measures how much we invest in these things but not how much we have. Satellites, schools, wind farms, and tractors all make up part of our collective wealth, and none of them are currently counted. This helps explain the woeful state of infrastructure in much of today's world. We measure the value we get from our infrastructure by its contribution to GDP each year, but our stock of infrastructure and capital which produces that value degrades over time. GDP measures the flow of maintenance expenses that would help maintain that stock but not the value of the stock itself. Spending on infrastructure costs the government money, and without a balance sheet the improvements are not recorded. Easier to let it fall apart.

Research suggests that current spending on basic infrastructure worldwide is *$1 trillion per year* lower than it should be and likely to grow.[15] That's more than the GDP of Australia (though not more than its wealth!). The American Society of Civil Engineers finds that many American roads, bridges, and dams are not up to standard and are often structurally deficient.[16] But who cares? None of this affects GDP immediately, though it does over time reduce productivity and will eventually reduce GDP. If a government borrows to repair roads, that increases the deficit (and leads to criticism), but only increases GDP indirectly and over time – hardly an election slogan. And when that infrastructure is key to mitigating natural disasters, the failure to long-term plan becomes particularly acute. Without a national balance sheet, there is no national measure of the strength of New Orleans's levees, the sufficiency of fire towers in Australia, or the resilience of European bridges to earthquakes.

Second, focusing on GDP misses natural capital. If a government cuts down a forest and sells the wood that boosts GDP, but it deprives future generations of the forest's benefits, whether felling it for wood or walking under its shade. GDP says we should always cut down the forest, whereas a balance sheet presents a more nuanced picture. The value of having extra homes built from the wood might well outweigh the benefits of a forest, but there is a trade-off. If we only consider GDP then the value of the forest is neglected beyond the annual value of any economic services it provides, such as enabling hunting. Doing so incentivizes us to deplete or exhaust the resource in order to maximize short-term returns.

Natural capital includes forests, oil deposits, and minerals, and also less tangible assets and the services they provide to us, such as clean air so that we can breathe easily, wetlands that reduce flooding, an ozone layer without holes to reduce cancer rates, or a sufficiently cool climate that supports human flourishing. Both the assets themselves and in many cases the value of the services they provide, such as supporting human health, are not well captured by GDP. Cleaning up the environment, though it does add to GDP because it is economic activity, costs the government and doesn't lead to a net credit on the balance sheet as a result of a better environment because we don't have a balance sheet to start with.

The concept of natural capital was popularized in 1973 by E.F. Schumacher in his book *Small Is Beautiful*.[17] There are two general types. One is stocks, such as minerals in the ground: they produce little until extracted, but once they're used up, they're gone. The other, such as forests, watersheds, or fish stocks, can provide a sustainable flow of returns. Every year, forests purify our air and provide people with the benefit of walking in their shade; watersheds help clean our rivers and provide an ecosystem for various species; fish reproduce, providing an important source of protein for much of humanity; and bees provide hundreds of billions of dollars in commercial value by pollinating food crops. All these have economic benefits, but they are treated by GDP as free gifts, their asset value neither counted nor weighed when making policy decisions.

Since natural assets and benefits do not appear in GDP, our damage to them is often ignored. As a result, a number of our natural assets have been depleted by overuse in recent years, from fish stocks in our oceans to the air quality in Beijing. A healthy fish stock can support many fishers, but if we do not pay attention to how our behaviour affects the fish then it is easy to collapse the population, making everyone worse off. This issue has become salient as environmentalists among others have become increasingly concerned about the finite nature of many of the resources humanity relies on. If GDP relies on a finite stock of resources that is running out, then growth is not sustainable.

Some of our losses of natural capital are more subtle, such as genetic diversity in crops. The Food and Agriculture Organization (FAO) of the United Nations estimates that in the twentieth century, 75 per cent of the world's crop diversity was lost, and three-quarters of the world's food comes from just twelve plants and five animal species: rice, maize, and wheat alone contribute over half of the calories obtained from plants.[18] Cambridge professor Sir Partha Dasgupta observed in his 2021 review of the economics of biodiversity that biodiversity is falling at a faster rate than any time in human history, with current extinction rates one hundred to one thousand times higher than the baseline.[19] Cary Fowler, former head of the Global Crop Diversity Trust, reports that in America in the 1800s farmers grew around seven thousand varieties of apple; today, all but a few hundred are extinct, with a handful of varieties dominating the field.[20]

Genetic biodiversity is an important natural resource. It often contains the elements needed to avert new diseases or pests, preventing starvation. When we lose genetic biodiversity, we lose the ability to respond to future crises. In the 1970s, for example, the brown planthopper migrated from Japan to the rest of Asia and the insects began destroying rice paddies by transmitting the grassy stunt virus, threatening enormous famines. Crisis was only averted after scientists screened over six thousand wild rice varieties, finally finding one in India that was resistant to the virus. Crossing it with Asian rice varieties meant they too could resist it, and this rice is now grown by millions of farmers.[21] As Dasgupta reports though, the rice blast fungus is still responsible for 30 per cent of global rice losses each year, enough to feed 60 million people; gains from developing more resistant varieties using existing biodiversity could be substantial.

Unfortunately, biodiversity is under-researched and under-preserved, while becoming increasingly valuable in the face of shifting climate patterns and increased risk of disease and pests from globalization. A single pest might wipe out an entire crop, with significant impacts on our food sources. Seed banks can help us combat this loss in diversity, but since we do not recognize their contribution to our national wealth, they inevitably suffer underinvestment. Any intrinsic value to life aside, this loss of genetic diversity makes us vulnerable to future crises, but GDP as currently measured ascribes no weight to preserving or enhancing that diversity. The more Red Delicious apples sold, the better.

Some countries have started to take action on natural capital. In the UK, for example, the Office of National Statistics assesses natural capital annually, in line with UN guidelines. The US announced in 2022 a major effort to develop natural capital accounts to record changes in America's stock of natural resources, from fish and forests to clean air and water. The goal is to create a single statistic to go alongside GDP that measures the country's natural wealth. The private sector also has started to consider their impact on natural capital as part of ESG (environment, social, and governance) considerations. Unfortunately, accurate counting of natural capital remains sporadic, and its use in government decision-making or national wealth statistics is not yet standard.

The third omission by GDP is what economists rather uninspiringly call human capital. Arthur Cecil Pigou, mentioned earlier, not only argued that we should give more weight to the needs of the future but was also an early proponent of the concept of human capital, the skills, abilities, education, experience, training, and even wisdom of people. Despite making humans sound rather like livestock, in the modern world this is perhaps the largest category of wealth of all: people allow us to innovate and create, developing and using new technologies and ideas. To some extent this can be measured by education, but doing so misses people like Steve Jobs, who dropped out of college but made an enormous contribution to the wealth of the US (and the world).

Human capital makes up a large share of the total wealth of many countries, especially wealthy ones. The United Nations Environment Program's *Inclusive Wealth Report 2018*, for example, found that in 93 of the 140 countries studied, human capital was the most important source of wealth, significantly outweighing natural capital or produced infrastructure (such as roads and bridges).[22] In 77 of those countries, it made up over half of the total capital the countries possessed, and on average across all countries it was almost 60 per cent of total capital.

The importance of human capital is also true of many individuals. When we think of a young woman just starting her career, for example, the value of her education and training in terms of potential future productivity far surpasses her net worth in dollar terms. In theory, it might make sense to let such young people borrow against that human capital in order to pay for education – could a student commit to repaying a percentage of future earnings in order to get a loan for an engineering degree today? Such discussions can come a bit close to indentured servitude, but it reflects the inherent value of human capital. Graduate taxes – where university degrees are subsidized but then graduates who make over a certain amount pay additional tax – follow much the same idea.

Human capital can also include the health of a population. A sick population, or one with a poor health-care system, is less able to innovate or contribute to national wealth. Since we don't measure health as an aspect of national wealth, however, the case for a strong health-care system is often weakened. This is true everywhere but particularly important in developing countries, where investing in health is often the single best investment governments can make: it is difficult to be a risk-taking entrepreneur when sick. Despite this importance, the health of our populations is neither measured nor reported in most government statistics, though it is partially captured by its impact on productivity.

This has been highlighted in the context of the COVID-19 pandemic. Lockdowns reduce GDP because they prevent economic activity from occurring: stores are closed and people stay home. Insofar as they protect human health, however, lockdowns also increase or at least minimize the reduction of human capital. Especially given concerns over long COVID, the potential long-term complications arising in some people, lockdowns create a much more nuanced trade-off on a national balance sheet than they do for GDP. Of course, as is often the challenge with crises, when lockdown decisions were being taken no one knew for sure the long-term impacts of the pandemic on either the economy or human capital, but if the focus is kept to GDP we lack the measurements even to consider the total impact on prosperity. Prosperity isn't everything – there is inherent value to people being healthy based on human rights and flourishing that has nothing to do with national wealth – but the absence of human capital in our national statistics doesn't help.

Finally, and perhaps most intangibly, we miss the health and strength of our institutions. Economists such as the 2024 Nobel Prize–winning Daron Acemoglu and James Robinson, known for their book *Why Nations Fail*, attribute much of the success or failure of countries to the strength of their institutions.[23] Countries with a long history of stability and the rule of law have an enormous advantage in development, even when other factors are identical. One striking example from Acemoglu and Robinson is the city of Nogales, in Mexico, which is divided from the city of Nogales, Arizona, by only a few metres of distance but also, crucially, the Mexican-American border. On the American side, crime is lower, life expectancies higher, and infrastructure is better maintained. The average wealth and well-being are significantly higher. Yet apart from the border, the two cities are similar in geography and demographic makeup: the difference is in institutions and cultural norms. Institutions aren't the only determinant of wealth or poverty, of course, but they do matter, and what takes generations to build may be damaged or destroyed in only a few years. North and South Korea provide another example at the national level. Colonial histories and individual leaders can profoundly shape the institutions of a country, with significant impacts on the national prosperity. Yet GDP, and government measurement in general, pay little heed to this.

Institutions set out the rules that shape human interaction. They include such things as a consistent legal framework, government openness and transparency, freedom of the press, individual rights, checks and balances on autocratic power, and high-quality government regulation and services. These can be supported through formal laws and regulations as well as more informal norms and customs, which bind a country together more with the force of habit than law. They are often the most challenging item on this list of the components of wealth to measure, and there is room for debate on exactly what good institutions look like. More work by Acemoglu and Robinson, along with co-author Simon Johnson, points out that institutions are typically determined by collective decisions of their respective society; different societies may make different choices, and different groups within societies may also have different preferences.[24] Institutions also sometimes need to change or lead to injustice; think of outdated laws and systems that were eventually identified as inherently discriminatory or racist.

Institutions are typically slow to change but once changed are also hard to change back. Many commentators have worried that Donald Trump's derisive approach to American institutions and social norms, including being the first president to be impeached twice, has permanently weakened American institutional quality. Trump has weakened both formal institutions and more informal norms previously common in American democracy with such actions as refusing to commit to a peaceful transfer of power, questioning the legitimacy of institutions such as the free press and the judiciary, not releasing his tax returns, not conceding defeat after the 2020 election, and alleging election fraud without evidence. During his first presidency, Americans expressed growing distrust of the press, with Republicans and Democrats putting their trust in almost entirely separate media universes, and many Americans lost confidence in institutions such as the courts and elections, some of them going so far as to storm the Capitol in response to claims the election had been stolen.[25]

Such violations damage institutions in ways difficult to repair; a norm, once broken, cannot be made whole again. As Edward Watts recounts in his book *Mortal Republic: How Rome Fell into Tyranny*, the end of the Roman Republic and its replacement with the Roman Empire can be linked to repeated violations of social norms.[26] Early figures such as the Gracchi brothers violated norms, including serving more than one term as tribune (a political role), and their opponents responded by violating norms themselves, ultimately including having both brothers murdered. For the preceding century and a half, political violence had been largely beyond the pale and forbidden by various norms and institutions. Following the Gracchi brothers, political violence became increasingly normalized, up to and including military leaders occupying the city of Rome with troops and executing thousands of political opponents. This would culminate in Julius Caesar crossing the Rubicon River – the boundary which Roman law and the Senate's orders had forbade him from crossing while commanding troops – and leading soldiers into the capital, starting a civil war that would end in the fall of the Roman Republic.

Roman leaders broke norms for various reasons, whether for their own power, to advance political goals, or sometimes because they believed it was the only way to save the Roman Republic. Watts himself says the purpose of his book is to help "readers to better appreciate the serious problems that result both from politicians who breach a republic's political norms and from citizens who choose not to punish them for doing so."[27] Since neither the Romans nor we kept reliable measures of the quality of our institutions, we undervalue institutional quality, encouraging our leaders to sacrifice our institutions to boost short-term economic growth or for other ends.

All four of these omissions – physical assets, natural capital, human capital, and institutional health – mean the current focus on GDP encourages a short-termist view. Governments don't keep track of what we're leaving for our children, so we typically ignore it. Since infrastructure, natural capital, human capital, and institutions add nothing to GDP unless we exploit them, it's challenging to make a case for saving them: the numbers are never in the future's favour. We may not be able to measure these factors perfectly, but we can do far better than our current decision to neglect them entirely.

There are more elements than just these four that we could include in national wealth, though many of them are even harder to measure. The accumulated knowledge of a society, for example, is surely an asset of significant value. A society that knows how to make electricity is better off than one that does not. Most of a country's wealth today is probably made up not of gold mines or strong institutions or human capital but rather the accumulated knowledge of past generations that allow us to feed, clothe, and house ourselves to a standard far higher than our ancestors could have imagined. This knowledge is captured as human capital through the skills and expertise of our population but also underlies the value of libraries, internet storage, and other mechanisms of passing on information. If we take policy decisions that hinder or enhance our ability to store and pass on knowledge (e.g., investing in long-term information storage devices or the study of history) we also affect our stock of wealth.

Social capital, such as the connections between individuals or habits of a population, also affects a country's wealth. Time could be thought of as part of wealth.[28] The report by Stiglitz, Sen, and Fitoussi for the French government, mentioned above, suggests adopting a dashboard of indicators rather than falling into the trap highlighted by Kuznets of believing any single number can capture the diversity of human development. I agree, and a balance sheet is no more a miracle cure than an income statement. It would, however, be progress and is the indicator perhaps most directly relevant to planning for the long term.

PROGRESS SO FAR

Some countries and economists have started to move beyond GDP and measure national wealth. The Inclusive Wealth report mentioned earlier, for example, aims to measure produced, human, and natural capital in 140 countries in order to build an Inclusive Wealth Index. Although it does not include institutions, some of the technical challenges in how to track and measure the wealth of nations have been addressed. The 2018 report finds that about 59 per cent of global wealth is made up of human capital, with produced capital (physical capital such as roads and buildings) at 21 per cent and natural capital at 20 per cent.[29] Only twenty-one countries had natural capital as their largest source of wealth, and those countries often had resource-dependent economies (such as Saudi Arabia).

When we think of global wealth, we may picture diamonds, or perhaps a corporate mogul with a private jet, but the true wealth of the modern world consists mostly of human health and education. Standard measures, which focus only on produced capital, miss 80 per cent

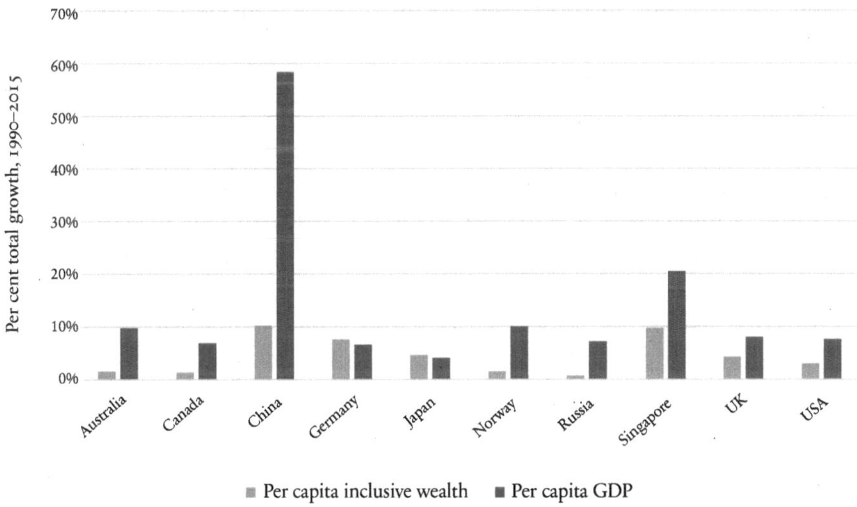

Figure 5.1 Selected countries' per capita growth rates in inclusive wealth and GDP, 1990–2015
Source: Data drawn from the UN Environment Program, *Inclusive Wealth Report 2018*.

of the wealth of nations. About a third of countries studied (44 out of 140) saw their inclusive wealth per capita drop between 1992 and 2014. This was mostly due to natural resource extraction: Iraq, Venezuela, Kuwait, and the United Arab Emirates all saw declines in their inclusive wealth per capita due to depletion of oil reserves, for example. However, GDP increased in almost all countries studied, even when inclusive growth fell. On average, inclusive wealth increased at about half the rate of GDP. Countries that used only GDP to assess their performance would have a misleadingly positive idea of how things were going.

Countries using a human development index, which usually focuses on variables such as education, life expectancy, and income, would in most cases also be overly optimistic. Of the countries studied, 139 of the 140 showed growth in their human development index, reflecting the steady increase in all three factors in most countries (though some countries have recently seen declines in life expectancy, including the US).[30] The difference between the human development index and inclusive wealth reflects the impact natural resource extraction has had on reducing inclusive wealth in many countries.

The graph in figure 5.1 provides several examples of this problem. Countries like China or Norway saw strong GDP growth over the past few decades, but relatively low inclusive wealth growth. Japan and Germany, in contrast, saw higher inclusive wealth growth than GDP growth. In most cases, GDP growth significantly outstripped inclusive wealth growth.

Concerningly, the relative size of produced capital and natural capital is changing. Produced capital grew the fastest at 3.8 per cent a year; human capital grew at 2.1 per cent a year. Natural capital, in contrast, decreased at 0.7 per cent a year, falling in 123 of the 140 countries. The rate of natural capital loss was five times larger in developing countries than OECD countries. Some types of natural capital were harder hit than others; only 15 countries increased their fisheries wealth, for example, while 55 countries increased their forest resources. In other words, a decline in natural capital was offset by an increase in produced capital and human capital. China has lost significant natural capital since 1990, but this loss is dwarfed by an enormous increase in produced and human capital. We are using up our natural resources, but becoming better educated and healthier and with more and better buildings. This is not inherently a bad thing, but there is clearly a limit on how long we can do so since we will ultimately run out of natural capital, not to mention potentially making our environment uninhabitable. Countries may wish to consider investing not only in buildings but also in the air they breathe.

There is significant variation across countries, of course. A number of former Soviet republics, such as Ukraine, Russia, Kazakhstan, and Lithuania, have seen declines in human capital as a result of falling populations. Other nations, such as South Korea and Singapore, have been on a sustainable path of increasing their produced capital without running down their natural capital. Some countries, especially a few in Africa, have very low levels of produced capital, suggesting there is a need for more investment there.

The Inclusive Wealth Index is hardly definitive, and much work remains to be done. However, it highlights an important concern: that many countries are replacing their natural capital with human and physical capital. This isn't always problematic, but it is an important trend we should be following carefully given its major implications for the future shape of our societies. At some point, no matter how educated or productive we are, we will likely regret the loss of our natural capital.

Another recent approach some countries have taken relates to quality of life. Countries such as New Zealand and Canada have introduced quality of life frameworks, webs of indicators meant to give a broad sense of their citizens' quality of life. Proposed policies can then be assessed based on their impact against the indicators. This approach seeks to capture other factors not captured in GDP, such as housing affordability, voter turnout, work-life balance, and crime rates, as well as factors such as environmental quality and health. The OECD presents a Better Life Index for their member countries that attempts a comparison based on these factors; helpfully, it provides the option of changing the relative weights of different components of their index to see how countries compare if the quality of social support networks in a community is more important to you than civic engagement, for example.[31] This is an excellent example of both a thoughtfully constructed index and one that has been designed to be as easy to use and understand as possible, unlike some of the more complicated constructs used elsewhere. That said, the quality-of-life approach may be useful on its own merits but does not necessarily better capture long-term considerations, though there can be some overlap.

As mentioned above, one promising sign is the 2022 announcement by the White House that the US government will be developing natural capital accounts for America's stocks of natural resources. It will be some years before any measures are ready, but they will hopefully strengthen policy development by the government as well as private sector ESG (environmental, social, and governance) efforts. The American effort is appealingly simple and clear, though sadly it only captures natural capital. Hopefully it can serve as a first step toward richer measurement of wealth across the board. For the moment, however, whether inclusive wealth, quality of life, or natural capital, these numbers are typically not reflected in either media coverage or political debates. The technical challenges are being solved. What remains is to start paying attention to the results and making judgments based not solely on GDP but on the country's balance sheet or inclusive wealth.

LESSONS

Unlike businesses, governments and citizens have so far largely failed to develop or track their balance sheets. What can we take from this chapter if we wish to plan as if the future matters? Most obviously, it matters what we measure. Henry VII's careful tracking of credits and debits enabled him to become one of the wealthiest monarchs in Europe. If we want governments to take the future seriously, we should be measuring their contributions to and detractions from it. No government should be allowed to ignore what they are leaving to the future.

What governments and the media currently ignore is our national wealth: the total value of our assets and liabilities, not just our short-term income or costs. This information has to become part of our political discussions, reflecting its importance to our long-term success. Introducing and popularizing some form of measure of gross domestic wealth could help advance the conversation and support long-term thinking. As the next chapter discusses further, having some measure of national wealth regularly reported in speeches such as the State of the Union or Speech from the Throne could help highlight how a country's wealth is changing, and encourage a more long-term view that values the total wealth of a country, not just short-term income from selling the family silver or using up natural and human assets. If we measure only yearly income, and that only from a specific subset of assets, then much of human wealth remains hidden and uncounted.

Particularly sobering are the recent changes in natural capital. Absent a record of how our natural resource endowments are changing, many countries have seen a steady decline in their natural capital endowments, making some of them poorer overall despite increases in human or physical capital. Even countries that have seen net increases in their total wealth may be concerned that their continued loss of natural capital and increasing dependence on physical and human capital may be harmful to their economies in the long run.

This is not just a government problem. The private sector, too, needs to take a hard look at how they define success: is it quarterly revenue growth and the daily fluctuations in stock price or long-term viability? Amazon has famously made a success of planning for the long-term and accepting short-term costs to get there, but many firms do not. Productivity, a usually ill-defined and hard-to-measure magic that increases GDP, requires an expansive view of what attracts, motivates, and enables talent. A broader measure of wealth might also mean a more thoughtful engagement with employee productivity.

Of course, it is not enough to simply talk about national balance sheets; governments must actually implement them, which requires the support of politicians as well as hard work from scientists, bureaucrats, and others. What incentive is there for politicians and leaders to do so? This is a complex question that will vary from country to country, but a few observations may help set out some of the power dynamics at play in implementation.

Since balance sheets may affect what decisions are made and what policies are popular, from a political perspective parties and leaders have a strategic incentive to support them when they align with their preferred policies and reject them when they don't. Anyone who wants to pursue projects that may be good for GDP but bad for long-term wealth, such a company that wants to open a new strip mine or a government that wants to go into debt to spend money on short-term projects, has little incentive to better measure long-term impact. Groups that benefit from the status quo may push back against national balance sheets and try to keep the focus on GDP.

That said, when it comes to measuring national wealth I am optimistic. Parties and leaders whose priorities do line up with the long term have an incentive to implement a balance sheet. A government that wants to justify spending on infrastructure, introduce policies that support productivity, or reduce the national debt, for example, could benefit from being able to demonstrate the long-term value using a balance sheet. Without one, the benefits in terms of national wealth are not captured anywhere, making the policy harder to defend or explain. A balance sheet also provides a way to critique the policies of political opponents if they would reduce national wealth, even if they are superficially good for GDP.

A crisis related to national debt, natural resource reserves, or crumbling infrastructure could also help spark a public conversation around measuring wealth and encourage a government to introduce a balance sheet, if only to make their predecessors look bad. Cynically, a government might choose to strategically time the requirement, introducing measures less beneficial to the future before announcing the launch of national balance sheet, in order to minimize the cost to the government in power while still implementing the policy.

What's more, measuring long-term wealth does not necessarily require government to play a role; non-profit and other organizations could also do the measurements. However, governments have an incentive to control the measures themselves, even if they would prefer it not be measured in the first place. At least if government oversees it, they have some level of control over how it is measured and communicated. Having the OECD opine that your country is getting poorer is not necessarily a message a government wants to hear.

A greater challenge may be keeping balance sheets in place. Once introduced, a future government may be tempted to abandon national balance sheets if they no longer align with their goals. In that situation, balance sheets hopefully benefit from the development of norms and expectations. It is almost unthinkable that a democratic government today might simply stop publishing information about how much they spend; any government that announced it would no longer be transparent about budget information would face significant criticism. We want to reach the same state when it comes to balance sheets. It should be a baseline expectation that governments release this information, or face a public and media outcry if they do not. At that point, abolishing them makes a government look bad, which of course they prefer to avoid. Wealth measurement by independent or international institutions can also encourage governments to continue their efforts.

Would national balance sheets change government behaviour? Once they are published, there are no guarantees the public will pay attention, of course. Governments may also choose to publish misleading or incomplete information to try to minimize the impact or simply frame the data as positively as possible. If the balance sheet does not garner much attention, then the impact on government incentives will be limited. Having independent institutions and actors that can assess and challenge the information released can mitigate this issue and provide a level of challenge and verification on what is released, much as the media as well as organizations like the Congressional Budget Office challenge budget numbers today.

Public attention might also increase if there is a crisis that requires the measure, as happened with the introduction of GDP during the Great Depression. A major infrastructure failure, for example, or ecological loss or species extinction, could focus attention on the declining value of our assets not currently caught by GDP. If the public or independent institutions do pay attention, then balance sheets can help shift the incentives for government by making the public more aware of and potentially concerned about impacts on national wealth, raising the political cost of government decisions that harm long-term wealth and making it easier for governments to justify and support decisions that increase it.

Overall, if international organizations and non-profits continue to push forward with their own measures of national wealth, I anticipate governments will come along, if only because such measures will strengthen the case for what some governments want to do anyway in terms of investing in long-term projects such as infrastructure or education. The challenge will be maintaining a measure of gross domestic wealth over time, which will require a change in how the public and the media think about national success and productivity. As is true to some degree for all the strategies we explore here, in the very long term public support is essential to preventing a future government from eliminating national balance sheets. Without a public that supports balance sheets to at least some extent, the nature of democracies means a future government can ignore or end the practice.

That cultural change may take time, but I think the timing is good, and the concept is sufficiently simple and intuitive to resonate with the public. A single measure of national wealth, while not as nuanced or informative as a dashboard of indicators, may be more likely to succeed given its ease of use and communicability, similar to GDP. Leadership, both from scholars and politicians, can also convince the public of the value of such measures and maintain public support over time. Economic growth has done a lot to raise people out of poverty and increase living standards, and for more than sixty years we have relied on it to measure our economies. The problem is that when we focus exclusively on the traditional measure of GDP, we're looking at growth *in the wrong thing* – we're ignoring how our wealth, whether physical, natural, human, or institutional, is changing. If we want to plan for the well-being of future generations and leave them a base of capital and assets from which they can flourish, we need to track how our wealth is changing over time. We need a balance sheet. Beyond that, we can also do more to make it easy for governments to consider the future and their impacts on the balance sheet. We turn to that next.

6

Make It Easy and Attractive

To show no model of extravagance to later generations, to leave all forms of life unaffected, to avoid embroidering ritual, to rule oneself by strict regulation in one's behaviour so as to be ready to deal with crises, thus helping other generations: this was what the ancients took to be the Tao.

Chuang Tzu, *The Book of Chuang Tzu*

If you start at the entrance in a rock face on a mountain in western Texas, there is a jade door rimmed in stainless steel, followed by a second steel door. You follow a dark tunnel, before ascending a spiral staircase up a five-hundred-foot shaft. Machinery gradually emerges from the darkness, and eventually you see a clock face, enriched with the cycles of astronomical time as well as the time of day. It sounds like something built by dwarves in *The Lord of the Rings*. In fact, it is a two-hundred-foot clock, built deep in the mountain. It is intended to keep time for the next ten thousand years, about the lifespan of human civilization so far. The design and engineering challenges are significant. At that time scale, gears start to grind themselves to dust, and the best batteries die. Instead, the clock uses temperature changes between day and night to power itself and ceramics instead of metals to minimize corrosion.

Why build such a clock? One could be forgiven for thinking it an act of hubris: a temple to time hidden in a mountain, funded by the largesse of tech billionaires. That's a fair point, but the creators, who have been working on it since 1986, have a serious purpose. Danny Hillis, an engineer and designer, is the inventor of the clock. He has worked with others, including biologist, writer, and environmentalist Stuart Brand, to set up a foundation devoted to long-term thinking, the Long Now Foundation.

Among the foundation's other projects are a digital library of all human languages; encouraging people to make bets on the future; developing a manual for civilization that records culture and technology for our descendants; using biotechnology to try to restore extinct species such as the passenger pigeon; and adding an extra zero to dates to remind us of the longer time frame (e.g., 02023). The purpose of the clock is to encourage people to think long term: to give them a lasting symbol of the need to consider not just today's problems but also tomorrow's. It serves as a tangible reminder of the need for long-term thinking, and its creators hope it will inspire people to change their behaviour toward the long term.

* * *

Unsurprisingly, humans are biased to follow the easy path. Not always, of course, but particularly if we are busy or focused elsewhere, our steps tend to turn downhill, not up. Taking a difficult path requires an effort; taking the easy path doesn't. Arguments for taking the harder path are long-standing, as the quote from Chuang Tzu above suggests (*Tao* translates as path, or way of being).

Chapter 5 focuses on making our impacts on the future obvious through thoughtful measurement. As mentioned, behavioural science shows that just measuring something can often help change behaviour. But sometimes measurement isn't enough. Even good measures may be ignored or insufficiently salient. This chapter explores how we can make the future tangible within our decision-making processes and steer governments toward future-friendly policies by making them easy and convenient. Most powerful of all is if the decision can be framed as a default.

Behavioural science has many examples of this bias of doing what is easy. Want to encourage people to save for retirement or increase organ donation? Make saving or being a donor the default. Want to eat less? Use smaller plates, so the easy option is to give yourself a smaller serving. Want to increase the number of taxpayers who enrol for a program? Send them the enrolment information directly, rather than to a website where they then have to find it themselves, or auto-enrol them entirely. Want to help under-represented groups attend university? Complete the application on their behalf. Want to reduce doctors' errors in writing prescriptions? Simplify the form they use so it is easy for them to fill out.[1] These nudges can help us achieve our long-term goals by harnessing our bias toward taking the easy path in the short-term. Without them, the deck can be stacked against us, with the easier option making us less healthy, less wealthy, and less successful. The same effect can be harnessed to nudge governments.

As discussed in chapter 4, one reason governments neglect the long term is distraction by short-term events and the political news cycle. Getting distracted is easy. Long-term planning is hard, requiring consistent focus and attention. It is much simpler for governments to get distracted by crises. Even when a government has multiple mandates in a row and governs for eight or more years, they may never get to their long-term priorities but instead ceaselessly respond to emergencies and crises.

Of course, governments also change priorities, and in a democracy the party in power will also change. That's why commitments can be powerful, as we see in chapter 7, which looks at encouraging governments to make commitments in the face of changing priorities or parties in power. In this chapter, the focus is on supporting governments that may believe they need to do more for the future but repeatedly fail at doing so because of the pressures of short-term issues. Fortunately, there are concrete steps governments can take to make long-term planning easier and distraction harder. Three behaviourally informed mechanisms can help us do so: guardrails, tripwires, and defaults.

As you read this chapter, it may also be helpful to remember that government is made up of (at least) two different groups: the elected politicians and the non-elected bureaucrats or public servants who serve them. Some of the strategies set out below will apply best to bureaucrats (e.g., setting up a delivery unit); some will apply best to elected leaders of governments (e.g., changing the State of the Union address or Speech from the Throne); and some are strategies everyone could be doing (e.g., increasing diversity in decision-making, designing policies to be defaults).

GUARDRAILS

Jeff Bezos, the founder and former CEO of Amazon, was at one point the richest man in the world, with a net worth of around $150 billion. Reportedly, at every meeting he attends he has an empty chair left in the meeting room to represent the customer. Why do this? It's to encourage attendees, when they go around the table providing their perspectives, to stop when they come to the empty chair and ask themselves what the customer would want. The empty chair helps ensure the customer's viewpoint is considered in every decision, a perspective that might otherwise be lost.

In their book *Decisive* Chip Heath and Dan Heath introduce the idea of guardrails and tripwires: systems that help us stay on track by guiding us back to the path we want to be on if we start to leave it or warning us if we go off-track.[2] The empty chair is a guardrail that reminds Bezos and other meeting attendees to consider the customer when they might otherwise forget. For individuals guardrails can be rules of behaviour, social norms, or decision heuristics. For governments they can include changes to institutions to allow for specialized teams and other ways to improve deliberative decision-making and warn when they are going off-course.

A first useful guardrail is what in the UK was called a delivery unit. The Prime Minister's Delivery Unit was set up under then prime minister Tony Blair within the UK Cabinet Office to focus on the prime minister's key campaign priorities: education, health, crime, and transport. When events or crises distracted the prime minister, the delivery unit was there to maintain focus on the campaign priorities and ensure their delivery, either bringing the prime minister's attention back to the issues or keeping focus while most of the government was distracted. The unit did not make policy decisions, but it helped ensure whatever decisions were taken were successfully implemented. A dedicated team devoted to long-term issues can play a similar function. As crises emerge, a dedicated team can stay focused on the long term and keep moving the ball forward. Particularly since long-term challenges tend to be complex and multi-faceted, consistent, incremental progress is often the only option, and that requires consistent and enduring focus.

The UK Delivery Unit has other lessons for how to stick with long-term goals. They used concrete, quantitative measures for progress, focused on a very limited set of key goals, and worked closely with the groups that could actually deliver on those priorities (hence the name). Too many governments try to do everything and as a result achieve little, which is as true for the long term as it is for everything else. A limited set of clear priorities with clear measures and accountability is far more likely to be successful.

Another useful guardrail is to introduce more diversity in decisions. We have already seen that individuals fall victim to biases in making decisions, including neglecting the long term. As Cass Sunstein and Reid Hastie point out in their book *Wiser* taking decisions in a group can sometimes make these biases worse, not better.[3] When groups are biased, they can fail to consider better options, miss key considerations, or make mistakes, leading to worse decisions and worse outcomes for everyone. Why do groups sometimes make biases worse? Groups can fall victim to what Sunstein and Hastie call in *Wiser* happy talk: team members go along with the group or say nothing is wrong rather than provide new information or challenge the consensus. When there is happy talk, a group doesn't learn what it needs to know, but everyone still feels better about the decision. As a result, groups tend to do better than their average member in making correct decisions, but not as well as their best members, and they can be more likely to converge on an extreme or initial opinion. The strongest effect of group decision-making is not improved decisions but rather greater confidence in the decision made, regardless of its quality. If members are biased – and we have already seen that many people are likely to undervalue the future – than the group decision is likely to be biased, but the group will have significantly more confidence in the decision and be less open to discussion or change.

Fortunately, there are steps teams can take to minimize the risk of happy talk and maximize the benefit of teams. At its best, group decision-making is a powerful way to aggregate information and bring together a lot of different perspectives, engaging a wide range of people in a decision and ensuring they understand the result and see it as legitimate. The optimal model is closer to the classic play and movie *Twelve Angry Men*, where one person overcomes the group's consensus to force a search for the truth (the whole thing is excellent – a fascinating psychological study and they never leave the deliberation room).

One important step is to increase diversity within the group taking the decision. Diversity in thought, background, education, socioeconomic status, ethnicity, and other factors can help strengthen decision-making in both the short and long term. Katherine Phillips, former professor of management at Columbia Business School, notes it does so through two effects:[4]

- Diverse groups have more information and skills. Adding more people to a group who are identical to those already there doesn't broaden the team's expertise, talents, or experience. Adding people who differ from current members brings new ideas to the table. In situations where no one person has all the information, diversity makes it more likely the group as a whole has all the pieces necessary to get the best possible solution. With less diversity, it is more likely that some people will have overlapping perspectives, and some perspectives or ideas may be missing, leading to errors.

- A greater range in perspectives can mean that ideas are dissected more carefully, with the consequences better analyzed and anticipated. Having a diverse group take a decision can encourage all participants to reflect a little more carefully on alternatives and other perspectives, because members anticipate some disagreement or differing perspectives. This awareness can make the group a little less confident in their decision and more open to new information. This can sometimes slow down a decision, but it also means mistakes are more likely to be anticipated and avoided. If a group comes to a consensus too quickly, it may rush to the lowest common denominator or the most obvious solution rather than the best one.

One study looked at how racial diversity affected the ability of small groups to solve a murder mystery. Each member of the team had different information, and all the information was required in order to correctly identify the murderer. Racially diverse teams spent more time on the problem and were more likely to outperform homogeneous groups, suggesting that having more diverse team members made it easier to share more information, which subsequently improved the decision-making process.[5]

Similar results have been found in mock jury trials. Social psychologist Samuel Sommers found that in simulated jury decisions, juries with racial diversity were better at almost every aspect of the task. They remembered information better, they deliberated more rigorously, and they exchanged more information. This wasn't just because the diverse teams brought new information to the table. The presence of racially diverse members helped the entire team be more contemplative and open to new ideas, and participants on juries with diverse members cited more case facts and made fewer errors relative to peers on non-diverse juries.[6]

Work by the UK's Behavioural Insights Team and Institute for Government suggests that in addition to assembling cognitively diverse teams, governments should formally introduce routes for diverse views to be fed in before, during, and after group discussions.[7] For example, an online form could capture views before and after policy discussions, helping share divergent views without the pressure of speaking in opposition to the group.

Recall that Sunstein and Hastie found that the strongest effect of taking decisions in a group rather than as an individual is that the group feels more confident in the decision, but the decision isn't necessarily more likely to be right. Research has found that not only the quality of decisions is higher in more diverse groups but also that the groups are less confident in their decision at the end.[8] Diversity can reduce confidence in the decision, which may be one of the mechanisms by which it increases the quality of decision; a little doubt and self-reflection can be good, if the alternative is overconfidence.

Thinking about how confident we are, not just trying to derive the right answer, is frequently useful. In 2010 the US government was exploring the possibility of a midnight raid on a compound in Pakistan where they thought Osama bin Laden might be hiding. The problem was they weren't certain: they had some partially obscured satellite photos of someone pacing the grounds, but they weren't sure if it was him or not. To make the decision, analysts were specifically asked to say how confident they were in their assessment not just provide a recommendation. Certainty levels varied from 60 per cent to 90 per cent. Perhaps unsurprisingly, the least confident were older analysts who had been involved in the Iraq weapons of mass destruction investigation.[9]

In this case, of course, it turned out that bin Laden was in the compound. Having a diverse group of analysts with diverse backgrounds helped ensure that more possibilities were explored and preserved a healthy level of doubt about the final finding. Doubt need not be paralyzing – Jeff Bezos reputedly takes decisions whenever he is more than 70 per cent sure that he is right – but it is healthy to remember we rarely have all the information, and there are usually multiple possible explanations for a given situation. Not taking a decision is itself a decision, one that perpetuates the status quo, which often has its own issues. Diverse perspectives can help us compare a wide range of options as well as the status quo to assess what might be best.

Diversity in teams may not always help improve outcomes. When a rapid decision is of the essence and there is no time for deliberation, such as during an emergency, a more authoritarian decision style might be more effective. Still, in most situations diversity can help teams and groups make better decisions.

What does that mean for government long-term thinking? Ensuring policies and programs are developed by diverse groups that include the perspectives of those who may experience the long-run impact (e.g., young people), can be a powerful way to ensure good policy design. Governments can also include a voice dedicated to representing the views of future generations, even if they are not around to represent themselves. Think of Bezos's empty chair concept, but used to remind policy-makers about future generations rather than today's customers. This serves as a guardrail, creating a group that will speak up on behalf of the future when relevant questions come up.

Of course, it is not enough to include young people or other groups within decision-making processes. Teams must also listen and give them space to bring up concerns or new perspectives, not provide happy talk. A key predictor of team success is psychological safety, the ability to take risks and be wrong without being condemned or criticized by the team.[10] If team members don't feel psychologically safe, they won't be willing to take risks or suggest new ideas and will be more likely to resort to happy talk, stifling the benefits of group decision-making.

Another way to reduce the risk of happy talk and boost diversity of viewpoints is to set up a red team: an independent team that plays the role of devil's advocate, exploring alternative futures or options from the mainstream view. This can challenge preconceived notions or assumptions and allow all perspectives to be considered. Unlike a delivery unit, it need not be focused specifically on the future but can provide an alternate perspective on any proposals made, helping ensure that consequences are thought through. Because members of a red team are formally tasked to disagree, they are more likely to avoid happy talk and raise concerns and less likely to feel insecure in doing so.

The origins of the role lie with the Catholic Church, which used to hire officials named Promoters of the Faith to argue against the canonization (recognition of sainthood) of nominees. They would look for evidence of character flaws or weaknesses in the evidence as reasons why a nominee should not be made a saint. For their hard work, they came to be known as *advocatus diaboli*, or devil's advocate, and they argued against the *advocatus Dei*, or God's advocate. One imagines they were not always popular with their colleagues, but they played an important role ensuring that the evidence was fairly assessed and weighed.

In a more modern setting, red teams have been heavily used by the American military, including after the September 11 attacks as a way to better prepare for future terrorist attacks. The Central Intelligence Agency (CIA) set up a Red Cell team to tell the CIA Director things other people wouldn't, and they are often used in war games and other military planning. Red teams were used in planning the raid on bin Laden, challenging both the likelihood of his presence as well as the raid's potential success or failure. Research suggests the benefits of red teams can be limited if they are seen as outsiders and thus have their findings dismissed, but if they can strike the right balance between being part of the team yet presenting a different perspective, they can help reduce groupthink.[11]

Using games or simulations to explore possible situations can help in other contexts too, though only if the results are taken seriously. As Bill Gates has pointed out, governments are bad at conducting exercises to prepare for pandemics, especially full-scale exercises, and worse at following any recommendations that may emerge.[12] Of the half-dozen or so exercises in the US simulating a disease outbreak between 2001 and 2020, all of them had roughly similar conclusions – the US was not well-prepared for a pandemic – but none led to significant changes in outbreak preparedness.

Many governments already have red teams of a sort in the form of opposition political parties. The opposition is usually explicitly intended to oppose the ideas of the government and to provide a check on policy proposals by presenting other sides. In parliamentary democracies, including the UK, the opposition is still sometimes referred to as the loyal opposition in recognition of the fact that it may disagree with the government of the day, but it remains loyal to the sovereign. The loyal opposition can play a useful role challenging the government and providing space for discussion and debate, although it can devolve into partisan showmanship. Red teams, however, can also be used within the government to support the development of policy proposals and anticipate future problems. Encouraging teams within the government to represent the long-term view and challenge status quo perspectives can help push against groupthink and ensure teams consider the implications for the future. Their value comes in part from the formal structure they provide. Simply asking team members to consider whether there are any weaknesses to a plan does not provide the space and time for discussion and deliberation that formally assigning someone as a red team member will.

Another possible guardrail is to include scenario planning in the decision-making process. Scenario planning is based on the insight that no one can predict the future that well. Philip Tetlock has found that the average expert is only slightly better at predicting the future than the average dart-throwing chimpanzee.[13] There are ways to do better than this, but scenario planning suggests avoiding the need to predict the future in the first place.

Instead, the concept is to come up with a range of scenarios that could describe the future: one that expects current trends to continue, one that expects things to get much worse, one that expects things to get better, et cetera. Then test the plans against all the scenarios, not just some of them. Because the future is uncertain, good plans should be successful in multiple possible scenarios. Similarly, top poker players don't try to predict exactly what hand their opponents have; instead, they "play the range," anticipating the range of possible hands their opponents likely have and then playing with that in mind. Like having diverse teams, this compels us to consider a wider range of possibilities. Scenario planning can be a powerful guardrail for organizations seeking to maintain focus on the long term by introducing a systematic way of considering and preparing for the future. If plans and priorities start to drift, they can be tested against the scenarios developed, providing an accountability mechanism as ideas develop.

In sum, guardrails can be effective for improving decision-making and focusing it on the long term. Delivery units, diversity, and scenario planning are all examples of guardrails to ensure multiple perspectives, including the long term, are brought to bear on any decision. Other approaches may also be worth exploring, such as pre-mortems, where decision-makers imagine the failure of a project and work backwards to identify why; increasing transparency of the evidence used to make decisions; and incorporating clear mechanisms for feedback and adaptation.[14] Sometimes, however, we also need a way to detect when we've already strayed off course. To address that, we turn to a second way of facilitating long-term planning: tripwires.

TRIPWIRES

Ian Ayres, a Yale professor of law and economics, uses what he calls a nagger. He has a spreadsheet online that he updates daily based on his progress on five goals: lose weight, exercise more, watch less TV, read more novels, and write more. His nagger is a student he has hired to check his progress on the spreadsheet. The student will first email him a reminder, then call him, and then physically visit him to ensure he ticks his boxes for the day. This combines two different incentives: there is the aspect of ensuring a reminder if he forgets or gets distracted, and there is also a strong social pressure element, since Ayres does not want to look unreliable in front of one of his students.[15]

Chip and Dan Heath refer to this practice as tripwires. If guardrails help keeps us on the path, tripwires are warning lights that tell us when are too far off-course.[16] Perhaps the simplest example of a tripwire is the alarm clock. Sleeping in may be appealing in the short term, but we know we'll suffer in the long term if we don't get to work. Still, almost everyone is tempted to stay in bed and snooze just a little too long. Alarm clocks let us know when we have slept too long, tripping us up when we succumb to the tendency to stay in bed.

As discussed above, guardrails play into the decision process itself: delivery units, diversity, red teams, and scenario planning can all ensure decisions are long term before they are taken. Tripwires kick in after the fact: if you're too far off the intended path, a tripwire tells you it is time to reconsider and change direction. The two mechanisms frequently overlap. Knowing you have a tripwire in place can impact your decisions up front. Knowledge that a student will be checking up on him no doubt motivates Ayres to avoid having to make an embarrassing confession in the first place.

What does this mean for government? Tripwires can alert governments and voters when their attention strays toward the short term, rather than staying on course with long-term benefits. Embedding tripwires in the systems of government can help check any accidental drift toward the short term. One high-profile example of a tripwire is the debt ceiling used in the US to at least in theory constrain spending. If the US government wants to keep spending beyond the debt limit, it has to seek authorization from Congress, bringing attention to the issue and that it may be time to change course. For much of American history increasing the ceiling was not particularly controversial, but in recent decades it has become more contested, sometimes leading to full government shutdowns and concerns about American financial stability. In effect it has evolved from tripwire to toll gate, with members of Congress who wish to slow growth in government spending using it as a political bargaining chip to extract concessions in exchange for an increase. The costs and chaos associated with the process may mean this tripwire is no longer desirable, although it does provoke public debate each time it is raised.

Another possible opportunity for a tripwire is the regular update governments provide to the country, whether the format is a Speech from the Throne in places like the UK, Canada, and the Netherlands, or a State of the Union address in the US, France, and the EU. The details vary and may evolve over time, as in the US where what was initially a written submission to Congress to avoid any pomp and circumstance has become a highly visible sign of the centralization of power in the US. For a government already measuring its impact on the long term, though, one tripwire could be a requirement to provide annual updates in those speeches. If the government has swerved off-course, the speech provides a warning for the public that change is needed. This also conveniently serves as a guardrail: the process of writing the speech and providing the update, particularly if it can be linked to concrete data, reminds the government to consider its impacts on the long term and reminds the opposition and public to do the same.

Of course, communication teams excel in taking updates of any kind and adding spin to ensure it supports the message of the government. To strengthen the tripwire impact further, key topics could be pre-set. For example, the government could be required to forecast the future tax burden based on its planned borrowing, the health of the environment based on its current policies, and the quality of the country's assets, such as infrastructure, based on current investment and maintenance.

This is what happens in Australia, whose government releases intergenerational reports on the long-term sustainability of current government policies every five years, as required by the Charter of Budget Honesty Act (1998). These reports focus on how demographic, technological, and other structural trends may affect the economy and budget over the following forty years. The most recent report in 2021 finds that Australia is recovering well from the COVID-19 pandemic, but pre existing structural trends, such as population ageing, remain an ongoing challenge: over the next forty years, the ratio of working-age people to those over sixty-five is anticipated to drop significantly. This approach also helps improve the measurement of potential impacts on the future, as discussed in chapter 5.

A more targeted version using an independent agency is the triennial actuarial report from the Chief Actuary of Canada, which assesses the financial health and sustainability of the Canadian Pension Plan. If the pension plan is insufficiently funded for future generations, the report calls attention to the issue. Similarly, the Canadian Commissioner of the Environment and Sustainable Development, part of Canada's independent Office of the Auditor General, audits the Canadian government's management of environmental and sustainability issues and reports the findings to Parliament. Chapter 7 discusses further how having these tripwires included in the mandate of independent organizations can be an effective way to commit to action when the government changes.

The UK goes further with their risk register, which was first published in 2008 and outlines the most serious risks facing the country. It gives each risk two scores from one to five based on how likely they are to materialize and how serious their impact would be if they did. A likelihood of five means a greater than 25 per cent chance of an event occurring in the assessment period, while a likelihood of one means a less than 0.2 per cent chance. An impact of one is minor and an impact of five is catastrophic. Risks range from the assassination of a high-profile public figure (likelihood five, impact two) to a pandemic (likelihood four, impact five) or an outbreak of African horse sickness (likelihood one, impact three). The risk register isn't perfect, but it takes what can be very abstract concepts and seeks to make them clear, simple, and communicable. It is updated every year, so that were a risk to suddenly change dramatically in likelihood or impact, authorities could respond. It is also a summary of a more detailed internal assessment done by the UK government, which serves as a tripwire for public servants internal to government who may otherwise not consider some of the risks listed. The public version can then serve as a tripwire for a public or media discussion, if one was needed.

Annual reports and speeches aren't the only opportunity to introduce a tripwire in government. Every government faces the challenges of allocating its scarce funding across the almost unlimited demands of stakeholders and lobby groups. This is typically done through the process of an annual budget, in which the legislature or congress gets to review and approve the spending and also often includes a forecast of spending for several years into the future. Requiring each proposed measure for the budget to include a brief analysis of the impact on the future helps focus both bureaucrats and politicians on the long term, and can alert the public if things are going amiss.

A similar requirement could be introduced for new legislation: if politicians wish to make a new law, they should ensure they have thought through the long-term implications, and the public can be warned if it will have a negative effect on the future. This could be done either before the legislation is introduced as part of the policy development process, or afterwards by an independent group such as the Congressional Budget Office. Michael MacKenzie, Jarislowsky Chair in Trust and Political Leadership at Vancouver Island University, in his book *Future Publics: Democracy, Deliberation, and Future-Regarding Collective Action* proposes a similar measure, requiring governments to issue "posterity impact statements" whenever they make decisions that affect the future (which he argues is all decisions).[17] As MacKenzie points out, publishing posterity impact statements is most effective if there is a clear sense of who will read them and how they will be assessed; otherwise, governments could say whatever they want. He suggests that representative and deliberative assemblies comprised of ordinary people be empowered to challenge the claims included in the statements and delay or veto unwanted actions. This could leverage some of the benefits of diversity discussed above. Another option would be an independent agency dedicated to the future, as we explore in the next chapter, or coverage from independent media.

Even absent external accountability, the requirement to publish analysis can still encourage attention from politicians and bureaucrats on long-term issues. That can add a warning light or tripwire to the system and encourage action. There is, however, a balance to be struck when it comes to publishing information: too much transparency can discourage concrete analysis or discussion of issues (governments aren't always keen to share their thinking), and sometimes space is necessary to consider issues privately too. Sunlight is the best disinfectant, but mushrooms need darkness to grow.

Internal tripwires can therefore also be useful. Introducing these can often mean changing the process or templates by which governments consider or make decisions. In the same way that you fill out paperwork to renew your driver's licence, processes inside government often have requisite extensive forms and paperwork every time a decision is made. Adding a section to these documents about the long-term impact of a decision, even if it is never made public, offers a tripwire both for the bureaucrats who fill it out and the leaders who read it. In Canada, for example, to create a new program you typically seek approval of an idea from Cabinet with a Memorandum to Cabinet; approval of funding with a Budget proposal; then spending approval from the Treasury Board using a Treasury Board submission. All three processes follow strict templates. One or all these could include sections asking about the anticipated long-term impacts of what is proposed or how the program can mitigate changes in priorities or attention over time. Other process changes could also be considered, such as requiring inclusion of a section on the long term in welcome documents provided to new ministers when they are appointed, or for departments to internally conduct regular long-term thinking exercises.

Finally, a government could choose several key indicators of the long-term health of their country and commit to making them public at regular intervals, whether in formalized annual messages such as the State of the Union, annual budget documents, or simply on a purpose-built website. Having worked through measuring long-term sustainability as set out in chapter 5, governments should then publish the results, informing the public with a sense of what is on track and what is not. The challenge here is to present enough information to be meaningful without becoming a sales exercise for a political side or presenting so much the website appeals only to policy wonks. Done well, such a transparency approach provides a powerful accountability mechanism for governments to stay on track.

A successful use of this approach in another context is the UK government's introduction of transparency in the gender pay gap. On 4 April 2018 every firm in the UK with over 250 employees was required to publish the average pay gap between their male and female employees. Firms were also permitted to post a narrative piece explaining their gap and what actions they were taking to address it. Unsurprisingly, the vast majority of firms paid men more than women, in some cases significantly more.

The UK's measures aren't perfect. Because it is the average gap, some of the findings are somewhat meaningless, such as the fact that male football/soccer teams have large pay gaps, since the comparison is between male players and female non-players. A more meaningful comparison would be between male and female players, where a pay gap also exists. The approach excelled, though, in starting a broader public conversation. Results were put up on an easy-to-use website hosted by the government and sparked a media debate about the size, causes, and consequences of the gap. It ended up as one of the largest stories of the year in the UK, rivalling the royal wedding between Prince Harry and Meghan Markle.

In the case of the gender pay gap, the UK government's hope is that the publicity will push firms to reduce their inequities. For more long-term indicators such as quality of infrastructure, disaster preparedness, or environmental sustainability, the same effect can be harnessed. Publishing both the absolute levels as well as highlighting when they cross certain predefined thresholds makes the information as easy to understand as possible, strengthening the tripwire effect.

DEFAULTS

We can do more than just try to prevent a slide toward the short term; we can seek to actively harness the human bias toward the easy path by making long-term decisions as easy as possible. Guardrails and tripwires help us stay on the path of long term-planning and alert us when we are leaving it. Sometimes, though, the best plan is to make staying on the path the easiest or default option, so that an intentional act would be required to move off it. This is often the most powerful of the three strategies outlined in this chapter.

The related individual bias is often referred to as status quo bias or the endowment effect: the tendency to go along with the easiest option or default rather than consider all possible options in a decision. Particularly when we are tired or distracted, decision-making is difficult and imposes a cognitive burden. Far easier to just go along with the status quo than make the effort to choose an alternative and risk an outcome we are less happy with. This is why we tend to stick with the same habits, shop at the same businesses, and keep our plans with the same phone company, rather than searching to see if there are better options available.

One way to do this in government is to make long-term policies automatic. Consider stimulus spending, which is spending that occurs during a downturn in order to boost the economy. The Keynesian argument (advanced by John Maynard Keynes) is that when the economy slows, the government is able to encourage it to pick up by increasing government spending. When the government pays a group of labourers to work on an infrastructure project, as was done in the Great Depression under Roosevelt's New Deal, the labourers then have more money to spend on food, shoes, and other necessities, thus farmers and cobblers are also better off. Farmers and cobblers then spend the money at farm supply stores and tanners, who spend the money at other places, and so on. The whole economy is strengthened by the influx of funds. Thus, counter-cyclical spending – spending that increases when the economic cycle is down and falls when the economy picks up – helps offset the economic cycle of booms and busts and bring more stability to the economy.

However, stimulus spending is often controversial. Increasing government spending during a downturn is not particularly intuitive: families usually do the opposite, tightening their belts when their income falls in order to get through the lean time. The case for it is based on the insight that sometimes the macroeconomic effect – the effect on the economy as a whole – differs from the microeconomic effect – the effect on a single individual or firm. If every family reduces its spending in response to a recession that might be sensible for them individually but worsens the recession because one family's spending is another's income. There are also limitations on the impact of stimulus spending: depending on the nature of the economy and household behaviour it may or may not be effective. For example, government spending may crowd out household spending, reducing the effect, or households may save the extra income they receive from government.

To afford stimulus packages during busts, governments also typically need to save when times are good. This is what makes the policy counter-cyclical: Keynesian governments should save when the economy is strong, and spend when it is weak. A high government deficit from borrowing when times are good reduces the fiscal room available to borrow next time, making it harder to respond to future crises. Unfortunately, the saving part can be a challenge. It is far easier for a government looking to get re-elected to justify stimulus spending in downturns than to justify reducing spending when times are good. Lobby groups point to the strong economy and argue there is no need to reduce spending; special interests defend their programs. Without saving in good times, however, it's hard to afford spending in bad times.

Here, then, we have a situation where the correct path for long-term planning is difficult (saving during boom times to spend during busts), while the problematic path is easier (choosing not to save for a rainy day). One option would be to set up tripwires and guardrails to alert politicians and the public when no saving is happening. More effective, though, is simply to swap the problem around: make saving, instead of spending, the default option during good times and spending the default during bad.

One way to do so is through automatic stabilizers, which are policies and programs that spend more when the economy is doing poorly and spend less when it is doing well, without intervention by politicians or bureaucrats. The most common examples are benefits such as unemployment insurance and welfare, as well as income taxes. In a recession, more people are unemployed, and the amount of money spent on unemployment insurance increases. When the economy improves, more people are employed, and spending on unemployment insurance falls. The same is true of taxes: when the economy is doing well tax collection increases, ensuring more money can be saved, but when a recession hits and incomes fall tax collection falls too (because the less someone makes, the less they pay in taxes). These effects serve to stabilize economic cycles automatically, without government action or decision.

The default effect helps prevent future governments from changing course: once a policy or program is in place and doesn't require further decisions, there are fewer triggers for a future government to change it. The next government may not approve of stimulus spending or prefer to spend the money differently, but unless it is a priority there is a reasonable chance that government will get distracted by other events or crises and not get around to changing the defaults. In response to the financial crisis in 2008, for example, the Bush administration introduced a $168 billion economic stimulus package, which had relatively broad support. Then the government and context changed. Obama's introduction of an approximate further $800 billion stimulus through the American Recovery and Reinvestment Act of 2009 was extremely controversial, with hard-fought battles playing out in the House of Representatives, the Senate, and the media. The Obama administration remained in favour of the stimulus package – the issue in this case was not that the new government was opposed – but Congress took a different stance on the spending after the election.

At the same time, largely without discussion or controversy, the Congressional Budget Office estimates that automatic stabilizers, such as unemployment benefits and food programs, as well as reduced tax collection due to lower incomes contributed $334 billion to the US deficit in 2009, followed by $389 billion in 2010,

$367 billion in 2011, $368 billion in 2012, $462 billion in 2013, and $464 billion in 2014 – over $2 trillion in total![18] Far less argument or debate was held over that $2 trillion, despite the considerably higher sum, than over the discretionary and non-automatic stimulus packages. When the economy improved, spending on automatic stabilizers fell without further debate or legislation.

Automatic stabilizers played an important role during the COVID-19 pandemic.[19] More attention was given to the generous benefit programs governments introduced to support household incomes, but billions of dollars were also distributed automatically by reductions in tax collection and increases in the total unemployment benefits paid. It is also often easier for governments to let automatic stabilizers wrap up naturally than to formally close new benefit programs, even if they were intended to be temporary. Many governments ended up extending their pandemic benefit programs once or several times under pressure from stakeholder groups, whereas spending from automatic stabilizers adjusted automatically as conditions changed. Reasonable people can disagree about the right amount of stimulus spending for a crisis, but if you believe stimulus spending is a good idea and want the next government to initiate it if a crisis emerges, it's far better to set up an automated policy than rely on government to make ad hoc policy decisions in a crisis.

Other policies can also be made automatic. A group brought together by the Brookings Institution and the Washington Centre for Equitable Growth, two think tanks, looked at how the US could better prepare for the next recession. They suggested introducing a payment to all Americans, to be automatically triggered when the economy is in recession. The total amount would be similar to the amount paid out in the Economic Stimulus Act of 2008.[20] This would establish a default stimulus package for the economy for use only when a recession called for it.

Another alternative would be to tweak spending programs such as food stamps, funding for medical care, unemployment insurance, or infrastructure investment in order to be more generous during recessions or more widely available. Automatic stimulus could also be introduced through automatic tax cuts: whenever a recession occurs, the rate of sales tax could temporarily fall, for example. In response to the 2008 financial crisis, the UK value added tax was cut by 2.5 percentage points for thirteen months, which economists found had a significant impact on the recovery from the crisis.[21]

A different automatic policy is dynamic pricing for electricity. There has been increasing public attention on the consequences of global warming, and it poses one of the most high-profile long-term problems today. One challenge is that renewable energy sources often have a very different energy profile that non-renewables. Solar power is most available when the sun shines, and wind when the wind blows, whereas coal is available whenever a power plant chooses to burn it. Since energy use tends to peak at certain times, such as when everyone arrives home from work, a system must have enough power available to meet the peak demand, even if that capacity is wasted the rest of the day. Unfortunately, that often means that coal plants keep running when there is plenty of solar and wind power available, because the coal can be relied upon at peak times.

One solution is to improve how well we store energy. Better batteries are a key part of the energy revolution. Another option is to encourage households to use more energy at off-peak times. Some things can't be moved – households are unlikely to cook dinner at midnight, for example – but tasks such as charging an electric car or running a dishwasher can be scheduled to run at midnight or other off-peak times. Dynamic pricing sets the price of electricity based on how much demand there is: households save money by using energy at non-peak times, discouraging use when demand and prices are high. This is good for the environment and, in places where the grid is not particularly strong, can reduce the likelihood of blackouts. Once dynamic pricing is introduced, the response is automatic. Rather than trying to adjust tax or subsidy rates as energy use changes over time, the cost is based on the level of demand and the amount of energy used. In this way, it smooths energy demand and reduces the amount of energy needed by the system, helping fight climate change. Conveniently, it does so without requiring active government intervention: the changes in pricing are the default, so it requires conscious action to change it. That's still possible, of course, but in a world where governments are swamped by competing priorities, it is less likely. As the controversy over energy pricing in many countries suggests, however, defaults are not magic; indeed, they can provoke significant controversy, especially if they or conditions change over time.

A third example of automatic policy is what are sometimes called sunset clauses. These are laws, regulations, or programs that have an end date built in: absent government action, they cease at a set time.

Governments are typically better at starting new things than stopping old things, and sunset provisions provide a way to harness the power of defaults to reduce that trend. Building in a fixed end date is hardly radical – the Romans did it when they chose someone to be a dictator in times of crisis. However, sunset clauses can make it easier to let a program fade away, since they change the burden of action from ending it to preserving it. In the US, for example, sunset clauses cover tax cuts to surveillance tools in the Patriot Act. Of course, nothing precludes these policies from being renewed – they frequently are – but at least it requires an active decision to do so.

The risk with automating policy is that automating too much can be as problematic as too little. Having too much of your paycheque automatically moved to your savings account can be detrimental if you end up paying fees because you accidentally overdrew your chequing account as a result. Governments that automate too much policy may be surrendering their ability to take the decisions that make differences in people's lives and making it harder to be flexible as things change. Making everything sunset can create instability and an inability to plan, as citizens and bureaucrats are suddenly unsure about what they can count on. This may lead to decision paralysis if dozens of low-risk programs require re-debating every few years. Governments must ensure they are automating where it makes sense, without minimizing legitimate legislative sovereignty over important decisions.

Finally, automatic policy and defaults may not be easy to introduce. Opponents to a policy may fight especially hard against policies they believe are likely to stay in place or pass unnoticed in the future based on being a default. The fight against carbon taxes has been particularly forceful in many jurisdictions, and shows little sign of being accepted as a default so far.

LESSONS

In short, there are concrete changes governments can implement to make it easier for them to focus on the long term. Pushing our governments to introduce guardrails, such as delivery units and scenario planning, can help guide them back to a focus on the future. Demanding that decisions be made by diverse groups, including young people or representatives of future generations, can affirm that the options for and consequences on the future are thought through. Implementing tripwires, such as regular updates in the Speech from the Throne or annual budget, can warn the government and the public when the government strays from the long term. Defaults, such as automatic stabilizers, can make the long-term policy the easy one.

Implementation of these strategies can be difficult. Like national balance sheets, any party or interest group that benefits from the status quo may oppose changes that increase the emphasis on the future, while those who believe their policies will be enabled by the measures may support them. Guardrails internal to the bureaucracy are less politically sensitive; an internal assessment of the long-term impacts of a policy by a diverse red team or a delivery unit does not create political risks in the same way a public one might. The bureaucracy has an interest in providing the best advice possible, and though it too is subject to short-termism, and as a large organization can be hard to change, strong leadership can do so without the kind of political constraints elected leaders face. Improving the quality of bureaucratic advice to include the long term can ensure forward-looking advice and considerations are available to elected officials.

The limitation, however, is that elected decision-makers may ultimately choose to ignore such advice, and if the elected government has no interest in listening to long-term advice, it can be challenging for the bureaucracy to justify dedicating resources or effort to it. Still, internal guardrails can be helpful in informing and shaping the bureaucratic advice and perspective, which can then influence decisions and play a role shaping how those decisions are carried out. In addition, guardrails may be effective in semi-independent regulators or other bodies with delegated decision power, such as a central bank.

When it comes to public-facing tripwires, such as including statements about the impact of proposed policies on the future in the annual budget, more opposition is likely. If voters or a government are pushing for a new policy that will dramatically increase the national debt or deplete scarce resources, publishing an impact statement describing the negative impact on the future is not helpful to their goals, and the incentive is to avoid introducing a tripwire in the first place.

As with national balance sheets, however, governments whose priorities do benefit the future may be more supportive of introducing new guardrails and tripwires. If a government is already planning to announce a long-termist policy, or it has just taken power from another party which has not done so, introducing a new requirement to publish an impact statement promoting its own policy and criticizing its opponent's policies holds appeal. Even if introduced, though, future governments may abandon public tripwires if they no longer flatter their preferred policies, or if they harm groups in the present or future that the government wishes to help. Public demand for these statements as well as support from the media or other organizations may help, but the risk of reversal is a challenge for such measures.

If tripwires are published, the public may ignore them. As Michael MacKenzie has pointed out, without a clear audience – ideally one empowered to challenge the claims in the statements – governments can say almost anything in a posterity impact statement without being held accountable, thus their introduction may have little effect.[22] His recommendation for representative and deliberative assemblies to challenge the claims of governments in their impact statements is particularly effective because it minimizes short-term electoral pressures and the influence of other powerful interest groups. Other forms of independent institutions, a healthy and independent media, and to some extent an active opposition party can also increase the political cost to governments of publishing misleading statements or neglecting the future, ensuring impact statements and other tripwires actually function and are not simply stepped over.

Defaults and automatic stabilizers are also vulnerable to reversal by a future government, although by their nature they may be sufficiently inconspicuous to not attract notice or warrant reversal, as occurs with automatic stabilizers in a recession. Their advantage therefore is that the political effort to implement them may only need to be made once, after which they are less likely to attract controversy or be reversed by future governments who may focus on higher-profile policies. Of course, there are no guarantees that defaults will stay low profile, and if controversy does arise then they too are subject to reversal.

Defaults may be difficult to maintain if by remaining low profile they reduce public debate and engagement and consequently lose democratic legitimacy. There can be a tension between the democratic values of debate and discussion and policies that intentionally avoid such debates. Building a public consensus on the value of guardrails, tripwires, and defaults is probably the best way to ensure their long-term survival, but doing so is not easy and may be counterproductive if it raises the profile of the defaults and thus reduces their default status. This is a precarious balance that requires thought on how to keep a default automatic while also maintaining sufficient democratic checks and oversight to preserve legitimacy and maintain public comfort with a measure.

Would guardrails, tripwires, and defaults change government behaviour? Measures internal to government are the easiest to implement but also potentially less effective, given that they impact the bureaucracy but only have an indirect impact on elected leaders. Still, they can help shift the narrative and improve long-term thinking within government. Similar to national balance sheets, public-facing guardrails and tripwires may be harder to implement and keep in place, but they have the potential for higher impact if they get sufficient engagement and support from the public or independent institutions. Ideally they can make it more politically costly for governments to announce policies with negative long-term consequences and make the public more aware when they do, changing the political incentives for governments. These measures may help steer action on less high-profile or polarized issues where the government is more comfortable taking the default or following the guardrail. However, this also makes them more vulnerable to cancellation, and without public support governments may ignore or eliminate them without much difficulty.

Ultimately, one plausible path for implementation of these strategies seems to me that they start with specific issues, where there is a clear case for long-term thinking and fairly broad political support. If a guardrail or tripwire related to infrastructure maintenance, for example, survives and is successful, it may build the case for future guardrails or tripwires for other topics, and eventually for governance in general. Such a path will likely be slow and intermittent as some governments introduce more measures while others eliminate them, but an advantage of these policies is that they can be self-reinforcing. Insofar as each new measure increases the space and motivation for governments to be forward looking and builds public support, they help make the case for future measures and defend existing measures from cancellation.

None of the strategies outlined in this chapter are foolproof. A determined government can crash through guardrails, cut tripwires, and overturn defaults. If some policies are introduced, they may be easy for a subsequent government to reverse. Governments don't just accidentally slip off the path of sustainable planning: as governments' priorities and goals change, governments also have a tendency to cancel the projects of their predecessors to score political points, sometimes playing off voter inattention. To keep governments on the straight and narrow as the party in power changes, it may therefore be helpful to create commitments, which we turn to next.

7

Commit

We choose to go to the Moon in this decade and do the other things, not because they are easy, but because they are hard, because that goal will serve to organize and measure the best of our energies and skills, because that challenge is one that we are willing to accept, one we are unwilling to postpone, and one we intend to win.

John F. Kennedy, "Address at Rice University on the Nation's Space Effort," 1962

On 12 September 1962, US president John F. Kennedy made his famous moon speech, after which he followed through on his commitment, approving an 89 per cent increase in NASA's budget that year and then doubling it again the following year. The lunar landing program, Project Apollo, was one of the most expensive peacetime projects ever undertaken, costing almost $200 billion in 2019 dollars.[1] (By contrast digging the Panama Canal in the early 1900s cost around $10 billion in 2019 dollars.) There was significant controversy, partly because of the program's cost. In 1963 Eisenhower called the project "nuts."[2] Republicans argued the money could be better spent on other military initiatives. Others argued that the money should be spent on different national priorities, rather than wasting it on going to the moon.

Shortly after JFK made the speech, in November 1963, he was assassinated. Lyndon B. Johnson succeeded him, at which point Johnson could have chosen to abandon Project Apollo and direct the resources instead to the Vietnam War efforts and his Great Society programs. The project itself faced adversity, including the death of three astronauts on the launch pad of Apollo 1 in 1967. Nonetheless, the project carried on, culminating in a lunar landing in 1969 and Neil Armstrong's famous small step on the moon but giant step for mankind.

There are many reasons for the project's success: the moment was ripe, the technical challenge was feasible, and the space race provided strong motivation. One surprising factor was the speech itself. The speech resonated with the American public, galvanizing action and bringing public attention and enthusiasm to the topic. With Kennedy's death, the project became almost a memorial to him, and it would have been difficult for a subsequent government to cancel it. Within a week JFK's successor renamed Cape Canaveral as the John F. Kennedy Space Center and named the space launch facilities there after him as well.[3] Once Kennedy's goal was achieved, though, the cuts came: in 1969 and 1970 Nixon cancelled three more planned trips to the moon as well as a subsequent planned space station; the entire space program slowed. At the time of writing, no human has left low earth orbit since the last Apollo mission in 1972.

Why does this matter? Kennedy's speech provides an example of a third strategy governments can use to improve their planning for the future: commitments.

MAKING COMMITMENTS

So far we have explored strategies to alert voters and governments when they are harming the future through better measurement and used guardrails, trip wires, and defaults to maintain focus on long-term priorities instead of short-term urgencies. If they manage to carry out all that, what about when the government changes? A new government, regardless of ideology, tends to reject the projects of its predecessor in order to demonstrate how it is different and better from the last.

As parties become more polarized, the decision about whether to cancel past policies may increasingly be based on a desire to fire up the base or signal change from the last administration rather than on evidence. Even if a new government doesn't actively cancel the last government's projects, they will likely have little interest in pursuing them, leaving long-term projects to languish or be started again in a different guise every time a new government comes to power, instead of building on what came before. Keeping the next government to the same path as its predecessor requires some form of pressure or incentive. In other words, sometimes it isn't enough to make long-term thinking as easy as possible, sometimes we have to make it hard to stop. For instance, if you want to stop spending so much time on social media, it may not be enough to make it easier to read books or spend time with your family. Additionally, you may want to have a friend change your passwords or delete the apps from your phone. In other words, sometimes you must commit.

We frequently commit ourselves to doing something, whether by taking a vow, promising a friend, or signing a contract. All these are decisions we take now that limit our freedom of action in the future, although the strength of the commitment or the cost we would pay to break it varies: signing a contract is very different than promising ourselves we'll do better next time. "Hard" commitments coerce us to behave in a certain way in the future. We can sign a contract with punitive terms if we break it, cut up our credit cards, or register ourselves with a rehab clinic that won't allow us to leave until the regime is complete. Though there might be a way to break these commitments, it wouldn't be easy.

Hard commitments make a lot of us nervous. If we could take a pill that would make us permanently allergic to chocolate, would we? What if we change our minds? Often strong commitments are simply not an option: our future selves are still us, and we can undo whatever commitments we've made. So the commitments we make are typically softer. When we go on a diet, we announce to our friends what we're doing, which doesn't actually stop us from having desserts, but it does discourage us lest we embarrass ourselves. We eliminate chocolate and other snacks from the house, ask our friends not to give us baked goods or sweets, or promise ourselves that we'll restrict sweets to the weekends. All these can be reversed, but there is a cost in terms of time, money, or pride. Commitments increase the barriers between us and what tempts us. If we are having a moment of weakness and there is no junk food in the house, it's much easier to resist. If we can set up those barriers in advance, then they can be hugely helpful in resisting temptation without doing something irrevocable.

Too soft a commitment is useless. Buying a gym membership is a popular January ritual as a way to commit to fitness, but in the vast majority of cases people end up going so infrequently they would have been better off skipping the membership and paying the drop-in fee.[4] Good commitments, in contrast, impose a cost on us if we change our minds.

There is an art to designing soft commitments to be as costly – and therefore effective – as possible. StickK.com, for example, is a commitment website set up by behavioural scientists. To use the site, you set up a contract where you commit to achieving a certain goal: lose weight, exercise more, quit smoking, or reduce your emissions, for example. You then agree to put a certain amount of money on the line and enlist a referee such as a friend or family member to observe your behaviour. If you do not meet the goal, the money is donated to an organization of your choice.

The extra clever part is the selection of the organizations that receive the money. You can select a charity you support, and many people do. If that doesn't provide adequate motivation, you can instead select an "anti-charity" – an organization whose objectives you oppose. A Democrat might choose the campaign to re-elect Donald Trump or a Republican political action committee, while a Republican could choose the opposite. The cost of failure isn't just helping out your preferred charity but rather actively contributing to goals you disagree with.

Commitments work. Consider some research that MIT professors Dan Ariely and Klaus Wertenbroch did with their students. They informed their students that they were required to submit three short papers during the fourteen weeks of class. Half of them had a commitment imposed upon them: they were given evenly spaced deadlines throughout the term, one for each paper. The other half were told they could submit all three papers whenever they wanted, including the last day of term. No feedback was given until the end of the course to avoid giving an advantage to students who submitted early.[5] If commitments didn't make a difference, then the flexible group, who could submit papers whenever they wanted, should be better off. Inflexible deadlines create the risk of a conflict with another course, or a student might get sick or have a ski weekend planned for the same time. Flexibility reduces this risk. This is the same reason we pay more money for flexible flights and hotel reservations that can be cancelled without charge; what if something comes up? If students wanted to have deadlines, they could always set their own internal ones without telling the instructor.

However, this is not what happens. Instead, students in the no-choice condition, those who were given evenly spaced deadlines for the papers with no opportunity for negotiation, had higher grades than those who were given flexibility. Though it might seem superficially appealing to have total freedom, the students fared worse when they had it. Sometimes having flexibility isn't an advantage.

That's not the end of the story. Some students in the flexible condition were also given the option of selecting earlier deadlines for each paper by letting the professor know. If they missed their self-imposed deadlines, their grades would incur a penalty of 1 per cent for each day they were late. The students could choose to have a commitment imposed upon them. Indeed, 68 per cent of the students asked their professors to impose earlier deadlines on them, before the end of term. Those who voluntarily committed to deadlines did better than those who did not, even though the other students could have followed exactly the same schedule if they wished. Interestingly, students who asked for the professors to impose evenly spaced deadlines on them did as well as those who had no choice in the first place. On average though students did worse if they could pick their own deadlines.

The same pattern appears in more meaningful examples (MIT students in classes taught by behavioural scientists aren't exactly a representative group). Banking customers who are offered the opportunity to have a locked-in savings account that they cannot withdraw from, for example, save significantly more than those who do not have the same opportunity – as much as 80 per cent more in some studies.[6] So being committed, even against our will, can be a good thing. If there is no external force that imposes a commitment on us, we can still try to find ways to create our own commitments, and improve our results accordingly.

Of course, commitments by governments are decidedly more complex than those by students, especially since the government in power can change over time. Commitments by governments are also not always appropriate. The whole point of democratic governments is to respond to the wishes of voters, and commitments by definition make the government less responsive to requests for change. It would not be fair for one government to suddenly lock in all their decisions so that after they are voted out the next government is unable to make change. As we shall see, however, governments can and do make commitments. Doing so requires striking a balance between leaving space to respond to the emerging needs of citizens and achieving long-term goals.

There are lessons to be drawn from the individual experience on how we can help our governments commit too.

HARD COMMITMENTS

Governments can also make hard and soft commitments. Hard commitments are powerful but can be difficult to establish: future parliaments or congresses usually have the power to reverse commitments made in the past, in the same way that signing up for a gym membership doesn't prevent our future self from choosing not to go. The most common hard commitments are institutions such as constitutions: governments create rules and then are bound by them, even if they would rather change their mind later on. The Indonesian constitution, for example, requires that 20 per cent of government spending be devoted to education. In Germany as of 2016 Article 109 of the German constitution requires that governments balance their budgets over time, and it sets a yearly maximum addition to debt of 0.35 per cent of German GDP. Temporary deficits are still permitted, and the German parliament has the ability to put the requirement on hold during an emergency (including during the COVID-19 pandemic).[7]

Many long-term constitutional clauses relate to climate change. In Ecuador, for example, as of 2008 the constitution requires that Ecuador "adopt adequate and cross-cutting measures for the mitigation of climate change, by limiting greenhouse gas emissions, deforestation, and air pollution; it shall take measures for the conservation of the forests and vegetation; and it shall protect the population at risk."[8] As of 2019 ten other countries also mention climate or climate change in their constitutions.[9]

Changing a constitution typically involves a high hurdle, such as a two-thirds majority of the legislature or a majority of the population and of the sub-regions. Governments can and do violate constitutional requirements, but doing so can require a coup or some other drastic measure. As a result, though not inviolable, constitutions serve as a strong restriction on government behaviour in democracies. In less democratic countries with single-party rule, however, changing a constitution may be easier. In 2019 Cuba added to its constitution a requirement to fight climate change, but the government could presumably change this if it wished.

Including some sort of requirement in a constitution to consider the future means that citizens can bring lawsuits against a government they felt was acting irresponsibly. This has already been tried in some jurisdictions by those concerned about climate change. A group of young people sued the US Government in 2015 for its inaction on climate change, for example, arguing that the failure to act on climate change had violated their constitutional right to be protected from it. Most lawsuits of this sort have been legally unsuccessful, though they draw public attention to the issue.

The challenge with constitutional requirements is their inflexibility. A high-level requirement to consider the future is more flexible, but also the least binding. The more general the requirement, the easier it is for future governments to ignore it or claim they are already in compliance. On the other hand, a specific requirement, such as a dedicated percentage of government funds to be spent on the future, precludes what may be necessary flexibility. There are times where harming future interests averts more significant harm to the present, and not knowing what challenges will appear tomorrow, we may be reluctant to impose a firm requirement on governments today. Had the German parliament not allowed for flexibility with their balanced budget rule, it could have weakened their ability to respond appropriately to the pandemic.

That doesn't mean a constitutional requirement is impossible or undesirable. It does mean it needs to be carefully thought out to be effective while also preserving some level of flexibility for future governments. In many countries, constitutional change is exceedingly challenging, and there is a risk that the time and energy spent fighting for amendments may be better spent on other measures.

Another version of hard commitments lies in how power is distributed within government. If power is highly fragmented, for example between national and subnational governments, it will be more difficult for any one government to reverse changes.[10] Similarly, if groups who will ultimately benefit from a policy are given a voice or a veto over its development, it will be tougher for future governments to reverse. Institutional and policy design can make it easier or harder for governments to change their minds once policies are created, establishing another form of commitment.

Ultimately, how hard this form of commitment is depends on what backs the distribution of power. A promise to give a voice to a stakeholder group in the future may not be upheld if the government changes, unless the promise is backed by a change to the constitution or some other commitment. It can also create costs. How power is allocated affects the structure of the government itself, and making it harder for governments to change direction can also make it harder to fix problems that emerge later or slow decision-making overall.

"Hard-ish" commitments can also be created by establishing independent organizations that will be difficult to reassert control over. There is a wide range of possible institutions that have been suggested, or in some cases created, to help support long-term thinking, as set out in Iñigo González-Ricoy and Axel Gosseries's volume *Institutions for Future Generations*.[11] Possibilities include specialized institutions, such as an ombudsman or representative for future generations, a global climate bank, or dedicated parliamentary committees, as well as adding long-term considerations to the mandates of existing organizations, including parliaments, central banks, or pension funds.

In Finland, one of the world's leaders on government long-termism, the Committee for the Future is a permanent committee of Parliament that was created in 1993 to generate dialogue on major future problems and opportunities. Each government must issue a *Report on the Future*, outlining Finland's long-term prospects and targets, at least once during their mandate.[12] The committee then prepares a response on behalf of Parliament. The committee also conducts projects of its own that relate to the future, including providing input to other parliamentary work, such as budgeting and the development of reports and studies focused on future issues. In a sense, they are the Finnish parliament's think tank, focused on long-term issues critical to the country.

This model achieves two things. First, it creates a dedicated constituency in Parliament for issues related to the future – the members of the committee – and commits those members to an ongoing role focusing on the future. Second, it commits the government to publishing the *Report on the Future*: a government could refuse, but that would require explaining why the future no longer mattered, which could be politically costly. It therefore pressures the government to spend time considering the future and to publish a report that can be judged by external groups, creating a measure of accountability. This is not as hard a commitment as a constitutional change, but it is considerably stronger than making a public announcement or setting up a team within the bureaucracy focused on the future.

The Committee for the Future is also embedded in a wider network of forward-looking institutions in Finland. This includes an academic institution called the Finland Futures Research Centre, established partly to support the committee, a dedicated group in the Prime Minister's Office as well as other departments that conducts extensive foresight activity, and a national foresight network established in 2005 to increase policy-maker access to foresight work from groups outside government. Members of Parliament often serve on the committee early on in their careers, helping shape their views when they take ministerial roles later on.[13] Research suggests that the Committee for the Future has had a significant impact in Finland.[14] It has agenda-setting power in the Parliament, helping determine what is prioritized for discussion, and the government frequently adopts the committee's recommendations. It is one of the longest surviving such institutions internationally.

Another successful model is Wales, which passed the Well-being of Future Generations Act in 2015 with cross-party support. It imposes a requirement on public bodies to support sustainable development and report on their performance. The act also establishes a Commissioner of Future Generations, who is empowered to advise public bodies on how to meet their sustainable development duty. The act roughly defines the broad concept of sustainable development as making sure the needs of present generations are met without compromising the ability to meet long-term needs.

Other versions of such institutions have been tried, not always with success. Hungary created a Commissioner for Future Generations in 2008 with significant power to protect the environment, reflecting environmental protections in the Hungarian constitution. Its powers were significantly reduced in 2011, however, when a new constitution was introduced, and it never had widespread support. Even constitutional change, as the Hungarian case underscores, is not a perfectly hard commitment: a sufficiently motivated government or sweeping changes can still reverse the commitment. Israel established a Commission for Future Generations in 2001, which among other powers had an effective veto on legislation that didn't meet the interests of future generations. However, it ended five years after it was established, due to budgetary constraints and concerns over the level of power it held to interfere with Parliament. Scotland's Futures Forum, in contrast, is less focused on Parliament and instead seeks to stimulate public debate in the country on preparing for the future. As of writing, it still exists, having been set up in 2005.[15]

There has also been discussion of multi-country bodies. At the EU level, the World Future Council has proposed setting up a Guardian for Future Generations, independent from other EU institutions but able to provide advice and analysis to policy-makers and legislators as well as review existing gaps in policy with impacts on future generations.[16] More speculatively, in Kim Stanley Robinson's climate fiction novel *The Ministry for the Future* (one of Obama's favourite books in 2020), a UN agency set up to advocate for future generations is charged with "defending all living creatures present and future who cannot speak for themselves, by promoting their legal standing and physical protection."[17] Creating a body that spans multiple countries could be useful for international issues such as climate change but also poses a host of new challenges, which may explain why such an approach remains theoretical.

More narrow models, focused on a particular issue or topic, can also be effective if that topic relates to the long term. In Canada, for example, the Auditor General, the Parliamentary Budget Officer, and the Commissioner of the Environment and Sustainable Development are all independent agents that report directly to Parliament instead of to the government. Like many of the other models we have looked at, their independence means they are relatively sheltered from the influence of partisan politics and have space to focus on long-term considerations related to their topics. None of their mandates focus on the long term in general, but within their area of responsibility they can still have an impact.

Simon Caney, a professor at the University of Warwick, builds on the Finnish model to suggest that governments each establish an independent Council for the Future whose role would be to produce reports looking at long-term trends and the likely impact of current and alternative policies.[18] To ensure that the council can have an impact, Caney recommends implementing a requirement that the government issue formal responses to the council's findings. For example, if the council finds a given policy will negatively affect the future, the government would be required to respond to set out why they believe it will not or why they believe a negative impact is justified. If needed, the council could also assess the quality of the government responses. Caney also argues for a dedicated parliamentary committee in each country, which could report on the adequacy of its government's plans for the future (plans which the government would be required to publish). All policies should go through this committee, he suggests, for scrutiny and evaluation of their impact on the future. Any parliamentary committee can choose to look at long-term questions, of course, but having a dedicated body can help serve as a tripwire and ensure the long term is not lost in the press of other issues. A dedicated day could be established for parliaments to focus on the governments' plans for the future and progress so far.

Other institutional commitments are possible. Researchers in the UK have called for the creation of an All-Party Parliamentary Group on Future Generations, the establishment of an expert advisory panel drawing on various UK research institutions and think tanks related to the future, and the inclusion of intergenerational rights if a British Bill of Rights is introduced.[19] In a different direction, Thomas Wells, at the Leiden Institute for Philosophy in the Netherlands, suggests giving charitable foundations, environmental advocacy groups, or non-partisan think tanks 10 per cent of the votes in Parliament, as trustees for the generations to come.[20] For this to work such trustees would themselves have to be given the space and incentives to consider the long term: it is not clear having bishops from the Church of England in the UK House of Lords successfully makes it a long-term organization, for example. Alternatively, Kristian Ekeli argues that a certain share of legislative assemblies should be reserved for elected representatives of the future; "political representation of posterity," as Ekeli puts it.[21]

Finally, there is significant work arguing that institutions in the tradition of deliberative democracy can help improve long-term thinking in democracies.[22] Mini-publics, for example, typically assemble a diverse group of randomly selected citizens to deliberate and decide on a public policy issue. They are perhaps most easily understood as similar to a jury but larger, more intentionally designed and facilitated, and focused on a policy question rather than a criminal one. There is evidence that mini-publics can be good for long-term decisions: the random selection means they are more insulated from short-term political pressures; they can be selected to be representative of the population and inclusive of different views, which allows for more inclusive decisions about the interests of the future; and they can be designed and facilitated to encourage deliberation about the interests of the present and the future.[23]

The firmer the commitment a government makes to these institutions, whether by tying its hands through constitutional change or legislation, securing independent funding, or building a base of popular support for the measure, the more effective it will be. Establishing institutions as independent minimizes the opportunities for governments to weaken them in pursuit of short-term goals and allows institutions to take a more future-focused perspective, away from the vagaries of the electoral calendar.

How these institutions are structured greatly impacts their stability. In the UK, for example, independent groups have frequently been established with their own endowment or funding stream that doesn't use government revenues. This removes the most obvious means for a future government to eliminate such a body, cutting funding. A future government can still eliminate such institutions, but not as easily. An equally important question is impact. Even if an institution is left in place, it may be ignored. Many countries have introduced some form of intergenerational role, but it is not always clear how much impact such changes have had on the national dialogue or policy-making. As we explore further in the section below, clear, concrete requirements, paired with some form of cost for ignoring recommendations, such as public attention or a robust legal framework, can strengthen institutions' potential for impact once they are created. Institutions must be designed for both stability and impact if they are to support long-term policy-making by governments.

SOFT COMMITMENTS

In many cases, legislative sovereignty limits governments' ability to make hard commitments. A congress or president has few options for binding the actions of a future one, because a future one can undo what the current one has decided. One government may choose to introduce a policy about the future or create a new institution; the next can reverse it or eliminate it. Absent the ability to change the constitution, most commitments governments make are fairly soft. There is always a risk of governments reneging. Multiple governments have passed laws requiring a balanced budget, for example. Only a few have held to that when things changed. One notable example is the UK's Fiscal Responsibility Act 2010, which declared that sound public finances were essential and set out rules limiting how much the government could borrow. The act managed to eke out a meagre thirteen months of life before being repealed.

A review of the various balanced budget rules in American states found that most versions of balanced budget limitations have little effect on government behaviour.[24] Only constitutionally enforced requirements – hard commitments – had any significant effect in increasing state general fund surplus; legislative requirements were not effective in changing government behaviour. Even constitutionally enforced requirements were relatively ineffective if they were enforced by a politically appointed court, suggesting that governments anticipated that if they could appoint the court there was little risk of being constrained by it.

Soft commitments can have an effect in some cases, though. When Kennedy announced that he believed "this nation should commit itself to achieving the goal, before this decade is out, of landing a man on the moon and returning him safely to the Earth," a statement he reinforced with multiple public speeches and statements, he was publicly committing to a goal.[25] If, five years later, he or a successor had wanted to change their mind, it would have been possible, but because of the public commitment, there would have been a cost in reputation to abandoning the plan, in the same way that abandoning your diet is harder after you've told all your friends. Even after Kennedy was assassinated, the legislative momentum for the announcement persisted (although the commitment was not the only factor in this).

Research finds the same pattern more generally. Robert Thomson and co-authors looked at over twenty thousand promises made in fifty-seven election campaigns across twelve countries and found that about 60 per cent were at least partially fulfilled by the winning party.[26] Countries and governments varied widely. Single-party governments were more likely to deliver on their promises, while coalition governments had a lower success rate, likely reflecting the need to compromise and negotiate priorities in those cases. Even single-party majority governments didn't deliver everything. One of the highest rates of promise fulfillment was in the UK at around 86 per cent of promises at least partially fulfilled, which is higher than some of us might expect, but hardly a perfect record. One also suspects parties promise to do things they planned to do anyway. Still the evidence does support the idea that governments face pressure to fulfill their commitments once elected, suggesting that convincing them to make relevant promises may at least softly commit them to delivering on a particular file.

MAKE SOFT COMMITMENTS HARDER

Fortunately, there are ways to make soft commitments more effective, for both individuals and governments. Commitments with the strength of changing the constitution may not always be an option, but working within the more everyday space of government policy, there are factors that affect how binding a commitment is on future decisions. In effect, this works by increasing the cost a government will pay if it reneges.

Voters appear to understand this. Research has found, for example, that voters are more willing to pay higher taxes to support spending on long-term benefits, such as education or the environment, when revenues are collected in a trust fund and legally dedicated to a specific purpose.[27] It appears they are more likely to trust that a government will deliver on its promise to spend the money on the long term if there are constraints on its use, even if a future government could amend the legislation to remove them.

Several factors can ensure soft commitments have long-term staying power: making them public, avoiding partisanship, and creating interest groups to support a long-term policy all strengthen a soft commitment. All these are still soft, and governments can and will renege sometimes, but these factors make it increasingly costly to do so. The 1969 moon landing provides one model: public commitments that rally voter support bind governments to some extent, though only in a soft way. This is why governments feel compelled to implement plans announced in their platforms or election campaigns, even if later on it emerges that such policies are probably not a good idea. First, therefore, we should encourage our governments to be as public as possible when they commit to taking action for the future.

Public commitments work for the same reasons that telling all our friends we're going on a diet encourages us to stick to it, providing extra monitoring (since our friends may remark if they see us eating chocolate cake) and increased accountability. When we've told others our commitments, we fear looking small in front of our friends if we fail, perhaps losing their respect. Governments have the same concern: telling voters one thing and doing another is possible, sometimes even desirable, but it can also alienate voters and encourage them to look elsewhere, which no government wants. The best public commitments are those which we can easily tell if governments are upholding or not. A legislatively created trust fund to hold money, for example, can be abolished by a future government but not without an explicit and public change to the legislation. Commitments should be clear and concrete, easy to assess whether they have been fulfilled or not, feasible, and have a well-defined timeline. That way, citizens can easily hold a government to account if its commitment is not fulfilled, and it is difficult for governments to declare victory if victory is not achieved.

The overused acronym SMART is a good start: publicly announced goals should be specific, measurable, achievable, relevant, and time-bound (there is some debate about exactly what each letter should stand for, but these are common). One reason Kennedy's announcement was effective is that it provided a specific goal ("landing a man on the moon") that was easily measurable (was there a man on the moon or not?), achievable (which is hard to know in advance, but with hindsight we can confirm it was indeed achievable), relevant (it was announced a month after the Soviet Union put the first person into space, Yuri Gagarin), and time-bound ("before this decade is out").

Second, good long-term public commitments are often made without partisanship. Partisanship is basically a preference for a particular cause or party and can be good or bad, but in some cases it can undermine support for long-term policies. The more partisan the announcement, the more likely a future government from a different party will repudiate it. Commitments made in a bipartisan way, in contrast, may be harder to reject or renege on, especially if everyone agreed at the outset they were for the public good. Unfortunately, particularly in today's polarized world such a cross-partisan option may not be available. In the highly partisan climate of countries like the US, it can be hard to avoid a decision becoming ideologically aligned.

The experimental evidence is clear: once people have a stance on something, they are far less likely to accept opposing evidence, an effect known as confirmation bias. In one famous study, subjects with a view on capital punishment – for or against – were given two different studies to read, each providing some evidence about the strength of the deterrence effect from capital punishment.[28] Half of the subjects were told one study supported capital punishment and the other undermined it, while the rest of the subjects were told the opposite. Subjects rated the study that they thought agreed with their perspective as more convincing and as higher quality research. The same study elicited completely opposite evaluations from people with different initial beliefs about the social issue. The net effect was more polarization, with each side believing it was more right than ever. Some research suggests that being more intelligent can just make you better at confirming your bias. In one study people who were more numerate, more adept at using quantitative information, were better at convincing themselves why information they disagreed with was incorrect by finding a way to interpret the data that suited them.[29]

The same effect has been found for political partisans. One study found that people could support either generous or restrictive welfare policies as long as the policies were branded with their political tribe's endorsement.[30] Similarly, an experiment with US municipal officials found that those who were ideologically predisposed against a possible policy were unwilling to learn from examples used in other cities.[31] This bias, however, could be overcome through increased emphasis on the results of the policy or its adoption by co-partisans in other municipalities. In other words, partisanship can close us off from good ideas by making us less likely to consider opposing evidence and more likely to simply believe as co-partisans do. It can encourage decisions based on ideological alignment rather than on facts or what is best for the future.

For commitments, aligning a policy to one ideological side makes the other side inherently less likely to support it. Worse, it may make the opposition more likely to cancel or annul the commitment when they are next in power. For long-term policies this is particularly damaging because by definition they are likely to span multiple governments. A policy that the opposition party supported when it was created is at least somewhat harder for it to reject later on, though such changes are obviously still possible.

That said, there can also be benefits to partisanship, including for the long term. Most directly, partisanship can have political benefits. Sharing credit for a policy with your political opponents may be generous but is not necessarily a good way to win votes or emphasize why your party is superior to your political opposition. Governments want to win elections, and it is not reasonable to expect them to constantly be acting in concert with the opposition. Policy disagreements are a chance for parties to highlight their differences and attract support from voters. Partisanship can also help rally members of a party to support the policy, even if they might otherwise oppose it. Firing up your base can build support and expedite bills getting passed, avoiding the need for endless negotiation and debate. If a bill benefits the future, partisanship can be harnessed toward passing it for long-term goals.

In some cases, therefore, a level of partisanship may be inevitable, given the political benefits. It may also be desirable, encouraging substantive debate on issues and rallying support for a policy. But for long-term policies, too much partisanship, or polarization, has risks. Although it may build short-term support for a policy, in the long run partisanship may increase instability and the likelihood a policy is reversed. Of course, if a commitment is so strong that future governments won't have the ability to reverse it, then partisanship makes little difference; however, it is rare for commitments to be that strong. Had Kennedy announced the moon landing as a purely Democratic initiative and something that Republicans should dislike, then the long-term health of the program could have been jeopardized. Instead, Kennedy reached across the aisle to all Americans, generating wide support for the program in the long term.

Building the legitimacy of a policy or program and avoiding partisanship is not easy. Transparency can help, as can ensuring inclusion of views from across the spectrum in the discussions. Reaching out across the aisle to ensure you have bipartisan support from the start, even if it means compromising on some of the vision, helps. Designing policies to avoid partisan controversy can be useful too, whether that means emphasizing benefits that appeal to both sides or avoiding using a long-term policy as fuel for offensive tactics against another party. Sometimes the simplest option is to avoid giving a specific policy too much profile. The more salient a policy is, the more likely a future government will hope to win political points by cancelling it, though less salience also means less political benefit for the party in power. Particularly when policies are easily reversible by future governments or will require sustained effort over many years, leaders should exercise caution in using them as wedge issues, since doing so may allow for short-term progress but lead to reversal in the future.

Minimizing partisanship applies to long-term thinking in general too. If planning for the long term becomes associated with one political tribe, it risks arousing opposition from others. We all have a collective responsibility to avoid labelling long-term thinking as belonging exclusively to our side, media and politicians included. Every time you tie a long-term policy to your in-group, you make it more likely out-group members will reject it without deliberation. Instead, argue for policies based on their results. Research suggests that tribal membership is most influential when people are unfamiliar with the policy in question. When they are given information about policy consequences, the partisan effects diminish and people focus on whether they agree with the policy rather than whether it comes from their party.[32] As the study of US municipal officials above found, increasing the adoption by co-partisans and making sure there are champions on both sides can reduce the likelihood of the future becoming a partisan football.

Ultimately, some partisanship can be helpful, as long as sides remain willing to listen to each other. Partisanship becomes a negative when polarization becomes too strong, and parties refuse to deliberate together or listen to each other. Addressing polarization is a significant challenge facing many countries. More work is needed around the effects of social media and AI recommendation systems, which allow for ideological bubbles to form where people are not exposed to other opinions, as well as the role of educational systems in preparing citizens to consider differing views, among other things. It is a challenging issue to solve, but increasing citizen willingness to support good ideas no matter where they come from and learn from each other seems critical to overcoming many of the challenges of our time. The issue could also benefit from a behavioural science perspective: like many of the long-term issues identified in this book, governments could likely do more to proactively engage and address this issue. Overcoming polarization is clearly possible, despite the challenges of modern technology. Wanting our grandchildren to have as good a world as we do is not a partisan issue.

A third way to make soft commitments more effective is to create public support for their continuation. If a policy or program creates a group dedicated to its success, either because they benefit from it in some way or are invested in its progress for some other reason, then it will be harder for future governments to overturn it without raising an outcry. Creating a constituency for a policy helps commit governments to it since any future change in direction would disappoint that constituency. In fact, this effect can often be an obstacle to good public policy, since it can lead to the perpetuation of policies that serve the needs of special interest groups, even if they do not benefit the country as a whole. For this reason economists often raise concerns about subsidies: even if subsidies make sense initially, they often continue long after they would be reasonable because of the recipients' ongoing demands. Sunset clauses can help by encouraging what are intended as temporary policies to stay temporary; however, when the sunset date arrives programs can often be extended due to stakeholder pressure.

To see how a government might build support for a policy, consider carbon taxes, which are controversial – most phrases that end in *tax* are. They have been the subject of hard-fought battles in a number of jurisdictions. They have also been repealed in various places, including in Australia where a carbon tax was nixed only two years after it came into effect. Two different strategies are often suggested to build support for a price on carbon. First is to use what's called a cap-and-trade system, which is similar to a carbon tax. Both impose a cost on polluting, one through a tax and the other through the purchase of permits in order to emit. A key difference of cap and trade is that some firms benefit from the regime based on how permits are initially allocated. Firms that are doing well in reducing emissions can choose to sell their extra permits, turning a profit from their reduction in emissions. It turns out that governments can choose to allocate the initial permits in a way that benefits some firms or interests, building a constituency to support the policy without reducing the environmental benefits because the overall cap on emissions stays the same, and firms can buy and sell permits as necessary.[33] Any subsequent government considering cancelling the policy finds itself somewhat committed to keeping it based on the support from benefitting firms.

Alternatively, there is the option of returning the revenues raised through a carbon tax to citizens as a kind of carbon dividend. Economists have not always been enthusiastic about this idea. Almost all taxes create negative effects of some kind for the economy. An income tax may discourage people from working as hard as they would otherwise, for example. A carbon tax is a happy exception: not only does it raise revenue, but it also discourages emissions, which are bad in any case. In theory, therefore, carbon tax revenues could be used to reduce other, more harmful taxes.

In practice, places that have implemented a carbon tax have sometimes also committed to making it revenue neutral, returning all the money raised to citizens in a form of carbon dividend. In part, this is a reaction to the carbon tax's regressive effects: since low-income households spend a higher percentage of their incomes, they end up paying a higher percentage of their incomes on the carbon tax as well. A second advantage of the carbon dividend model is that it can create a constituency for the policy. If someone is lukewarm about the idea of a carbon tax, having received regular cheques for the past few years may make them more apt to support it. Carbon dividends are still too new to determine if this strategy will be effective, but it is conceivable that future governments will find their hands at least loosely tied by the policy.

In short, when it comes to building public support for a measure, as well as the success of a measure overall, the how matters. The details of how a carbon tax is implemented may not be as glamourous as the headline announcement introducing it, but the nitty-gritty of how revenues are collected and what is done with them can determine whether a program succeeds or fails. This lesson on the importance of delivery, not just decision, is one that governments frequently overlook and one we examine further in the next chapter for its consequences for long-run success.

All three strategies – making commitments public, minimizing partisanship by seeking cross-partisan support, and building a public constituency for their support – can be effective. In the best cases, soft commitments can solidify into a widely accepted norm. For example, the preceding chapter proposed requiring an assessment of the impact on the future in the annual updates provided by governments, such as the State of the Union address or Speech from the Throne. If carried out over a long period, the requirement can become established as a norm, the standard way of doing business. A future government is not forced to include the assessment but once established, norms can be costly to change. A government that suddenly stops including a future assessment after it has been done for many years may worry about negative media coverage or criticism, based on the idea that the impact must be truly terrible if they are unwilling to make it public.

Norms are only so strong, however. George Washington stepped down as America's first president after two terms not because he had to, but because he chose to. Future presidents followed that norm until it was eventually written into the constitution as a hard commitment in 1951. Before then, a strong-willed president who refused to step down could have broken the norm. Franklin D. Roosevelt did so, serving four terms, but the exigencies of World War II provided a clear justification for the break, which did not extend to future presidents. Nonetheless, one reason for the change to the constitution was to prevent Roosevelt's choice from setting a precedent for the future. Ultimately, norms are vulnerable to a single strong-willed naysayer in the same way that the norm of the emperor wearing no clothes was accepted until a single child destroyed it. This is what pundits sometimes worry about with leaders like Donald Trump. Regardless of his actual policy decisions, Trump's way of doing business when in office, whether declaring national emergencies or not releasing his tax returns, broke social norms and weakened the social fabric upon which the American system is based, making future abuses more likely by all parties. American socials norms are a function of their history and culture, as is the case in any country, and violations can set a precedent that weakens or eliminates the norm going forward.

All these strategies, even if they gradually solidify into something more durable in the form of a social norm, remain soft: in many ways they are about shifting the narrative of a given policy or program. A future government with a strong narrative in a different direction can override or change the policy without significant difficulty. Still, the harder soft commitments can be made, the more effective they will be. In the real world, of course, there is no reason to choose a single strategy. Governments keen to advance long-term policies can mix and match, using the strongest options available to them, potentially including constitutional changes and establishing dedicated institutions to promote long-term policies that are independent of government, as well as softer measures, such as public announcements and designing policies to minimize partisanship and maximize public support.

COMMITMENTS IN ACTION: NORWAY EDITION

Different countries have set up a variety of independent institutions, from independent research groups and blue-ribbon panels to independent commissions and central banks, with varying levels of autonomy, resources, and power. They are not always successful. Their independence may not be strong enough to protect them, or they may remain independent but have no success influencing government policy. A government may choose to influence or ignore them, or with enough public support and determination, abolish them altogether.

One particularly interesting example is sovereign wealth funds. Norway has led an increasing trend toward independent sovereign wealth funds, using both hard and soft commitment techniques. Sovereign wealth funds are established by governments as investment funds that invest in assets such as stocks, bonds, and real estate. They vary in purpose and goals but commonly focus on long-term returns while investing money from a natural resource boom or other temporary influx of funds. Knowing that natural resources, such as oil or diamonds, don't last forever, a sovereign wealth fund is an attempt to take an unsustainable resource and turn it into a sustainable one – an investment account. Their creator government sets how it will be funded, how and if money can be withdrawn, and the overall investment strategy. Then the government steps back.

Norway's Government Pension Fund Global, established in 1990, has well over $1 trillion in assets. That's enough to own approximately 1.5 per cent of the entire world's listed companies, and over $200,000 per Norwegian citizen. It has been built through the profits from Norway's oil sector, and the Norwegian government has limited itself to withdrawing on average only the real return of the fund, around 3 per cent of the fund's value each year, to ensure that it does not get overdrawn. That 3 per cent contributes almost 20 per cent of the Norwegian government budget.[34]

Oil was discovered in Norway in the 1960s. At the time Norway had no experience or expertise in developing and marketing oil reserves. It wanted to encourage international oil companies to help develop its reserves while still ensuring it secured revenue for itself. The solution was a special tax on oil companies, set by 2019 at 53 per cent and making the total tax on profits from oil 78 per cent. Initially, the money raised was simply treated as tax revenue, but by the 1990s the scale of revenue meant the idea of a fund was taken more seriously.[35] The goal of the fund was simple and explicitly future-oriented: allow for the sustainable use of oil revenues so that even if oil reserves ran out the fund could continue to benefit

Norwegians. All net revenues from the petroleum sector were to be transferred to the fund, and withdrawals would be integrated into the Norwegian budget. The fund is formally owned by the Norwegian people, but it is managed by the independent central bank to provide a level of independence from short-term pressures, and the fund invests in equities, fixed income, and real estate around the world. As the central bank describes it, the fund "serves as a financial reserve and as a long-term savings plan so that both current and future generations get to benefit from our oil wealth."[36] The government has also set out criteria for blacklisting individual firms if they break certain ethical rules, such as violating humanitarian principles, producing tobacco, and some kinds of weapon production. In essence, Norway has institutionalized self-restraint in how it uses its oil revenues.

Contrast this with standard practice in most countries. Natural resource revenues rush in and out of the system at almost equal speeds. Typically, massive private fortunes are made but almost no money is set aside or used for long-term purposes. A few decades later, all that is left are some faded once-wealthy towns, testaments to former riches. Many countries have little if anything to show for resource booms once they are over. A sovereign wealth fund can ensure resources are set aside for future use. There are also indirect benefits, including minimizing the effect of natural resources on the economy. Economies that are overly reliant on exports of natural resources can find that those exports increase the value of their currency so much that it weakens other domestic industries. This is a phenomenon now known as *Dutch Disease*, a term coined by *The Economist* after manufacturing in the Netherlands declined following the 1959 discovery of the Groningen natural gas field. When the natural resources run out, an economy can find itself with few other industries to rely on. A sovereign wealth fund that invests abroad reduces this risk by letting revenues into the country slowly. Of course, for countries that are themselves short of investment capital, such as some lower-income countries that desperately need more infrastructure, it may still be better to invest domestically.

There is much debate over the fund in Norway, as is appropriate given its scale and importance to the country. Remarkably, however, there has been a high degree of consensus throughout its history on both the left and right regarding the need for the fund and upholding the fiscal rule to limit withdrawals to ensure the fund is healthy in the future.[37] Debate has largely focused on specifics, such as whether more companies should be put on the blacklist due to unethical activities or whether it should invest less in the stock market to avoid volatility. In 2014, for example, the fund divested from a number of coal companies, and in 2022 it announced it would stop holding Russian assets.

The consensus on the long term is helped by the fact that the fiscal rule – on average, withdrawals should be limited to the real returns of the fund – was designed to allow some flexibility. To help defray the cost of the pandemic response, for example, Norway withdrew almost $40 billion in 2020 and $50 billion in 2021 – around 4 per cent and more than the real returns in both years. As long as they are more moderate after the pandemic, they can still follow the fiscal rule of not withdrawing more than 3 per cent of returns on average. So far, the 3 per cent withdrawal rule has held. It is quite possible a future government will change it, or abuse the flexibility it permits. Still, the creation of the fund makes it harder for that to happen, and any future government looking to make changes would be forced to justify them and convince Norwegians of their value.

Similar funds have been set up in many other countries, not all of them with oil. Singapore's US$500 billion Temasek Holdings, for example, was set up to manage the major investments of the Singapore government, originally including businesses such as Malaysia-Singapore Airlines and Singapore Telecommunications. It brands itself as a generational investor, investing with tomorrow in mind. In 2006 Australia set up its own sovereign wealth fund with the idea that funds could be devoted specifically to its multi-billion-dollar unfunded public servant pension liability, a long-term need that it was struggling to pay.

The funds do not exist solely in wealthy countries. The Pula Fund in Botswana was established in 1993 using revenues from diamond mines, again with the goal of preserving some of the wealth for future generations. Pula, in addition to being the name of the currency, means "rain" in Setswana. Botswana has literally set up a rainy-day fund. Rwanda, with no large natural resource deposits of its own, asked its citizens to donate money to build its fund.

* * *

Sovereign wealth funds are commitments. They prevent the government of the day from spending money on short-term priorities by assigning the money directly to the fund and creating safeguards or limits on how the money can be withdrawn or reallocated. In Norway's case, though the fund does not have a constitutional guarantee of independence, since it is managed by the independent central bank it has a degree of independence. In addition, the announcement of the fund and the emphasis on transparency make it harder for individual politicians to divert the funds to a short-term need. The models in other countries vary, but they typically have some degree of independence from the government, especially when it comes to the management of the assets they control. As long as other checks are also in place, such as the rule of law and independent courts, it can be difficult for a government to reclaim control once they have given it away.

At first glance this seems a triumph of government long-term planning, and it is. But such funds don't always work; to succeed, they require ongoing support from both the public and governments. A sovereign wealth fund in the Canadian province of Alberta, for example, though set up in 1976 in anticipation of considerable oil revenues to come, remained basically empty for the following thirty years as subsequent governments either declined to contribute or spent what little had been saved up. The Alberta Heritage Savings Trust Fund was set up with good intentions: save for the future, strengthen and diversify the Albertan economy (which relied heavily on oil and gas, and still does), and improve the quality of life for Albertans. Unfortunately, it was not set up to be independent of government, and its terms were easily reversed. Initially, 30 per cent of Albertan non-renewable resource revenues flowed to the fund, while the rest supported government spending directly. The amount allocated to the fund quickly dropped, however, first down to 15 per cent and then to zero in 1988. Worse, in the 1990s and early 2000s revenues were steadily withdrawn from the fund for immediate spending. Due to this pillaging, between 1977 and 2011 the net income of the fund was $31.3 billion, but $29.6 billion was transferred out of the fund in the same period.[38] If Alberta had followed Norway's example and required that all resource revenues be deposited in the fund, then between 1982 and 2011 total contributions would have been almost $170 billion.

As a result, for much of its history the value of the Alberta fund was basically flat, with money taken out almost as quickly as it came in, despite tremendous oil revenues in the same period. Only an economic boom in 2005 and 2006 would lead to new deposits to the fund, the first deposits in nineteen years. And only in 2008 was an independent organization set up to manage it. In 2012 a new law was passed requiring a certain percentage of oil, gas, and mining revenues be deposited into the fund. Whether these changes will be effective remains uncertain.

What makes sovereign wealth funds succeed? Obviously, having clear rules about when withdrawals are permitted and what should be deposited is important. But how do we ensure governments comply with those rules? As we see in the Norwegian case, three factors can contribute. First, institutional independence is key, including the ability to prevent subsequent governments from using resources allocated to the fund. If the fund is drained as soon as the government changes, there is little value in setting it up. As in Norway, governments can make hard commitments to do this by setting up independent institutions, or giving control of the fund to existing independent institutions, such as central banks. This also delegates day-to-day decisions and avoids daily struggles, removing the need for a full discussion in Parliament every time the fund takes a decision. This independence also reassures the system that decisions will not be made for political reasons. This is particularly important for institutions like central banks, for whom independence assures investors that money will not be printed whenever the government asks. When investors expect that the central bank will act to prevent inflation that expectation itself can stabilize prices. Of course, to maintain democratic accountability it is important Parliament retain some level of oversight and control. Stronger yet would be creating a constitutional guarantee, which typically requires specific conditions, such as a supermajority (e.g., two-thirds support) to change and is enforced by the courts.

Second, even relatively hard commitments may be inadequate without a complementary soft commitment, namely, getting public support for the measure. Some political consensus on the fund is necessary to keep it going. As we saw above, a non-partisan announcement of the sovereign wealth fund, and when possible securing a clear constituency that supports its continuation, can help fortify the commitment effect of its creation. If the government is unable to make the institution independent, public support can provide at least some protection from short-term meddling.

In this respect, sovereign wealth funds benefit from a bias that can also encourage individuals to save for retirement. Cass Sunstein and Richard Thaler, originators of the behavioural nudge movement, recommend a program called Save More Tomorrow to assist people trying to increase their retirement savings.[39] Rather than taking money from today's paycheque to put in savings, people decide in advance to take some of their next raise and send it automatically to their retirement savings. Because there are no immediate costs to do so, their present selves don't mind the idea, and though in theory their future selves could have a change of heart when the pay increase arrives, in practice the money usually goes into retirement savings. In the same way, governments typically prefer to avoid taking current spending and reallocating it to the future. A government that attempted to do so would likely face considerable opposition. Instead, governments tend to promise new or future revenues to a sovereign wealth fund, such as from a natural resource find or expected government surplus. The effect on current spending is relatively minor, with only future revenues dedicated to the fund. This helps build popular and political support for the measure, strengthening its foundation.

A final factor is to allow some flexibility. Providing clear requirements but allowing flexibility within them, as Norway does with its limit of 3 per cent withdrawals on average, helps strike a balance that allows for short-term crisis response and reaction while staying within the rules. If too strict a rule is set, then as soon as it is broken due to emerging events the whole foundation of the project may crumble, with different parties trying to abolish or change the fund and limiting its long-term value. Flexibility within a frame clarifies what is and is not permitted, while avoiding a need for violations as soon as the fund is created.

These principles apply to other institutions where commitments to the future may be beneficial. Pension plans, for example, are funded by the contributions of employees and employers and invest money on behalf of future retirees. As the deeply underfunded state of many American pension plans demonstrates, they too can have problems with government underfunding, risking an inability keep up with the promised payouts.[40] Pension plans also have less flexibility to adjust spending than more general funds do, given the need to make sure retirees receive regular and predictable income. When designed successfully, however, with professional, independent management and funding separate from government accounts; strong public support and regular external audits; and assessments to highlight issues, they can remain well funded and well operated.

LESSONS

What, then, should we as voters demand from our governments to assure they are committed to the future, not just the present? The strongest commitment would be a constitutional requirement to consider impacts on future generations or avoid undue harm to them. Absent the impetus to change the constitution again later on, this would bind future governments, with court decisions able to back them up as needed. The challenge arises in finding language that strikes the right balance between a meaningful requirement and not tying the hands of the future such that future leaders are unable to adapt to future crises. Ultimately, it seems likely that constitutional change is an approach that will work in some countries and not others, particularly given the difficulty in changing the constitution in some jurisdictions.

A less strong but still effective commitment is to set up an institution with responsibility for the future with either direct decision-making power, similar to an independent central bank in many countries, or the resources and capacity to monitor government decisions and provide assessments of their impact on the future. Direct decision power can be particularly valuable when there is a series of decisions with important implications for the long term that are at risk of short-term political interference, as is the case with central bank interest-rate setting. Monitoring government decisions can provide a valuable accountability mechanism, particularly if funding is sufficiently independent that it will be difficult for a future government to end it.

Having an institution or group with responsibility for the future creates a dedicated group interested in the subject, which can make concerns and impacts on future generations more immediate and give voice to the interests of those not yet born, even if said institution does not have direct decision power. Such a group helps ensure that policy decisions are scrutinized from the perspective of the future; however, it doesn't directly force a government's hand in the way a constitutional amendment might. A government could simply choose to ignore such a group's reports, preserving its sovereignty.

If the need is to balance spending over time, independent sovereign wealth funds can also be effective, although they need to be designed to support long-term thinking, not just assumed to do so. Such funds are most useful when a country has a large inflow of wealth, such as from natural resource development. Since natural resources will by their nature run out, a sovereign wealth fund allows for future income sources to be developed before the resources are gone. Some countries may also choose to create an independent institution focused on the future and allow that group to run the sovereign wealth fund. If the institution identifies an underinvestment in infrastructure, climate change adaption, or other long-term projects, the sovereign wealth fund could help steer resources toward those gaps.

Weaker yet, a country could choose to create a government department or designate a member of cabinet devoted to the future. This measure is less costly than creating an independent institution but also more subject to change or elimination under future governments. Nonetheless, such a project could be effective if complemented by soft commitments, such as a high-profile public announcement of the need for more future thinking, and a clear statement of both its goals and how specific groups, such as the young, will benefit, to create a more solid base of support.

Finally, governments can make entirely soft commitments. Public announcements like JFK's that the US was going to the moon still have value, even if they are not binding, especially when the goal commits the same government to action later, as in election platforms, rather than binding future governments. In this light, the trend for political parties in democracies to make their platforms public has some appeal as a way of binding them to then take action on the long term, provided their platforms reflect long-term values. As every voter knows, an announcement while running for something is one of the weakest commitments available. Still, if parties make announcements in a clear, concise, and easily measurable way, they may find themselves committed to at least responding to the issue. The higher profile the commitments are, for example if they are included in a Speech from the Throne, the more politicians may feel politically bound to fulfilling them, even if there is no institutional or legal obligation.

What about the political incentives for the implementation of commitments? By definition, commitments generally involve a decision by a present government that will restrict or shape the options of a future one. For that reason, they are likely to be appealing to the government in power, since it is either unaffected by the commitment or is committed to doing something it intended to do anyway. In effect, the current government gets to announce the measure and garner any political points, but any costs of the commitment only apply to subsequent governments, once conditions change. The challenge is therefore whether the commitments survive changes in government. When the next government arrives and is bound by the commitment, they have a strong incentive to remove it even if it is costly to do so, as we saw in the case of balanced-budget commitments.

In the very long term, future governments and generations will make their own decisions. There are no options available to governments to fully commit a future government to a specific option, such as a climate change agreement or level of national debt.[41] If there is no public support for something, constitutions can be changed, institutions shut down, public promises reneged on. Disinterested voters may not be willing to pay to end commitments, insulating commitments that have a cost to undo (such as dismantling infrastructure that is already built), but active opposition can threaten any commitment. Persuading the public, today and in the future, of the value of a commitment is probably the best method to support commitment survival.

In my view, commitments have the best chance to survive in the long term if they have clear democratic legitimacy, and correspondingly public support. If an independent institution is too powerful or seen as overstepping into political decisions about the allocation of costs or benefits, then it is more likely to lose public support and be unable to survive a government that opposes it, as occurred with Israel's Commission for Future Generations. Having a clear mandate established by elected officials that focuses on a specific area, ideally one that is seen as technocratic rather than political, can help maintain public support. Committed leadership and careful design, as seen in the case of the Norwegian fund, can help establish these conditions.

In addition to being too powerful, commitments can also be too weak. Nothing shields against criticism like success, and if an institution is too weak to achieve its mandate, then it will be unlikely to survive or matter. Long-termist institutions can also be inherently vulnerable to public criticism because by definition, the group who benefits most from their existence is young or not yet born and unable to express their support. This is hard to mitigate entirely, but transparency can help reassure the public about both the value of and limits on the institution, a factor which perhaps underlies the recent trend of central banks to publish more information about their deliberations. If their design can be done well, however, and their foundation sufficiently strong that future governments do not reverse them, then the advantage of commitments is that once in place, they can have a sustained impact over time.

Often commitments are also set up in response to a crisis, which helps establish their rationale and justify their existence, further legitimizing them. Independent central banks were set up in part in response to the inflation crisis in the 1970s, for example, which helped convince the public of their need (and they risk facing increased criticism as memories of that crisis fade).[42] Constitutional requirements are often easiest to change when a crisis forces action. No one wants a crisis, of course, but scholars and practitioners can help be ready for them when they arrive by designing thoughtful institutions and proposals in advance.

Policy wonks sometimes refer to the concept of the Overton window, which suggests that politicians typically pursue ideas and policies with a level of mainstream support. The window captures the range of policies that have mainstream support and are therefore feasible. Over time the window can shift, often as a result of events, individual leaders, or structural factors such as demographic change; new policies can become acceptable to the public and old ones lose favour. The prohibition of alcohol, for example, was at one time well within the Overton window in the US. It is hard to imagine prohibition having enough mainstream support in America to be politically viable now. Part of long-term policy-making, commitments included, is considering policies and programs which may not be realistic today but could be tomorrow.

Countries should also remember the disadvantages of commitments. More so than the other strategies explored in this book, commitments can sit in tension with democratic principles. The more we outsource decisions to independent bodies or predetermined constitutional rules, the more we limit the ability of future governments and voters to fulfill their democratic role and make their own decisions. Democracies already do this, of course, but the more power is delegated to unelected bodies, the greater the tension. The same political pressures that can drive short-termism can also reflect the legitimate democratic preferences of voters, and in a democracy, future governments are not supposed to be constrained by past ones, even if they are inevitably impacted by their decisions. There is a balance to strike between independence and politicization, with political considerations particularly important when it comes to ensuring the representation of interests of everyone affected, distribution of costs or benefits, and navigation of potential conflicts between groups.[43]

If independent institutions diverge too far from public preferences or create too much tension with democratic principles, their legitimacy may be challenged, which can in turn reduce their effectiveness or lead to their elimination. Central banks are not famous for their responsiveness to the needs of voters, and though that is an intentional design choice and a benefit of the model, it has also exposed them to criticism. Of course, just because such institutions are imperfect does not mean they are not worth having, but threading the needle of independence and politicization will help build their legitimacy and increase their likelihood of survival. Most behavioural interventions are relatively limited in their impact in this regard; they are meant to be reversible if the leader or voters care enough, and while this makes them less directly powerful it also means there remains some level of democratic control.

For commitments, however, there is a clear trade-off between the democratic objectives of flexibility and steadfastness, which governments will need to balance.[44] Governments should take care to preserve democratic legitimacy where possible, whether by keeping the institutions relatively limited in scope and scale or providing specific checkpoints where democratic accountability is maintained, such as a periodic review of the institution's mandate and rules by the elected government. We already have independent institutions of various kinds and other commitments in most democracies, and in my view, they are appropriate. However, there is tension there that should be acknowledged when they are considered.

Introducing dedicated institutions to represent future generations can have its own challenges. The future cannot hold their representatives accountable in the way that voters today can vote against their leaders.[45] Independent institutions may also make mistakes about the interests of future generations, particularly because benefits are likely to be distributed across different groups within future generations, with some groups winning and some losing both today and tomorrow rather than a clean reallocation between generations. What if a policy makes wealthy households in the future richer but lowers the income of poor households today? Independent, unelected institutions may struggle to weigh those costs and benefits and may be seen as illegitimate. Another risk is that conflicts of interest may lead institutions to make decisions in their own interest rather than the future's, or the public may see them as too biased for or against the future, reducing the institution's credibility. If institutions are not striking the right balance between representing the needs of present and future generations or are perceived as not doing so by the public, then they may lose public support and be eliminated by a future government.

In my view hard commitments, perhaps more than the other strategies we look at, are likely to be motivated by a crisis of some kind. A debt crisis justifies a government imposing restrictive borrowing requirements on future leaders; an environmental crisis prompts the addition of environmental protection of the environment into a constitution. No doubt such crises will continue to emerge in the future. Norway seems to be an exception, having successfully set up their fund as a proactive measure on the discovery of their massive oil wealth, rather than in response to a crisis after the wealth was largely spent. Such proactive measures seem uncommon, disappointingly.

Overall, for me it is less about convincing governments to make commitments and more about finding ways to help commitments survive over time. Public support will be crucial in convincing future governments to accept limits on their behaviour, and they should be established in ways that maintain public support and do not provoke complaints over democratic illegitimacy or abuse of power while still being effective. This will require constant work. Institutions inevitably weaken over time, whether due to a particular scandal, political opposition, or simply entropy. Thus, new ones will likely be continually needed or old ones continually renewed.

The bottom line is that though hard commitments have some intuitive appeal, there is no reason to use only one type of commitments. Countries can use hard and soft commitments to motivate an emphasis on the future. As we've seen, commitments also limit flexibility. A commitment may not be appropriate in situations where the right decision is unclear, more information is needed, or a commitment risks reducing democratic legitimacy or support. In the next chapter, therefore, we turn to iteration and experimentation as ways to address those challenges while still preparing for the long term.

8

Iterate and Experiment

The country needs and, unless I mistake its temper, the country demands bold, persistent experimentation. It is common sense to take a method and try it: If it fails admit it frankly and try another. But above all, try something.

Franklin D. Roosevelt, "Oglethorpe University Address: The New Deal," 1932

The American constitution famously lists three unalienable rights: life, liberty, and the pursuit of happiness. This is a classic example of commitment: Jefferson, who wrote that line, was seeking to commit future governments to a vision of human rights, binding future government policy. There is a second important aspect to this declaration, however. What the constitution does not include is exactly how the state will get its citizens there. It doesn't prescribe tax rates or details of what social supports will be provided. Jefferson didn't pretend to know all the answers on how to deliver those rights, and what was needed might well change over time anyway. Instead, he gave space for future governments to experiment, adapt, learn, and innovate, while still aiming for a constant goal. This need not be complicated. Governments, as well as businesses and individuals, benefit from taking Roosevelt's advice above: if you face a problem or challenge, systematically try possible solutions on a small scale and see if they work. If they do, scale them up. If they don't, say so and try again.

This idea has a number of different names, including randomized control trials, A/B tests, trials, lean start-up, agile methodology, experimentation, and prototyping. Trying new things is what allows for innovation and finding better ways to do things. There is no magic to this; in some ways it is simply the scientific method, dressed up in modern clothes. In the long term though it is innovation that can bring the largest rewards, transforming how we think about or solve a problem. No matter how well the telegraph was used or integrated in operations, a cell phone is better.

This approach is already standard in many industries. Products are tested and iterated a thousand times before the final is released. Those Facebook, YouTube, or TikTok videos you watch? Some are sincere, but many are the results of thousands or millions of tests to find out what works, scripted and produced to exact specifications to maximize views and engagement. Governments, however, are still unused to the concept, usually taking decisions once and for all rather than in an iterative way. Yet an iterative approach is only more important today. The long-term problems we face require bold new ideas, and iteration and innovation are an important part of how we can get there. The rapid rate of change in the modern world also means that even if today's government is doing well, by tomorrow its policies and programs may no longer suit the need.

One obvious benefit of an iterative approach is that it lets us test things to find out what works best, basing decisions on clear evidence. An iterative approach can also help governments avoid the bias toward short-termism and improve how they plan for the future. There are three channels for this effect. First, as discussed in chapter 4, one reason governments fail to prepare for the future is that they worry present-biased voters will punish them for doing so in the short term, while in the long term another party will reap the benefits. An iterative approach mitigates this problem: it gives governments something they can announce immediately that has the potential for long-term benefits. Done right, this can harness the power of present bias for long-term success. If people care more about the present, then design policies to provide small wins immediately.

This works because experiments are in some ways a success no matter what happens. If government tests something and it works, then great! Scale up and roll out. If government tests something and it doesn't work, then great! Save taxpayer money and avoid doing it at scale. Either way something is learned. If government is testing multiple things at once, one option is almost guaranteed to work best, so a winner can always be declared if a policy is required. Experiments create small wins that can be turned into announcements and positive news stories, helping fight government present bias by giving good news today.

A second benefit of iteration and experimentation when it comes to long-term thinking is reducing governmental fear of failure. Governments are typically not good at bold, daring action. The media and opposition are quick to punish any government for a project that does not go well. And failure can cost politicians their jobs. As a result, it is safer to stick with traditional, tried-and-true options. Unfortunately, the only way to avoid ever failing is to do what we have always done, and that is usually a path to fiasco or at best mediocrity. Risk and failure are inescapable parts of innovation and transformative change.

The fear of failure is particularly problematic when it comes to addressing long-term problems. Many of the complex, multigenerational problems we face today require transformative change to address. Climate change or demographic shifts, for instance, are not one small tweak from being solved; they require potentially profound changes to our economy and society. It is almost impossible to achieve these changes without some failures along the way. Luckily, long-term problems are also just that, long term. Though some require immediate action, most are slow moving, and there is time to iterate and test possible solutions, failing a few times in order to find the best solution.

An iterative approach allows governments more space to try for moon shots, because no one failure is mission critical; instead, it is all just part of the testing process. Many options can be explored at a small scale and the best pursued further. Even if a hundred moon shots fail, it can all be worth it if one succeeds. Iteration and experimentation minimize the cost of failure by testing things before scaling up. Trying things out on a small scale can help avoid large-scale problems and embarrassing debacles. This embrace of failure can be particularly helpful because of the role government can play supporting innovation. Mariana Mazzucato has pointed to the major role the US government has played in that regard, from its support of the internet and GPS to the US National Science Foundation's funding for the algorithm that helped create Google's search engine.[1] The challenge, of course, is that in many cases these benefits were unexpected, and not all investments work out, making tolerance of failure essential if government is going to take on early stage, risky investments that the private sector would otherwise not pursue.

Importantly, taking an evidence-based, iterative approach does not mean failures will never happen. If anything, they will be more frequent – the more you try the more you fail. And failure or perceived failure can have political costs, making it uncomfortable for leaders. However, this aversion to failure misses a key point: though a small failure can be costly a large failure is worse. Not learning from a weak pilot or experiment means the program may be expanded, with a potentially greater cost later on. Committing relatively few resources to experiments also reduces the perception of sunk costs and a large and costly failure.

Governments can also mitigate the perceived risk of failure by being up front about it. By framing things as trials, tests, or pilots, they give themselves more space to change course if things do not work out. Admitting ignorance is not easy politically; however, doing so early and then setting out a plan to test solutions and discover what is best means the government is less likely to be perceived as having failed if some of what is tested doesn't work.

The design of experiments also matters. If you test one thing and it doesn't work, it is hard to avoid having the experiment branded as a failure, even if learning what doesn't work is just as important as learning what does. Savvy governments may prefer to test multiple things at once to increase their odds of success and have at least one option work better than all the others. That way, the experiment can be declared a success in almost any scenario.

The final and perhaps most significant benefit of iterating and experimenting is the ability to mitigate uncertainty. Most of the challenging, long-term problems we face are uncertain. Yes, we're worried about nuclear proliferation, antibiotic resistance, resource exhaustion, and a potential existential threat from AI, but none of us knows exactly how those problems will evolve or, worse yet, interact in the coming decades. Perhaps a global AI will solve antibiotic resistance, or maybe resource exhaustion will intensify the risks from nuclear proliferation. This uncertainty has only grown as the pace of technological and societal change has accelerated. Humans and governments have never been good at predicting the future, and it isn't getting any easier. Worse, humans and governments show a consistent bias toward overestimating how good they are at it and how correct their predictions are. As the saying goes, prediction is difficult, especially about the future. Iteration lets governments test what works and what doesn't while evolving as events do, rather than guessing and hoping for the best.

In seminal work on predicting the future by University of Pennsylvania business school professor Philip Tetlock, a group of experts was asked to predict geopolitical events. They were not much better than dart-throwing chimps, and were consistently less accurate than basic algorithms. "Foxes," who knew a little about a lot of different topics and were humble in how accurate they were, did best, but almost no one did well. Concerningly, "hedgehogs," who focused on one big idea and were aggressive in pushing it, were particularly bad at predictions, and particularly likely to be famous and successful pundits, since audiences liked how certain they were.[2] This overconfidence isn't limited to predictions about the future. Research has also found that government officials can be overconfident about their own knowledge and expertise, asserting that they are well informed about subjects but incorrectly answering questions when asked.[3] More experienced bureaucrats were actually the most overconfident in assessing their expertise, and the more overconfident an official was the more likely they were to take risky decisions. Similar results have been found for politicians.[4] Overconfidence of any kind can make projects more likely to fail.

There are a number of related behavioural biases and fallacies that relate to our inability to anticipate and predict the future. The planning fallacy describes our tendency to underestimate how long it will take to complete a task, from finishing an assignment to building an Olympic stadium. The illusion of validity is a bias that convinces us our ability to predict something is better than it is. Optimism bias leads us to overestimate the probability of success of a given policy or program. These biases mean managers overestimate the returns to investment projects, and policy-makers are too optimistic about the likelihood of their programs' success.[5] Sometimes the incentives are more straightforward, too. Politicians may be rewarded electorally for claiming to be certain about something, even if they are not.[6]

Some of the most important events are also the hardest to predict. Black swans, as Nassim Nicholas Taleb memorably coined events that are outside the realm of regular expectations, have a significant impact.[7] By their very nature, rare events provide few opportunities for policy-makers to learn and improve their predictions. Anticipating future events is easier if we are given repeated opportunities to make predictions and learn from our mistakes. If a global pandemic or the emergence of a transformative technology occurs only once in the life of a policy-maker, there is no opportunity to learn from error. We might have been better prepared for the COVID-19 pandemic if policy-makers who had lived through the 1918 Spanish flu were still around.

Forecasting the future isn't doomed. Later work by Tetlock and others has found ways to improve it, and it is an ongoing area of research. Some individuals are good at forecasting. In one exercise Tetlock oversaw, and in which I participated as an experimental subject, some forecasters could beat intelligence analysts at predicting global events despite not having access to confidential information, and they improved over time.[8] Teams outperformed individuals, especially after training on how to eliminate biases and make more accurate predictions, and more open-minded people made better predictions. Governments can and should do better at harnessing the power of forecasting and other future-looking exercises to better anticipate future risks. The point, though, is that iteration allows governments to sidestep many of these problems in the first place, by minimizing the need for hyper-accurate forecasts.

Iteration and experimentation avoid the need for perfect forecasting by allowing for small-scale action today, even if not all the answers are known. In fact, experimentation is at its best when much remains uncertain: if you don't know all the answers, then testing things first can help tell you what works without taking a huge risk. For long-term problems, where there is often significant uncertainty about the best way to resolve them or what the problem will look like in the future, an adaptive, iterative, and experimental approach is ideal for making progress.

Iteration thus counteracts human and government overconfidence about the future. There is no need to provide accurate forecasts of the future when we experiment and iterate; instead, we can adapt over time. Governments and voters may genuinely not know how to address a long-term problem or which solution will prove most effective. Systematically trying new things can help answer those questions. The challenge is how to make governments – large, bureaucratic organizations – adopt a more adaptive and nimble approach.

GETTING NIMBLE

In 1997 Harvard's Clayton Christensen published *The Innovator's Dilemma*, a seminal work on how organizations can better innovate.[9] Christensen argues that firms can get trapped by their current customer base and demand for the highest possible returns. In trying to please their customers, firms fail to consider new markets with initially lower returns, despite those new markets potentially being the most profitable in the long run. Only when it is too late and a competitor has already seized those markets do they start to respond. Since innovation is a sideline to the organization's traditional core mandate, executives and the overall culture of the organization tend to stifle it as secondary or unimportant. A multi-billion-dollar organization will struggle to invest time or attention into a project for a few million dollars. Thus, short of a crisis, new ideas and markets never achieve enough importance relative to the current work to get off the ground. Paradoxically, the very attributes that make a firm successful in the short term – a focus on customers and a drive for profits – are what prevent it from innovating in the long term. That is the innovator's dilemma.

To solve this dilemma, American entrepreneur Eric Ries has argued for firms to take a "lean start-up" approach.[10] Ries points out that if the key driver of innovation is thinking not only about current products and markets but also future ones, then firms' fundamental focus should be how to learn quickly. This is quintessentially true of start-ups: by definition, they are new businesses that don't know their potential product and customers well. Rather than picking a particular path and charging down it at full speed, small businesses should stay flexible. They can try small versions of their products, often called prototypes or minimum viable products, and see how customers respond. If customers don't like them, then the firm should move to the next prototype. If customers do like them, then the firm should start to scale up, sticking with an incremental approach that gives them the space to adapt as they learn more about what customers want and what they are good at producing. In effect, organizations should implement the scientific method: when they come up with an idea, they should figure out the testable hypothesis behind it, and then run the test. Ries describes the desired end state as a loop of build-measure-learn, with the goal being to repeat that cycle as often and as quickly as possible.

Many organizations fall into the trap of trying to preserve rigid and inflexible systems and policies. If the world stays static that can be sufficient; you find what works and you stick with it. The modern world, though, is defined by change, not consistency. Businesses, governments, and other organizations looking to flourish in a world of unceasing change need to be open to change themselves. The way to succeed is not to fixate on a particular product or process but instead fixate on learning: on applying the scientific method to every project and proposed vision to find out if it works and how it can be made to work best. Teams should race to test their initiatives and present the results to management, refocusing on what is found to work best while accepting failures with an appreciation for the learning they provide.

We typically think of this rapid cycle of build-measure-learn in software development, but it can have very practical applications. Zappos was established in 1999 as one of the first online shoe retailers. At that point, no one was sure if people would buy shoes online; wouldn't they want to try them on, first? The founder took a classic lean start-up approach. He went around to some shoe stores in town, took pictures of the shoes, put them up online on a website he built, and waited for orders. When someone ordered a pair on his website, he'd go to the shoe store where he'd taken the picture and buy a pair for full price. Not a great business model, and impossible to scale, but it gave him what he needed: it told him whether people were willing to order shoes online without investing millions of dollars in building a shoe-making business. Once he'd proven people were indeed willing, he found an interested investor, and the rest is history. Zappos sold to Amazon in 2009 for around $1.2 billion.[11]

The lean start-up approach isn't limited to start-ups. The same advice can help large organizations. Rather than spending all your available capital on a single big idea, a lean start-up approach recommends trying small versions of many ideas and learning from their relative successes to keep iterating and improving further.

WHAT ABOUT GOVERNMENTS?

Governments, too, suffer from a form of the innovator's dilemma. They can't be outcompeted and go out of business, but their traditional businesses do consume resources and attention, making it difficult for new ideas to flourish. Innovation ends up "side of desk," a side project for someone who already has a full-time job. Elected leaders and bureaucrats may be in favour of innovation in principle, but in practice it is challenging to prioritize in the face of tight deadlines and urgent deliverables. Yes, digital transformation of services matters in the long term, but in the short term getting people the passports they've requested is pressingly urgent. Just as in the private sector, governments end up neglecting new markets or ideas, realizing only decades later they now need to catch up.

Access to expertise, funding, and time can all be significant barriers to experimentation in government. Often, though, the biggest barrier is cultural. Despite individual public servants' enthusiasm about experimentation, it can be hard to get support from others, especially if experimentation is seen as optional or outside their day jobs. In my time leading an experimentation team with the Government of Canada, we often saw good experimentation ideas stymied not by a lack of funds or a technical issue but by reluctance, risk aversion, or simply a lack of prioritization by managers or colleagues whose support was needed to advance the project. Work from the OECD echoes this experience, highlighting how often innovation is not seen as part of core business or how things are done.[12]

Partly as a result, governments have not typically adopted an iterative approach. They are better known for trying to keep ideas secret until the last minute and then announcing a fully formed initiative, instead of carefully testing and improving as they go based on feedback. At best, governments may seek to consult the public by asking their opinion in a general way but not actually test or trial a policy or program. Such an approach tends to lead to disaster, in part because one of the major weaknesses of government is implementation. A key issue is frequently operational disconnect: politicians rarely have experience putting programs into place or ensuring they work. As a result, they focus on writing laws and making policy but leave the question of implementation to the bureaucrats.

Anthony King and Ivor Crewe in their book *The Blunders of Our Governments* highlight how this differs from the military maxim that the general who writes the plan should also be charged with carrying it out to ensure it is feasible and informed by operational considerations.[13] Blunders, they argue, are situations where a government had set objectives but failed to successfully implement or achieve them. This may be based on incorrect assumptions or failures of design or implementation that neglected facts on the ground or missed key issues. Information technology projects provide particularly rich examples of implementation failures, from the high-profile crash of the US government's launch of HealthCare.gov to the UK's introduction of a new system for the National Health Service, or Canada's introduction of the Phoenix pay system, which didn't work and cost billions more than anticipated. As King and Crewe's book makes clear, a common source of problems is the pressure for speed in modern policy-making, which also underlies many of the challenges in getting governments to think long term.

Implementation often attracts less attention in the media, unless it turns into a high-profile failure. Politicians and the media turn to the next big thing. The implementation phase, however, is critical: thousands of small decisions may remain that help define the policy. In some cases, the decisions can make or break the success of the policy. For the Canadian Phoenix pay system, poor implementation decisions helped derail the whole initiative. Even at a smaller scale, and as behavioural science frequently illustrates, everything from the timing of when citizens are engaged to the language used to describe a policy can impact a program's success.

An iterative approach in government helps address this issue by bringing operational considerations into the policy process. If the prototype fails, the full program probably won't work either. Iteration helps ensure policies are well designed, it builds support for policies by engaging people early and letting them influence the outcome, and it mitigates risk by trying a small version first instead of rushing to a large and costly error. At heart, it is about seeing what works and then doing more of that for the same reason an engineer might build multiple models of a new bridge design and test them with toy cars before building the full bridge.

Governments have started to recognize the value of iteration, though there remains a long way to go. Rather than betting the house on a single policy approach or intervention, they can try small versions of many possibilities and see what makes a difference and what voters respond to. The correct answer when presented with multiple policy ideas is not to ask which is best but rather to ask whether all of them can be implemented on a small scale at once and their respective results measured. At first glance, this approach can seem to be in tension with commitments. If governments are making commitments to bind the hands of future leaders, then that can limit flexibility in the future to learn and adapt. The way to square that circle is to realize we do not need to commit to specifics, in the same way that a start-up does not need to commit to a specific product. Instead, we should commit to outcomes. Kennedy committed to having a man on the moon but not to the technology that would get him there.

This is easier in theory than in practice, of course, and there will always be some programs of direct interest to voters that governments choose to campaign on. It also means governments must be prepared to abandon approaches that do not work. Even when an iterative approach is taken and the sunk costs are low, it can be politically difficult to admit something doesn't work. Focusing on outcomes gives governments more space to adapt while focusing on what ultimately matters to voters. Outcomes, not dollars spent or number of laws passed, are what affect the common welfare. Cynically, that may be why it is more popular to campaign on policies than results, since it is harder to deliver results than to set up ineffective policies. Voters deserve better and should do better at holding their governments to account not for individual actions but for actual results, whether it is reducing unemployment, fighting crime, improving public health, or other issues. A focus on results rather than means – the what and why rather than the how – strengthens long-term planning on the part of governments.

ITERATION IN PRACTICE

To see what an iterative approach looks like in practice, consider China. Deng Xiaoping allegedly described managing the Chinese economy as crossing the river by feeling the stones – have a direction but be adaptive in how to get there, and feel out the path step by step rather than going all at once. That philosophy has reappeared in various forms in Chinese governance, including experimenting with fairly fundamental ideas like testing ways of empowering farmers to sell the right to use their land for agricultural purposes, a pilot begun in 2014.

China is not a democracy, of course, which makes it easier for the government to launch grand projects or national experiments without worrying about the impact on those affected. Few countries can compare to China in breadth, depth, and duration of policy experiments, and researchers have argued that institutionalized policy experimentation is a critical part of China's economic success over the past few decades. Shaoda Wang and David Yang, from the universities of Chicago and Harvard, outline the most common form of experimentation in China as the selection of experimentation points, a limited set of sites where a policy is first tested, sometimes over multiple waves.[14] If the experiments are successful, they are then rolled out more widely. Wang and Yang identify 633 experiments between 1980 and 2020, covering everything from rice production insurance to anti-poverty programs and carbon emission trading. Eventually, 54 per cent of the experiments were rolled out nationally, while the others were quietly let go. Many of the successes were cited in the central government's Five-Year Plans.

One notable example is special economic zones (SEZs), which were set up in the 1980s under Deng to allow more flexibility to approve foreign investment and waive economic controls. By 2010 the initially small pilot had expanded to seven comprehensive SEZs, sixty-nine state-level economic and technological development zones, fifty-four high-tech industrial development zones, fifteen free trade zones across thirteen coastal cities, and sixty-one export-processing zones. By then, the seven national SEZs contributed around 22 per cent of China's GDP and 46 per cent of total foreign direct investment.[15]

Initially, the SEZs were deliberately set up far from the centre of political power in Beijing and close to coastal areas with a history of contact with the outside world, at once minimizing the risk of affecting the rest of China and creating more space to try new things. The once small thirty-thousand-person fishing village of Shenzhen, for example, was chosen partly for its location next to Hong Kong. Among other things, it was given the same powers as a full province and exempted from submitting taxes to the provincial or central governments for its first ten years. With its new freedoms, it introduced a minimum wage and increased social security: workers started to flock there from other parts of China. Shenzhen also sought to attract foreign investment to boost worker productivity and provide long-term employment and growth by streamlining administrative control and planning procedures, introducing tax breaks, and reducing duties. Having started in 1981, by 1998 it accounted for 14 per cent of the world's output of floppy disks and 6 per cent of PC motherboards. Domestically it produced close to 70 per cent of LCDs and 30 per cent of personal computers.[16]

The point is not that SEZs are a panacea – Shenzhen was next to Hong Kong, and would likely have grown regardless of government policy – but that Shenzhen provided a lab to test ideas that could be applied elsewhere in China. It was the first city in China to have a stock exchange, have a centre to monitor exchange rates, and permit the entry of foreign banks. At each stage, China has learned from the results of the existing SEZs to inform later iterations, with the project overall serving as a pilot for market-oriented policies that have since been implemented more widely. Scholars have cited China's ability to adapt and learn as critical to its success, enabling the country to adjust its governance to public demands while still maintaining an authoritarian state.[17]

Of course, China also has room to improve. Wang and Yang find that Chinese policy experiments are often done with unrepresentative samples (e.g., testing an agricultural productivity program in a region where agricultural output is already high), and local politicians allocate additional resources to ensure the experiments' success, likely due to bureaucratic incentives; after all, successful experiments look better on an aspiring bureaucrat's CV.[18] Since these conditions are not replicable when the project is rolled out nationally, the results may be misleading.

Experimentation and iteration in democracies will differ from that in China. Democratic governments will need to spend more time building public support for the experiment, for example, rather than imposing it on certain areas or groups, and they will face pressure to compensate groups who lose out. Property rights, privacy, and other legal requirements will all need navigation. Transparency around the ethics of the experiment will be crucial, perhaps including a formal review by an ethics review board or similar body. Democratic governments will also have to acknowledge the reality of elections and in some cases design their experiments to accommodate the electoral cycle, as we discuss later. Still, democracies can benefit from this approach and may have an advantage in identifying promising projects given their emphasis on citizen input.

Countries with a federal system like Canada or the US, where individual provinces or states have considerable autonomy, are implicitly creating space for experimentation by allowing for different subnational governments to take different approaches. Long term, other regions can assess and learn from these experiments. In Canada, for example, Quebec was the first province to introduce an affordable child-care system, Saskatchewan was the first to introduce universal hospital care, and British Columbia was the first to introduce carbon pricing. All three helped inspire and inform similar policies that were introduced at the national level. A similar dynamic led US Supreme Court Justice Louis Brandeis to refer to the American states as the laboratories of democracy, though the benefits rely on subnational and national governments learning from each other, which cannot always be taken for granted.[19]

Contrast the success of experimentation in China with the total failure of individual learning accounts (ILAS) in the UK, introduced in 1996 and eliminated in 2001. These aimed to help adults improve their technology skills in recognition of the increasing need in the modern economy. The idea was to help people access skills training by offering a government subsidy to those taking courses: prospective trainees could deposit a small sum into the account in their name, and the government could top it up. By the time it was abandoned in 2001, it was widely regarded as a fiasco due to the total lack of controls to prevent fraud. As many as six thousand applicants turned out to originate from the same address, and there had been multiple arrests. Of the £290 million spent, about a third was lost to fraud. Of the remaining two-thirds, some of the major beneficiaries seem to have been wealthy executives taking MBAS, since those are some of the most expensive degrees, rather than the low-income people the program was meant to help.

The UK scheme failed because of a failure to anticipate problems, which had it been tested would have been obvious. The program unwittingly made fraud almost trivially easy. There was no verification of trainees or trainers that registered for the program, and trainers could simply take money directly from trainee accounts. Fraudsters would set up an account in someone's name, create a trainer account, and then transfer the money from one account to the other, defrauding the taxpayer of the subsidy. In the words of one participant investigated by the audit team, "We saw the ILA scheme as money lying on the street – so we went and picked it up."[20]

An experimental approach could have identified these problems before rolling out the program more widely. For example, the program could have been introduced in a single region initially, with results compared to other regions to assess whether the program worked. This would also have averted other problems with the policy and made sure it was benefitting the targeted groups, not just MBA students.

Governments have started to learn from these mistakes. The UK has started taking an experimental approach to policy issues with the leadership of the Behavioural Insights Team, which has led experiments in tax collection, organ donation, army recruiting, education, pensions, charitable giving, and a range of other topics. Though originally set up by David Cameron in 2010 as part of the UK Cabinet Office, it was spun off as a private organization in 2014 and has opened offices in New York, Australia, New Zealand, and Singapore, among other places.

In the US, the Foundations for Evidence-Based Policymaking Act in 2018 required departments develop learning agendas, setting out what the department is seeking to learn, how it plans to learn the answers, and what it will do to disseminate the information. In the US Department of Labor, for example, 0.75 per cent of its funds was set aside for evaluation, supporting a chief evaluation officer who coordinates and builds capacity for evaluation across the department. This provides dedicated resources and support for trying things at a small scale, as well as public accountability for publishing what they learn and using it to improve their operations.[21]

Unfortunately, progress remains slow. Iteration often remains a side of desk or boutique project, rather than a core part of how a government delivers services. It is typically not yet integrated into the key services governments provide or used as a way to fundamentally assess the strength and viability of programs. Instead iteration is left for shiny demonstration projects or minor updates to websites and delivery approaches.

LESSONS

One of the biggest barriers to an iterative approach is the demand from voters for instant solutions. It is easy to be in favour of pilots and testing in principle but difficult when it comes to issues we care deeply about. You may well agree in general with prototypes and experimentation. If you think of the two or three political issues that matter to you most, though – the ones on which you might be willing to change parties or actively volunteer for a candidate – how willing are you to see delay on those priorities in order to learn more about them?

There's nothing wrong with demanding instant solutions: policies can be too slow as well as too fast, and prototypes can be an excuse for delay as well as a way of testing what works, so there is no right answer to the question of when to stop testing and scale up. It is a question of how confident you are about what the future will look like and what will best benefit citizens, and that can vary by case. In some instances, a priority is so pressing that immediate action is necessary, even if information is incomplete; a timely imperfect solution is better than a perfect solution that is never implemented. When COVID-19 struck in 2020, for example, many governments reached for imperfect or insufficiently studied solutions, reasoning that some chance of success was better than none. As the research has developed, some things that seemed like priorities early on were de-emphasized based on ongoing research (e.g., hand-sanitizing), while the evidence for others grew stronger (e.g., good ventilation).

When it comes to long-term problems, though, we frequently have time to pause, test, and learn. The aging of populations in developed countries has the potential to become a significant crisis, but it is a slow moving one. This is true of many long-term issues. Taking the time to iterate and innovate can help us solve long-term problems in the most effective way, saving us money and time overall. Four concrete steps could help governments be more experimental and iterative.

First, as mentioned the electoral cycle can create unfortunate incentives in terms of long-term planning by governments, but at least in countries where elections occur at fixed times, it also sets out a clear schedule for implementation. Governments naturally want results immediately before the next election, when they are most in need of successes to demonstrate their value to voters. In the first year or two successes are still valuable, but without an election looming there is also more flexibility to test and try things on a small scale. Governments could set out in their platforms, budgets, and annual plans what small-scale policies they plan to test that year and how they would use the results to inform eventual national projects. This could be done both by mandate and by year. The party running could set out the small-scale experiments they would run in their first year in office in their platform, and then they could update the plan and announce the results in their yearly reporting to the public.

Scheduling tests and trials this way also mitigates the risk that future governments will cancel the experiment before findings are available, as happened with the Basic Income Pilot Project in Ontario. Having been introduced under one government, the project was cancelled ten months later, after an election brought a new government into power, making it difficult to learn anything from it (as well as proving enormously disruptive for the participants, who had expected it to run for three years). Such cancellations can earn political points but are frustrating from the perspective of learning what works. Where experiments do run the risk of running over changes in government, they should also be designed either as commitments, using the principles chapter 7 discusses, or in ways that do not attract partisan opposition. Some cancellations are inevitable, especially for experiments with a high partisan charge, but most experiments can likely be designed to provide results within a single government term. Where they cannot, making sure to design and frame them in a neutral, non-partisan way may help increase their chance of survival.

A second step draws on an insight from David Halpern of the UK's Behavioural Insights Team, who has remarked that he knew he had succeeded when a minister in the UK brought several options to the Cabinet table, and instead of choosing one, Cabinet decided to try them all and see what worked best.[22] Governments could focus less on setting out several options and then selecting one, and more on trying all the possible options and integrating what they learn into an eventual policy. To reach this point, iteration must be normalized in governments. One fundamental insight from behavioural science is that people do things when they are easy. Governments must shift so that iteration and innovation are the easy path, not an add-on that requires extra effort from teams. Building experimentation into the policy process (e.g., make it a standard part of the process to access funding) can make it easier for bureaucrats and politicians to iterate by default. The American requirement for departments to have learning plans is a nice example of this integration, since departments must consider experimentation and evidence as part of their yearly planning.

Third, governments need to build internally the infrastructure required to experiment. An agile, iterative approach would require significantly more data literacy than is currently found in many governments, requiring skill-building and targeted recruitment for bureaucracies. Governments are typically slow to hire or adapt to changing demands, and when it comes to data and computer science skills, that weakness is particularly painful. This means more experts are necessary, both to do data work themselves and to oversee and manage contracts with the private sector, but it also means a general increase in data literacy across all public servants.

If public servants of all kinds are not broadly familiar with how to use and think about data, the public service's ability to produce and use data thoughtfully, getting maximum value from it while respecting privacy, will remain limited. Good use of data will not only supercharge the governments' capacity to test and iterate ideas but also transform how services are designed and delivered, making them more user-friendly and effective as well as providing better information about what works and what doesn't.

Finally, voters and legislative assemblies can demand iterative or experimental evidence before accepting policy decisions. This applies when deciding who to vote for but also more generally in how the media and the public engage with and respond to new policies and programs. If a government knows that the public reception of an idea will depend on how well they can demonstrate it based on evidence and iteration, it will be more motivated to do so. The best kind of evidence will depend on the questions being asked. As we saw with commitments, establishing a parliamentary committee or independent body to publicly assess the quality of the evidence the government presents for a policy could incentivize governments to test ideas and confirm the evidence supports them before pushing them through. Evidence drawn from actual attempts to implement the policy or trying it out on a small scale is particularly compelling, and governments could be encouraged to generate this evidence whenever possible. An independent evidence review body would at once encourage governments to take an experimental approach and provide a quality check on the evidence produced, while also acknowledging that in some cases experimentation might not be possible or appropriate.

Such a review body would be different from most discussions in parliaments, which focus on whether the policy is desirable or helping the right people. Instead, a check on the evidence is about assessing whether a policy would work or not. Whether the objective is liberal or conservative, left-wing or right-wing, checking the evidence is about identifying whether the proposed policy or program will achieve that objective. In that sense, evidence need not be a partisan question. Even if a supporter agrees with a policy objective, if the proposed policy won't work then more thought is needed. An iterative approach and gathering evidence are needed to identify what will work.

Doing all this isn't easy and would require change on all sides. Governments would need to be explicit on the results they want to achieve and the small-scale prototype policies they plan to test. Citizens would need to give their governments the space and time to do those tests without demanding immediate results. Bureaucrats and the politicians they advise need space to have frank discussions about shifting direction, capacity, and likelihood of success and to take risks and fail. If leaders feel unable to test new ideas that may not work, or they are so rushed that they are unable to deliberate or test sufficiently, then the risks of negative outcomes rise. Policies that are implemented may lack legitimacy. There are some proposals that should be implemented as quickly as possible, but where there is space to try multiple solutions to see which ones work best, we should do so.

Ultimately, I see iteration both as one of the most powerful strategies to improve long-term outcomes and one of the hardest to implement from a political perspective. Success requires a cultural change among voters and governments to better tolerate and even seek out failure, as well as structural changes and, in some cases, access to technical expertise. Unfortunately, the political incentives to support iteration are relatively limited. If a group likes a policy, they often just want it implemented immediately; no need for testing or starting on a small scale. If a group dislikes a policy, they are also often uninterested in testing it. Politicians in turn will be reluctant to test things if the public sees a negative result as a failure and means they lose support. There are groups who argue for evidence-based policy and politicians who support it, but such groups are relatively few in number.

That said, iteration and experimentation can be an important part of democratic legitimacy. The philosopher John Dewey argued that democracy was in some sense the social embodiment of the experimental mindset by allowing for discussion and exchange of views as a way of testing new ideas and solving problems.[23] Testing new ideas, including the new forms of governance we explore here, is how democracy can deliver results and how governments can justify their decisions to voters.

Building political support for iteration and experimentation means emphasizing the value it can provide to elected officials. For example, reframing iteration to highlight that it can bring forward wins and reduce the risk of large-scale failures can make it more appealing to governments regardless of their priorities. The role of bureaucracies can be particularly crucial. They can help emphasize the value of testing ideas to elected officials, proposing tests and encouraging an iterative mindset. If a government is unwilling to experiment with key parts of their agenda that they have already committed to, there are likely still opportunities to iterate with other, less central and less polarizing, priorities.

Encouraging governments to launch experiments when they first come into office so they can be completed before the party in power changes can also be effective. An advantage of iteration is that as long as a test is completed and the results released, even if it then sits unused while another party is in power, the results can be picked up when the government changes again. A party that launches an experiment early on can claim the credit for doing so, even if the results are not implemented before they lose office. Not all policies or ideas can be iterated in such a defined time period, but many can be. New institutions could also help increase the demand for and visibility of iteration, for instance by assessing the quality of evidence behind policy proposals set out by the government. The public and the media can play a role in asking for what evidence underpins various policies. But normalizing iteration will be a challenge.

More positively, and unlike most of the other strategies we consider, iteration can be effective even if it is entirely internal. Ultimately it may not matter politically whether something was tested, and governments may not inherently care about iteration or its absence. What does matter is whether the policy works or not and whether all the possible consequences have been considered. To some extent, iterative policy design can help meet this need and improve policy decisions, even if public and political interest is limited regarding the actual methods used. However, the more high-profile or controversial the policy, the less space there may be for iteration, limiting the potential applications and benefits. Ultimately, mainstream adoption of iterative methods likely requires widespread public demand and tolerance of failure, which will not be easy to achieve.

Perhaps the most likely path to implementation, in my view, will be an incremental one. Governments adopt iterative approaches for small or largely inconsequential policies first and gradually build up the iteration muscle internally. The public slowly becomes more accustomed to seeing prototypes and early iterations, perhaps helped by the widespread use of such methods in other sectors. Over time, especially as other strategies such as national balance sheets are introduced, governments will see increasing value in iteration as a way to mitigate political risks and maximize the chance of their policies succeeding, and the public starts to ask for more iteration, leading to further adoption. Perhaps the public becomes more tolerant of failure by governments, though that seems a distant goal today. As with all things political, we get the governments we deserve. If we are unwilling to wait for governments to learn and adapt, then we condemn ourselves to having short-term, knee-jerk policies inflicted upon us.

PART THREE

Putting It All Together

9

Climate Change

When you think about "the future" today, you don't think beyond the year 2050. By then I will, in the best case, not even have lived half of my life. What happens next? The year 2078 I will celebrate my 75th birthday. What we do or don't do, right now, will affect my entire life, and the lives of my children and grandchildren.

Greta Thunberg, *No One Is Too Small to Make a Difference*

In 2018 the Intergovernmental Panel on Climate Change (IPCC) released a special report assessing the potential impacts of global warming of 1.5°C above pre-industrial levels and comparing them to the impact of 2°C of warming.[1] The levels chosen reflect the assessment that humanity has already caused approximately 1°C of global warming, and warming of 1.5°C or 2°C was likely by between 2030 and 2052 at current emission rates. The IPCC's findings were clear. They were highly confident that global warming was already having an impact and that some impacts could be long-lasting or irreversible. By 2050 climate change is expected to have negative effects on biodiversity, human health and livelihoods, food security, water supplies, and economic growth. These effects are already particularly acute for vulnerable populations, such as low-income communities or those living in remote regions. All these impacts are significantly higher if warming were to be as high as 2°C instead of 1.5°C.

The IPCC estimated that in order to avoid 1.5°C of warming, current emissions would need to decline by 45 per cent by 2030, reaching net zero emissions by around 2050. To keep the increase to 2°C of warming, emissions would need to decline by around 20 per cent by 2030, and reach net zero by 2075. There are different ways of reaching these levels of emissions (e.g., reduced energy use can be combined with cleaner energy or carbon capture). However, almost all transitions that led to sufficient reductions in emissions involved significant changes in energy production, land use, infrastructure design, and industrial systems. In other words, the panel found that we had just over a decade to take action on climate change. If emissions don't start to decline by 2030, the world is highly likely to experience increasingly adverse effects from climate change.

More recent work by IPCC identifies a sweeping set of impacts already occurring from climate change, some of them irreversible.[2] Their report outlines effects of human-induced climate change that include heat- and drought-related human, coral, and tree mortality, increased burn areas from wildfires, adverse impacts of tropical cyclones, sea level rise, the loss of local species, regional decreases in precipitation, and reduced agricultural productivity. These changes have exposed millions of people to insecurity related to food and water, and roughly half of the world's population currently experiences severe water scarcity during the year. The changes increase the risk of new animal and human diseases emerging, and will have significant impacts on human health, livelihoods, and welfare. Overall, the panel estimates that roughly 3.5 billion people live in contexts highly vulnerable to climate change.

All this is widely known and well reported in the media. It is no surprise to governments. In 1992 at the Earth Summit held in Rio de Janeiro, countries made commitments to reduce their greenhouse gas emissions; developed countries agreed to help developing countries do so. Since then, emissions have steadily increased. Half of the total carbon dioxide emitted since the Industrial Revolution has occurred since 1990. The world is already more than 1°C hotter than it was before the Industrial Revolution, and though it is difficult to attribute specific climate events to an overall trend, it is also difficult to deny that heat waves, once rare, now seem common; weather in the Arctic is changing, with vast sheets of ice melting and contributing to increased sea levels; and violent storms are increasing. The IPCC estimates that at 1.5°C of warming, as many as 14 per cent of terrestrial and freshwater species may be at high risk of extinction. Nonetheless, action has been feeble, and 1.5°C of warming now seems almost inevitable.

The 2022 IPCC report observes, despite the existence of feasible and effective adaptation options, that "many initiatives prioritize immediate and near-term climate risk reduction which reduces the opportunity for transformational adaptation ... Most observed adaptation is fragmented, small in scale, incremental, sector-specific, designed to respond to current impacts or near-term risks, and focused more on planning rather than implementation."[3] The problem has been kicked to tomorrow, when the costs will only be higher. Governments are thinking too short term.

CLIMATE CHANGE AND SHORT-TERMISM

Climate change is a complex problem, which includes technical and scientific issues as well as the multi-faceted political challenge of navigating entrenched special interests and power dynamics that may seek to preserve the status quo. Nudges alone will not solve climate change, but government short-termism makes it even harder to address.

One challenge in fighting climate change is the tragedy of the commons: no country can stop climate change on their own. If one country makes the requisite changes to reduce their emissions, and no others do, then they have sacrificed without solving the problem. As a result, no country has a particular incentive to take action on their own emissions, no matter how much they want the international community as a whole to do so.

The tragedy of the commons was named for the English commons, based on a hypothetical example from British economist William Forster Lloyd about unregulated grazing on common land.[4] To see it in action, consider the experience of the Hakka people in China. In the 1600s the Hakka were pushed out of their homes in the mountains of Fujian, Guangdong, and Zhejiang by coastal people fleeing fighting between the failing Ming and incoming Qing dynasties. To survive, they deforested the hills and planted maize, both of which increased erosion by exposing more of the soil to rain. The consequence was a dramatic increase in floods. In the Song dynasty (960–1279 CE), major floods occurred once or twice a year. By the 1800s the Qing dynasty was facing thirteen or more major floods a year – the equivalent of a hurricane Katrina every month – targeting key agricultural sectors in China.[5]

The problem was one of collective action. Most Hakka rented from landlords, whose property did suffer from the floods. However, any one landlord who stopped renting out their land would not make much difference to the flooding but would lose out on rental profits. Since they received all the benefits but the costs were shared across the region, they continued renting out their land. The result, as a Chinese official in the nineteenth century put it, was, "Now the waterways are filled with mud, the fields are buried under sand, the mountains reveal their stones and the official and the people know of the great disaster, but they do nothing to stop it."[6] Constant floods led to famine and unrest, weakening the Qing dynasty and contributing to its eventual collapse in 1912, the end of the final imperial dynasty of China.[7]

Short-termism worsens collective action problems. Modern governments are supposed to help solve such problems by taking action to ensure that resources are managed sustainably; commons are not overgrazed; and our lands, waters, and skies are not polluted. In ancient China, the emperor could have restricted deforestation, reducing erosion and flooding. A short-termist government, however, has little incentive to solve the problems, since doing so would likely be unpopular with polluters or deforesters in the short term.

The already meagre incentives for countries to take action on climate change or prioritize international discussions on how to address the collective action problem are diminished by the fact that the consequences will likely occur after our current leaders are voted out of office (or die). Politicians are more likely to be re-elected when the economy is strong: it is hard to get excited about weakening the economy to address a problem in the distant future. Voters, too, may behave the same way: absent visible evidence of the consequences of climate change, many of them may punish rather than reward politicians who impose current costs on the country in the form of a carbon tax or cap and trade system in pursuit of future gains. The result is what we see in many countries today: a low emphasis on or neglect of international discussions and mechanisms for reducing climate change, and a population divided on what should be done. When countries do sign up for the Kyoto Protocol or Paris Agreement, they frequently fail to deliver on their commitments.

Short-termism makes governments less likely to reduce emissions or adapt their economies to be more sustainable. Those strategies are typically referred to as mitigation, since they serve to mitigate the scale of climate change that will occur. Short-termism is if anything more acute, however, when it comes to the second way of responding to climate change: adaptation. Adaptation is about anticipating that climate effects will occur and adapting our societies to minimize the harm, whether by water conservation, flood defence, development of drought-tolerant crops, or other measures. One of the most-cited effects of climate change, for example, is the increase in catastrophic events, such as floods or hurricanes. There is no tragedy of the commons in protecting a country's own communities from floods, but governments have still been bad at doing so.

Regardless of whether one is worried about climate change, the US was woefully unprepared for Hurricane Katrina. Hurricane Betsy, the first tropical storm to inflict $1 billion in damage, hit Louisiana in 1965, causing eighty-one deaths and injuring almost eighteen thousand people. Major changes to the hurricane protection system were recommended immediately after Betsy; some were made, some were abandoned, and after multiple delays the full hurricane protection system was not scheduled to be complete until 2015, *fifty years* after Betsy had hit the state.[8] When Katrina hit in 2005, not only were the improvements incomplete but individuals struggled to take it seriously, since many of them had not been born when Betsy hit. The result was a catastrophe, with property damage close to $125 billion, 2,000 people dead, and thousands more displaced.

A hurricane hitting Louisiana is not a surprise. Given its location, officials at the city, state, and federal levels of government could be almost certain that Louisiana would get hit by another major hurricane, even if they couldn't know when. Nevertheless, both the hurricane preparations and the crisis response were roundly criticized as poorly planned and mismanaged. Responding to a crisis is never easy, but this was not some unforeseeable event but rather a clear risk that governments should have prepared for.

Minimizing the harm of natural disasters is a core responsibility of governments. In countries where the issue of climate change has become polarized, there is generally a consensus that floods and hurricanes are bad and should be prepared for. Climate change makes these extreme weather events more probable, but even without a consensus on climate change, we need governments able to look to the long term and plan for adverse weather events.

RECOMMENDATIONS

The strategies outlined in this book can help our governments rise to the problem. Consider five key steps our governments could take. The first is to measure how we're doing on climate change, a common gap. How much do you know about your country's response to climate change? How much has been invested in defences against floods, storms, or droughts? Does your country have an infrastructure gap relative to potential natural disasters, as New Orleans did in 2005? Knowing the current status of your country's investments against climate change can help you assess whether we are making progress or not and has important implications for our national wealth. If we are unprepared for floods or hurricanes, voters and parliamentarians can push for different policies. Being aware of natural disaster preparedness gaps or failures is also the foundation for many other nudges for government long-term thinking, since without the data it is hard to assess what problems need solving.

Measuring natural disaster preparedness is a good first step. A second step is more thoughtful measures of emissions. Most countries measure their total emissions to some extent, but many could improve how well they measure emissions of particular policies or programs. Governments announce many new initiatives every year, but only rarely do they link their announcements to the potential carbon impacts. This process has begun in some countries through what the OECD calls green budgeting, but more can be done to encourage its use as well as ensure that citizens can assess progress and hold their governments accountable for the results.[9]

Knowing the impact of an individual policy lets us assess how meaningful it is relative to the problem. If a proposed policy would save a gigatonne of greenhouse gas, knowing that is around 2 per cent of world emissions each year lets us assess whether the policy is worthwhile or not. If we're looking for ways to stop climate change on a world scale, we probably want to be looking at impacts of at least a few percentage points of national or world emissions, if not immediately at least when the solution is scaled up. Regrettably, considerable government, public, and media time is currently spent on relatively ineffective climate change policies. Campaigns against plastic straws make for good Instagram photos and slightly reduce plastic litter but make little difference to carbon emissions.

In some cases, such campaigns can make things worse: paper bags have higher emissions that plastic bags given their increased weight and so emissions from transportation, as well as the use of water and trees for production. Cotton bags are worse, needing to be reused at least 131 times to be worthwhile from a climate change perspective relative to plastic bags, which at one shopping trip a week is around two and a half years of use per cotton bag.[10] If the plastic bag is also used as a garbage bin liner the needed uses of cotton bags soars to 327 times, or about six years. Evidence and data on emissions, not Instagram, is the place to go for identifying how to reduce carbon emissions in a meaningful way.

This isn't always easy. Governments will frequently be forced to make best-guess estimates of carbon emissions from such policies or simply admit they don't know. Even that would be progress, relative to the current status quo, where policies are implicitly assumed to have no consequences at all for emissions or are not compared to the status quo. Without those measures, it is difficult to have meaningful conversations about trade-offs.

Remember, what gets measured matters. Measuring the gap in disaster preparedness and how individual policies and programs affect emissions would help incentivize governments to pay attention to the consequences of their decisions for climate change. However, even if all that is measured, governments and voters may both just choose to ignore the information or focus on other things.

To make it easier for governments to focus on climate change, a third step is to build in guardrails, tripwires, and defaults. An obvious guardrail is to include those who will be affected by decisions in the deliberation. This can be informal, such as inviting representatives of younger generations to summits or policy discussions, or formal, such as establishing a parliamentary committee, which could represent the views of future generations in policy discussions. Similar changes could be made within governments, for example having a cabinet minister represent the views of future generations at the cabinet table or identifying a red team within the bureaucracy to challenge policy proposals based on their impact on the future. These changes still rely on the parliamentary committee or cabinet minister for the future convincing others, but the changes help raise the profile of the future and give it a voice it otherwise often lacks.

It also helps to include at key points tripwires using the data on how we're doing regarding sustainability. Governments that have to annually publish the total emission implications of their budget, as well as the level of climate-related disaster readiness and other sustainability statistics, would have more incentive to consider these issues to avoid negative media coverage or a critical public reaction.

Making policies automatic or the default can also make a difference. As discussed in chapter 6, if electricity is priced based on demand, it encourages people to use electricity when demand is low, reducing total energy use and making it easier for renewable sources to provide what's needed. Since the rates for electricity use adjust automatically, there is less need for government intervention and more chance of consistent policy. A more controversial policy could do the same with emissions: a dynamic carbon tax with an automatically adjusting tax rate could encourage reduced emissions. Some countries may choose to return the tax revenue to households, which helps create a constituency that may defend the policy in the future.

That said, given how partisan an issue climate change is, automatic policies may be difficult to establish and may well be reversed anyway. In addition, the cost of energy is an important part of household spending; if rates go up too much, there will be understandable pressure on governments to provide relief to struggling households, as has been seen during the energy price spike from the war in Ukraine and subsequent rise in inflation. Thus, tripwires and guardrails, rather than defaults, may be a better choice.

A fourth step is to implement commitments. Given how polarized climate change is, public announcements that a given political party or government is committed to achieving a certain target or level of emissions are probably insufficient. Many governments have announced emissions targets only to renege or see their commitment reversed by a subsequent government. Even international agreements such as the Kyoto Protocol have been relatively ineffective at promoting compliance or action.

International agreements have worked for other environmental issues. The 1987 Montreal Protocol, for example, a landmark agreement that has helped reduce ozone depletion, has been a major success. There are many reasons for that success, including clever treaty design that provided incentives for other countries to participate and allowed flexibility for the treaty to be adjusted as the science developed. Importantly, ozone depletion also presented a relatively straightforward set of issues focused on a narrow set of products and industries that could be incentivized to stop their use without significant disruption either to the industry or the world at large.[11] Substitute technologies quickly became available, whereas for climate change technological solutions are still in development. Nonetheless, the success of the Montreal Protocol does suggest that in situations where the problem is relatively clear and requires little disruption to resolve, international agreements can be a powerful element of change.

Public commitments may have value in more narrowly scoped and less partisan areas, such as announcing new investments in technology development or better preparations for a natural disaster. Technological innovation can play a major role in any solution to climate change, from better batteries to energy production that creates fewer emissions. The more these commitments can be made specific, measurable, achievable, relevant, and time-bound, the better governments can be held to account for meeting them. Announcing a new public commitment to improve hurricane defences in the Eastern United States by a specific date and starting the investment immediately will create jobs and build momentum that may be harder for a subsequent government to reverse, unlike emission targets. Defining these announcements not in the context of climate change but in terms of disaster readiness or other less partisan topics can mitigate the likelihood of cancellation.

A more binding form of commitment would be creating institutions related to climate change. A diverse, independent committee for future generations could help respond to government announcements with a view to highlighting implications for climate change and provide a voice for future generations that will be impacted by proposed decisions. The government could be required to publish a regular report on the future, perhaps as part of the budget process or other cycle, outlining their plans for and impacts on the future, to which the committee could respond. The committee could then publish regular reports on progress and provide a voice for activists concerned about the future as well as unborn generations. This model has been implemented with some success in Finland, as described in chapter 7.

Other independent institutions could be established. A sovereign wealth fund could specifically target green investments, for example, although too much interference with the mandate of the fund may do more harm than good. Such institutions are harder to ignore or reverse than public announcements, but they are not perfectly binding, especially if they still rely on the government funding. That said, independent institutions increase the pressure on governments to respond. The more independent they are the more difficult they will be to abolish and the more they may be able to pressure the government or engage the public in a discussion on the future.

Some countries may choose to commit to action by including climate change in their constitutions, as with Ecuador's constitutional requirement.[12] This is a binding commitment. Regardless of whether a future government dislikes the constitutional requirement, unless they can summon the political power to change the constitution back or weaken the rule of law, the courts will hold the government to that commitment. Whether this is worthwhile will depend on the country: in places like the US, where climate change is a heavily partisan subject, seeking a constitutional change may become a costly distraction rather than an effective policy tool. In less democratic countries, changing the constitution may be relatively easy for the government, making the commitment less meaningful. Frequently a constitutional change is also only possible when most of the country already agrees with the policy. However, it may still have value in terms of binding future governments to a specific course.

Fifth and finally, governments can iterate and try new things. Climate change is by its nature a problem that requires crossing the river by feeling the stones, sometimes both literally and figuratively depending on flooding. Requiring government to explain what it is trying to learn in order to address climate change would be a useful first step. Governments need not and cannot know everything, and they, like everyone, should spend time thinking about what they don't understand but need to. Our independent committee for future generations could also help demand the evidence behind government decisions. If an announcement claims that a policy will reduce emissions by 30 per cent, the government should clearly explain why and if they have tested the policy to confirm the estimate.

Most of all, though, we as voters can do more to give governments space to admit they don't know everything, and let them take time to better understand the problem and possible solutions. That isn't always easy with a topic such as climate change where emotions run high; no matter how much (or little) you care about climate change, consider giving the government space to try things and learn what policies will work best. Of course, you should also hold them accountable for actually doing so, and as the problem becomes increasingly pressing the time available for experiments will shrink, but demanding immediate action may take longer in the end if the actions taken are incorrect.

Ultimately, in my view a promising path for implementing some of these strategies may be to harness the urgency around climate change to establish national balance sheets that help measure our disaster readiness and the impacts of climate change. Governments that want to take action on climate change can benefit from using balance sheets to justify investments in adaptation and mitigation measures. Following that, independent climate-focused institutions could be established to address and advise on specific issues identified through the national balance sheets. This could also encourage changes within governments to support ongoing dialogue between government and the institutions, much like what happens in Finland between the government and their parliamentary Committee for the Future. If successful, these changes could then motivate and create space for further such changes, perhaps targeted at long-term thinking in general.

That said, the reality of the polarization around climate change suggests measures such as tripwires and defaults that require sustained government support are likely to be at high risk of reversal or elimination by future governments. Even national balance sheets, institutions, and other commitments may be at high risk of reversal in some countries or at minimum of being ignored or neglected by some governments.

* * *

Climate change is a tough problem, as our repeated failures to address it indicate. Short-termism is part of the puzzle, but even if all the above was implemented or cognitive biases disappeared, climate change would remain challenging to solve. Many individuals and government officials already agree that climate change is an issue; the problem is navigating the dynamics of politics and power that result from the potential impacts of reforms to material and partisan interests. Significant reductions in emissions could impose considerable costs on individuals and businesses, all of whom have an incentive to resist change. It may also require sweeping structural changes to our economies, our built environments, our patterns of land use, our lifestyles, and the allocation of power across society, all of which are likely to meet resistance. These problems are ultimately political and solving them will require governments that can engage citizens in a meaningful way while navigating the entrenched special interests that may oppose change. Behaviourally informed governance will not solve these issues, but it can complement other, more structural changes and help reduce the pressure on our governments to focus on the short term.

Nevertheless, I am guardedly optimistic. Scientists are right that climate change cannot be said to cause any given climate event, but there is evidence that the increase in natural disasters, such as hurricanes, is helping change attitudes.[13] Public concern about climate change has started to rise: polling in 2020 found that as many as two-thirds of Americans believed that climate change is real, and that the government was doing too little to stop it.[14] There are also some private companies, even oil giants, that seem to be moving faster than governments. As opinions change, the key will be ensuring our societies take concrete steps toward solutions, and do so in ways that have tangible impacts. The more our governments think about the long term the better, although much hard work will remain if we are to minimize the harms from climate change and leave a healthy planet to future generations.

10

Infrastructure

Those who can, build. Those who can't, criticize.

New York City Parks Commissioner Robert Moses,
quoted in Caro, *The Power Broker*

In 2017 the consultancy Oxford Economics and G20-sponsored Global Infrastructure Hub published a report on the state of global infrastructure investment. They estimate that between 2016 and 2040, global infrastructure investment needs will be around $94 trillion. Unfortunately, the world will invest only around $79 trillion, a $15 trillion gap, or almost $1 trillion per year. Investment would have to increase by about 20 per cent – from 3 per cent of GDP to 3.5 per cent of GDP worldwide – to meet the need. The largest infrastructure needs, over half the world's total, are in Asia, but the largest investment gaps are in Africa and the Americas. An additional $3.8 trillion in investment is needed in the US alone. Most of these gaps exist in roads and electricity, with the bulk of the remainder in telecommunications, rail, water, airports, and ports.[1]

Governments underinvest in building and more so in maintaining infrastructure. This systematic underinvestment has concrete consequences, with apologies for the pun. Bad infrastructure denies people basic services, including clean water, sanitation, and electricity. It harms economic growth by denying businesses the roads, bridges, ports, and reliable electricity they need to produce and move goods. And it makes countries more vulnerable to other disasters, from tornadoes and hurricanes to terrorism and pandemic-related supply chain issues.

When we do invest in infrastructure, the projects are often fiascos. Bent Flyvbjerg, quite possibly the world expert on megaprojects

(projects over $1 billion), observes that based on a study of 16,000 megaprojects across 136 countries, only 0.5 per cent of them score the hat trick of being on time and on budget and providing the expected benefits.[2] Less than half are on budget, and less than 10 per cent are both on time and on budget. If you think about any recent infrastructure projects in your own city or country, these failures to deliver projects well probably sound familiar. Once infrastructure is built, we are also typically stuck with it: decisions governments take today on infrastructure will reverberate through decades. A building with high carbon emissions built now doesn't just emit today but for decades to come.

Infrastructure underinvestment is particularly salient in the US, though there has been some progress from the Biden infrastructure bill. In 2021 the Infrastructure Report Card from the American Society of Civil Engineers (ASCE) gave US infrastructure a C-. That is better than usual, and the first time in twenty years it has not been graded with a D.[3] What does a C- mean? As the report card notes, a water main breaks every two minutes in the US, wasting 6 billion gallons of treated water every day. Forty-three per cent of American roads are in mediocre or poor condition, representing almost 20 per cent of miles travelled, and as a result the average motorist pays almost $1,000 every year in wasted time and fuel. Almost fifty thousand bridges are deemed structurally deficient, despite being crossed 178 million times each day, and they need $125 billion in repairs. There are approximately 1,300 hazardous waste sites where cleanup activities are either incomplete or not yet begun, and progress toward dealing with legacy sites has stalled. Stormwater, which results in $9 billion in damages annually, has a growing annual funding gap of $8 billion per year just to comply with current regulations.

By 2039 the overall shortfall in American infrastructure investment is estimated to cost every US family $3,300 a year. The situation is worst in aviation, dams, hazardous waste, inland waterways, levees, public parks, roads, transit, stormwater, and wastewater. To address these issues, the ASCE recommends "increased, long-term, consistent investment … from all levels of government and the private sector" with the aim of spending 3.5 per cent of US GDP from the current 2.5 per cent by 2025, and making maintenance a centrepiece of the plan.[4]

The ASCE estimates the investment required to get to a score of B is about $2.59 trillion over ten years, approximately 10 per cent of US

GDP, or around half of the typical spending by the US federal government in a year. By 2039 this investment gap is estimated to cost the US economy $10 trillion in GDP and 3 million jobs. And even a B grade is defined as "Good, Adequate for Now": more investment would be needed were the US to truly have infrastructure ready for the future and be resilient to disasters or severe weather events. After so much neglect the scale of underinvestment is enormous. Were Congress to simply stop all discretionary spending, including military, education, training, transportation, science, and some health spending, it would still take several years to make up the shortfall.

As discussed in chapter 9, the most visible consequence of this underinvestment pertains to natural disasters, such as Hurricane Katrina. Cities at risk of weather events, such as New Orleans, are desperately in need of investment, and the number of cities included in that list may continue to increase as global warming affects world climate patterns. Cities and farms in the Midwest could require emergency investment in drought or flood-resistant systems, for example.

More pernicious is the ongoing underinvestment that affects households. Poor irrigation systems lead to small harvests for farmers. Poorly constructed or run-down school buildings impede learning for children. Slow internet access inhibits starting businesses or working from home. Poorly designed or maintained road systems extend commutes, increase stress, and lower productivity. The problem is not only that insufficient money is spent but also what money is available is misallocated.[5] Spending is focused mostly on new projects and initiatives, while existing infrastructure suffers from neglect. The political incentives for maintaining existing infrastructure are low, since maintenance doesn't come with ribbon-cutting ceremonies, major press announcements, naming rights of a new bridge or road, or other politically useful opportunities. Politicians get little if any credit for good maintenance, unlike the accolades for new builds.

Similarly, fixing a pothole provides much less publicity than building a new road. As a result, many US states focus on new road construction. Existing roads, which represent about 99 per cent of the road system, get less than half the total spending.[6] Existing stocks decay while new roads receive all the attention, only to decay in turn. However, maintenance is a much better deal: researchers from the World Bank estimate every dollar spent on infrastructure maintenance in OECD countries is as effective as $1.50 of new investments.[7]

Even when it comes to building new infrastructure governments may encounter difficulty. The party in power that launches the project may be criticized by local residents who oppose construction near them, and projects can have significant environmental and regional costs, although the benefits are worthwhile in the long term. Such projects are therefore a classic victim of government short-termism: costs fall on the current government, and benefits are likely only evident after another party is in office. Even if the short-term costs are minor, since the benefits will not be recognized for many years, the party in power has an incentive to divert the spending elsewhere.

Before Abraham Lincoln ran for president he was a member of the Whig Party. In addition to supporting the rule of law and protecting minorities, a key plank of the Whig Party's platform was internal improvements, meaning expanding the road and canal systems as well as strengthening public schools, charities, and cultural institutions as a way to fortify and enrich the entire country.[8] The goal was to build a morally and economically improved nation, or in other words provide long-term benefits to the country, despite potential short-term costs to investing in them. The same goal applies today.

DICTATORSHIPS AND USER FEEDBACK

Confronting this challenge, a natural assumption is that dictatorships must be better at infrastructure. With more centralized power and more certainty they will be in power long-term, there is much greater incentive to build. To some extent this appears to be true. China famously used more cement between 2011 and 2013 than the US did in the entire twentieth century, and China has almost no shortfall in infrastructure investment. The foreword to a book by Robert Moses, one of the most successful builders of infrastructure in modern history and the builder of most of New York City's roads, parks, bridges, and other major infrastructure projects, pessimistically remarks that "pure democracy has neither the imagination, nor the energy, nor the disciplined mentality to create major improvements."[9] Moses's ability to force through change while avoiding democratic process meant he in many ways built modern New York City, as the driving force behind modern Central Park, the UN building, 2 world's fairs, 658 playgrounds, 669 kilometres of expressways, 13 bridges, and a host of other projects.

There are also disadvantages to such an approach, however. Robert Caro recounts in his compelling and Pulitzer Prize–winning biography of Moses, *The Power Broker*, how the builder's actions led to the displacement of hundreds of thousands of people and many minority communities, the destruction of multiple neighbourhoods, and an underinvestment in public transport that continues to haunt New York City.[10] Moses's heedlessness in prioritizing more roads over the need for public transit meant the city's traffic problems steadily worsened, and his dictatorial style meant he actively eliminated diversity of opinion that might have checked his error.

Dictatorships are almost always marked by a disconnect from the needs of individual citizens. Even if they start out with such interest, the realities of ruling a country without the need to pay attention to citizens leads to difficulties. In the case of infrastructure, this frequently means white elephant projects. Dictatorships around the world are known for their grandiose and frequently useless infrastructure projects, dreamed up without sufficient consultation or familiarity with the facts on the ground. The inclusive, deliberative process in democracies, though not perfect, can do significantly better at understanding and responding to citizen needs.[11]

The same problem sometimes occurs in poorly designed development projects. In one infamous example, the PlayPump, a pump was designed to have a merry-go-round attached. As children played with the merry-go-round, water was pumped into a storage tank. The plan was to improve access to water in the developing world. Investors and the media were hugely excited when it was introduced, with millions of dollars pledged to help install the units. Pictures were circulated of smiling children playing while supposedly solving Africa's water accessibility problems. Unfortunately, the project suffered from significant flaws, including high cost (several normal pumps could be installed for the cost of a single PlayPump), complex maintenance requirements, and crucially a reliance on children playing with them that did not materialize. Journalist Andrew Chambers pointed out that children would have to play on the merry-go-round for twenty-seven hours per day to meet the target water output levels.[12] The project culminated in desolate pictures of older women struggling to push the merry-go-rounds to pump water, using them as very inefficient hand pumps. Millions of dollars had been wasted. Although the marketing was excellent, it failed for the same reason many projects conceived by dictatorships fail: ignorance about what users actually needed.

Local needs are not always easy to balance against collective benefits. Locals can be understandably frustrated with or opposed to projects that will impact their neighbourhoods, even if the national impact is positive. Many governments are wrestling with this when it comes to densification of communities, for example. House prices are sky-high in many places, and a key part of the solution is to increase the number of homes available for people to buy in places they want to live. Building more homes is challenging, however. Increasing the number of homes available means increasing density, which current residents frequently oppose.[13] Local regulations are often designed to prevent increased density by requiring authorities' approval to build or using zoning laws to limit multiple residences on the same lot. These rules serve a noble purpose, trying to preserve the character of neighbourhoods and avoiding overcrowding, but in practice they are frequently invoked by locals to prevent needed increases in housing density. It is often the most desirable neighbourhoods, which are also the wealthiest and frequently the least diverse, that are best at using these limits to deny newcomers. As a result, house prices continue to increase, affecting the quality of life of younger and future generations and leaving them with long commutes or grotesque housing costs.

Riding roughshod over local opposition, as dictatorships often do, can be appealing in the short term but ultimately often galvanizes opposition or alienates people from government altogether. Before starting an infrastructure project, talking to locals, understanding local impacts, and doing as much as possible to address and mitigate those impacts can help reduce opposition, build long-term support, and simplify construction, though it may be impossible to entirely eliminate local resistance. It may make sense to compensate locals for any adverse impacts, as governments often do when building new highways. And as we saw in the case of Robert Moses, local concerns may be right! Sometimes building for the national good means negatively affecting local groups, but it may also be a white elephant project, inflicting more harm than good. Democracies are far more likely to take the time to talk to citizens and find out what projects are genuinely needed, even if the price of doing so is delay. All politics is local, as they say, and this is especially true for infrastructure projects.

Building infrastructure without a clear sense of what users need and what they will use can lead to expensive failures.

RECOMMENDATIONS

As with climate change, the strategies discussed in this book can help governments take a more long-term perspective on infrastructure. First, better measurement through a national balance sheet is fundamental. Has a government let its nation's assets tarnish and age or has it maintained or improved the infrastructure for the next generation? Most governments do not report with any regularity on the quality of infrastructure in the country. Reporting occurs only in response to a crisis: when a bridge breaks or a water system fails, citizens and the media are outraged. When the Morandi Bridge in Genoa, Italy, collapsed in 2018 killing forty-three people, it provoked a wider conversation about the quality of infrastructure in Italy and across Europe. Attention is usually temporary, though, and gaps in investment are not addressed systematically. It should not fall to international NGOs or engineering associations to track the quality of a nation's infrastructure. Doing so is a fundamental responsibility of government.

What could this look like in practice? Imagine a country where an independent body makes a regular estimate of the current infrastructure stock and future needs of every region. This could be based on both the depreciation of current stock as well as changing circumstances that might lead to new infrastructure needs, such as changing demographics or an increased risk of weather events due to climate change. A summary of the findings, perhaps projected onto a national map, could be included in an annual update from the government such as the State of the Union address.

It could go farther. The city of Boston, Massachusetts, introduced an interactive website that allowed residents to see the location of service requests such as potholes and broken street lamps and track progress by the city's government in addressing them. Research found that the website increased resident confidence in the government, even when it was apparent the government was failing to meet the growing backlog of requests.[14] Sometimes transparency can make people happier, even if results are poor. Governments, regional or national, could enable residents to see where investment in infrastructure is occurring and report where investment or repairs are needed. As underinvestment becomes acute, citizens would be able to identify the gaps and push their governments to act by making reports themselves and through media attention to the issue.

Establishing this transparency could encourage long-term confidence in government and provide a feedback loop that could inform future infrastructure investment as well as provide incentives to keep up with maintenance. In other words, it could help not only measure the scale of the problem (chapter 5) but also make it more salient and make government responses more automatic (chapter 6). To ensure inclusion of other viewpoints, a red team could be set up to develop scenarios of possible infrastructure needs and challenge governments' predictions about project costs and where infrastructure would be needed. Projects should involve significant user engagement to minimize the risk of potential users rejecting them after they are built, as occurred in the PlayPump fiasco, and should engage end users as well as representatives for the needs of this generation and future ones.

What about the third strategy, commitments? We frequently see commitments to individual infrastructure projects: governments announce they want to build this massive hydro dam or that large light rail system, for example. Governments could go farther, committing not only to individual projects but also to a broader investment strategy that involves maintaining and improving infrastructure for future generations. Or they could commit to a level of quality or service as provided by the infrastructure, the ultimate outcome that infrastructure is intended to achieve.

A stronger commitment could be the creation of a fund dedicated to infrastructure or the creation of an independent infrastructure bank, which has happened in Australia, Canada, Colombia, Mexico, Poland, and the UK. Infrastructure banks typically allocate funds to projects with high long-term benefits and attract private investment while remaining relatively independent from political pressures. The advantage is that even if governments or priorities change, the infrastructure bank's independence allows it to continue investing in long-term infrastructure needs. Success for an infrastructure bank is not automatic, though. A bank would require a clear mission related to addressing long-term infrastructure investment gaps and metrics to assess progress. It would also need to strike a balance between supporting valuable projects that would not otherwise occur and avoiding unnecessary or inefficient investments.[15]

Commitments can be harmful if they are too specific. Sometimes, the best option is to avoid construction altogether. Rather than building new infrastructure to extract more water from our lakes and streams, it may be better to introduce measures to reduce water use, for example. Committing to an infrastructure project too early can do more harm than good if it turns out there are other policy options that can achieve the same goal more effectively. Flexible options are often superior to committing to individual projects.

Finally, complementing national infrastructure balance sheets and a commitment to infrastructure investment can be a more iterative approach to infrastructure projects. Such an approach can be beneficial in two ways. First, it can help infrastructure stay relevant to evolving user needs over the following decades. Second, it can strengthen the design and construction process, reducing costs and increasing efficiency. Bent Flyvbjerg, the megaproject expert mentioned earlier, is a strong proponent for experimentation, even when it comes to billion-dollar-plus projects. He argues that "whatever the project or technology, it's the most effective path to a plan that delivers."[16] As Flyvbjerg observes, Frank Gehry, one of the most successful architects in history, leaned heavily on experimentation to deliver masterpieces like the Guggenheim Museum Bilbao, often identified as one of the greatest architectural achievements of the twentieth century. Before starting construction on the Bilbao, Gehry spent two years working through hundreds of iterations, starting with actual wooden models before moving to design software.

One of the biggest challenges of infrastructure projects is that they are almost always long term. Large projects can take decades to build and then last for decades or generations more. Choosing which projects to prioritize is challenging because it requires guesswork about the needs and goals of the future. A national balance sheet encourages governments to maintain current infrastructure, but how do we encourage governments to think about what the next generation will want or need? This is where an iterative, experimental approach can help.

It can be challenging to anticipate how infrastructure will be used decades or generations on. A public transit system may be too small if the population of a city grows, or too large if the population shrinks. It may end up travelling to the wrong place if the city grows in a different direction. Schools are built without knowing the birth rates of the future. Office buildings designed pre-COVID did not anticipate the sudden move to hybrid work. Climate change has rendered a whole generation of infrastructure awkward or no longer fit for purpose, designed as it was when energy use was less of an issue, and climate-driven floods or storms were not on the radar of urban planners, leading to high-cost retrofits or removal.

Some infrastructure ends up making a problem worse. The classic example of this is road building. Traffic congestion is a major complaint in many cities, and though the increase in remote work after the pandemic helps, commutes can take hours each day and cost the economy billions.[17] People hate commuting; it is often rated as one of our least enjoyable activities. Policy-makers have drawn the obvious lesson that the world needs more roads, and adding highway capacity has been a consistently popular political priority for the last century. Unfortunately, the strategy often doesn't work. What is sometimes called the fundamental law of road congestion is that the more roads you build, the more people drive. It rarely reduces congestion.[18] In technical terms, the demand for driving is highly elastic when it comes to the number of roads; when you build more roads, people choose to drive more. A little more humility from policy-makers and a more iterative approach that included measuring congestion levels before and after highway projects could have highlighted this truth decades earlier and enabled a more thoughtful exploration beyond laying asphalt (such as congestion charges or public transit).

Instead of guessing what the future holds and building accordingly, a better approach is to build infrastructure that can suit a wide range of possible futures. Projects need to be built anticipating that they may only be the first phase in an ongoing process of adaptation and changes in use and not locking in a particular way of doing things. Building in flexibility minimizes the risk of the future inadequacy and allows projects to adapt over time. When it comes to infrastructure, as with many things, humility about what we do and don't know and a corresponding project design that allows for agility when conditions change is the way to go. In other words, where possible, current infrastructure projects should not preclude alternatives in the future. At best, they can be designed in advance to accommodate many possibilities. In an example of what not to do, Caro suggests that Robert Moses built overpasses in New York that were too low to accommodate buses, preventing expansion of transit lines as demand rose and harming poorer families.[19] Whether this was intentional – to prevent low-income minorities from visiting popular beaches by denying bus access – is debated; however, overpass height is a clear example where a small design change of a few extra inches of height can make the difference between having the flexibility to accommodate increased population and demand by running buses on a road or not.

To future-proof roads today, we might want to design them to accommodate electric or autonomous vehicles. Among other things that can mean ensuring lanes, signs, and curbs are well-marked for cameras to identify and read; planning for space to install eventual charging stations or building charging systems into the roads themselves; reinforcing parts of roads that will receive increased use given that autonomous vehicles will likely be better at centring themselves in lanes; and accommodating increased curb use for autonomous vehicles to pick people up and drop them off, as is already needed with Uber and other ridesharing firms.[20] It is typically far cheaper and easier to build in such considerations from the start than to introduce them later. For example, reserving land for charging stations or adding a few inches to increase overpass height is relatively cheap when a road is first built but costly afterwards. When governments commission or build infrastructure, rather than trying to get the cheapest price or the largest number of jobs, they should think about how they can make the project as robust as possible to changing conditions. Obsessing over the cheapest price to start, though understandable, can mean large bills later.

The need for future-proofing infrastructure is perhaps most obvious when it comes to climate change. Indeed, many of the short-term challenges described in chapter 9 are replicated and reinforced by short-termism when it comes to infrastructure. To successfully adapt to the long-term impacts of climate change, we will also need to change our infrastructure. To take one example, since we do not know exactly how climate change may affect extreme weather events, having infrastructure that is resilient to a range of such events is increasingly important. Building systems that can be updated and adapted easily mitigates the risk.

The SMART tunnel in Malaysia, for example, is designed to allow for traffic but can transition to stormwater management during flash floods, which are common in Kuala Lumpur. China's sponge cities have increased their capacity to absorb and store rainwater, thereby mitigating floods, reducing runoff pollution, and increasing water supply.[21] Sponge cities modify underground parking lots to serve as emergency reservoirs, for example, as well as plant more trees and cover the roofs of buildings in grass. Sponge cities are presumably easier to implement in a non-democratic state with less emphasis on property rights. Still, if storms and flooding increase as a result of climate change, Chinese cities will be better prepared. If the flooding is less severe than expected, then the cities still function well; after all, having more roofs covered in grass doesn't limit habitability.

Even climate change infrastructure can fall victim to short-term thinking. As the International Panel on Climate Change sets out in their 2022 report on the impacts of climate change, some responses can be examples of maladaptation, projects that do more harm than good due to a failure to consider unintended consequences or to plan for the potential rate and magnitude of climate change.[22] Seawalls, for example, can reduce space for natural ecosystems that help reduce wave intensity, such as mangroves and reefs, and increase coastal erosion by changing patterns of water flow, worsening the problems they were meant to avert.

At the extreme, large investments can lead to what is referred to as lock-in effects, especially carbon lock-in.[23] Once an infrastructure system is built, it can create barriers to transitioning to anything new. Once a society has built its energy network around coal or oil, for example, the cost of using those sources falls: the upfront costs of the mines, power plants, and distribution networks have already been paid, and power from coal or oil is cheaper than wind or solar, which require new infrastructure to be built. Households become accustomed to and plan around the cost of energy at coal-based prices, perhaps by choosing to buy homes in the suburbs and own cars, and are reluctant to change. This discourages a transition to other energy sources, which seem expensive and inconvenient in comparison.

Large-scale infrastructure projects can thus discourage future innovation and adaptation by locking-in current technology, even if the ultimate outcome would be an improvement. An iterative approach to infrastructure can mitigate this issue. A distributed power grid, for example, makes the system easier to adapt over time in response to changing economic conditions and reduces vulnerability to unexpected shocks, such as natural disasters, system failures, or terrorist attacks.

There is a trade-off. It is usually more expensive to build something that can be adapted and evolved in the future. Making a road suitable for use by self-driving cars in the future will cost more than not doing so and may lead to waste if technologies change in the meantime. Government procurement processes often create pressure to choose the lowest-cost option, which almost by definition will have the least adaptability to future needs. Sometimes the additional cost will not be worth it. But often some humility and acknowledgment that a project will need to stand the test of time can mean small investments up front make life far easier for our descendants.

An iterative approach to infrastructure doesn't just help address lock-in effects and changing future needs. It can also help support the actual design and construction of infrastructure projects. Building a project in phases allows designers to learn from each phase of the project, adjusting course as necessary. Depending on demand and use, future phases can then be tweaked to better suit the needs of the population. This iterative, flexible approach has its roots in software development, where it is known as agile project management. Most interesting from an iterative perspective, agile methods typically include breaking work into smaller pieces that can be delivered sequentially, seeking customer feedback on each one.[24] This allows for rapid user feedback and testing at each stage, ensuring the product is functional and meeting user needs.

Large physical infrastructure projects cannot always be done iteratively in the way software can, of course. It is hard to break a bridge into component parts that can be delivered in sequence; a bridge either crosses the river or doesn't, and the final product, a successful bridge, is usually delivered only once. Safety considerations mean that delivering the minimum may not be appropriate. A minor glitch in software may mean a website is down for a few days; a glitch in a hospital building or school could have serious consequences. Moving fast and breaking things, Facebook's infamous slogan, is not a goal when it comes to bridges or nuclear power plants. Regulatory oversight is understandably tighter to ensure projects meet the necessary safety, environmental, reliability, and other standards, and the resources required for physical infrastructure are often vastly greater than those for software.

Nevertheless, there are some lessons from agile software development that can apply to physical infrastructure projects. Many of the lessons of agile project management do apply to the design phase of a project. Before any shovels hit the ground, short cycles of design and user testing can ensure infrastructure projects engage and consult stakeholders well. Researchers from the consultancy McKinsey suggest that using an agile approach for capital projects can reduce costs and time to completion by 10 per cent.[25] On a billion-dollar, multi-year project that is considerable savings. During the initial design phase, for example, agile teams spend more time on framing the right questions and identifying which options are most likely to succeed, rather than dedicating too much time to options that ultimately are not used. Such a process can be helpful when procuring large projects, avoiding a single catastrophic failure of a project by breaking it into smaller pieces.

During the construction phase there are some infrastructure projects that can be rolled out in pieces. For example, if the goal is to provide free Wi-Fi to an entire city, the project can start by providing it in targeted blocks, measuring demand and usage to inform the project's eventual expansion. Such an approach helps preclude white elephants: building a smaller version that can be expanded means that if no one likes or uses the small version, the big version can be avoided entirely. If an initial pilot achieves success, it can quickly be scaled up and expanded. Tesla introduced a similar approach to the automotive industry, rolling out regular updates and improvements to their vehicles rather than the more traditional annual update cycle for vehicles. Products get up to twenty engineering changes a week, and cars are designed to be modular so that teams can iterate on different parts over time.[26] This approach isn't always possible. If the goal is to connect two cities by roadway, then building 10 per cent of the road and seeing how many people use it will not be informative. That said, there is frequently a way to test at least parts of the infrastructure on a smaller scale before committing to a full project that may or may not work as hoped.

Digital technology can also help divide projects into more manageable steps. McKinsey's report describes one mining company that built a digital twin of a major construction project. The comprehensive model allowed them to visualize and test different approaches, accelerating the project by more than six months. As technology continues to advance, it will be increasingly easy to use this approach for other projects, providing more space to take an iterative tactic.

Agile, iterative methods are no miracle cure. In a study of over twenty-five thousand IT projects, only 11 per cent of standard-managed projects were entirely successful, and 29 per cent were complete failures. Projects done using agile methods fared better: 39 per cent were successful, and only 9 per cent were complete failures.[27] However, 39 per cent is still poor, although it helps to remember Flyvberg's finding that most megaprojects aren't successful either. Agile methods will be most useful when user needs are evolving or unclear, so there is a need to iterate and adapt over time. The point is not to copy and paste agile methods to physical infrastructure, which have a very different context and constraints, but to learn from them in order to make physical infrastructure projects more iterative and more successful.

* * *

Infrastructure offers a promising case for the implementation of several of the strategies we have discussed. A government that wants to invest in infrastructure, as many do, has an incentive to introduce a balance sheet of some kind in order to point out the failure of their opponents to maintain the infrastructure stock and build their own case for investment – especially if they are considering borrowing to do so. Institutions to support infrastructure investment and iterative methods can have short-term benefits by improving the implementation of their infrastructure goals and thus may also hold appeal.

Once infrastructure is built it is to some extent a commitment, since dismantling and starting over can be expensive. Infrastructure is usually less polarizing than climate change, making sharp reversals in policy by future governments less likely. However, infrastructure and infrastructure maintenance do face a risk of dwindling interest over time, as future governments focus on more visible priorities. National balance sheets and other such measures are particularly crucial to render infrastructure investments or gaps visible and keep public interest and political motivation focused on the issue.

Good infrastructure is a key part of a nation's wealth. In the same way that a household is likely to have a lower income without a functioning car, such infrastructure as roads, bridges, water purification plants, and power grids are fundamental to a healthy and wealthy economy. Many of the same lessons apply for investing in things less traditionally included under the heading of infrastructure: strong health, education, sanitation, and other systems are all long-term investments, and frequently suffer from neglect by short-term governments. Measuring how well a country is doing, ensuring diverse perspectives are engaged in planning, having governments commit to improvements, and encouraging an adaptive, iterative approach to projects can all push governments to take a more sustainable, long-term view to problems, supporting the country as a whole.

11

Conclusion

If your plan is for one year, grow rice. If your plan is for ten years, grow trees. If your plan is for one hundred years, educate children.

Proverb attributed to Confucius

When I lived in the UK, I had several opportunities to admire the roof of the New College dining hall. New College is (confusingly) one of the oldest member colleges of the University of Oxford, itself the oldest English-speaking university in the world, and over the last seven hundred years New College has endured wear and tear. The roof is made up of huge oak beams, and according to the Long Now Foundation, an organization devoted to spreading long-term thinking, about a century ago someone noticed that beetles had almost eaten through the beams.[1] Large oak beams are not as readily available as they were in 1379, and someone proposed searching the college lands. (When an institution is around for centuries and teaches exclusively the children of the rich for most of that period, it acquires a lot of land.) As the legend goes, the college called in their forester, who pointed out that when the roof was built the founders planted a grove of oak trees to replace the roof beams as they wore out. For the next few hundred years, foresters would tell their successors that those oaks were not to be cut until the roof needed replacing.

A lovely story, but it probably isn't true. The reality is likely that it was standard practice for foresters to plant a mix of woods and harvest the other woods while leaving oaks to grow large so they could be used in major construction projects. Thoughtful management over the generations meant the college didn't need to predict the future but instead was prepared for a wide range of possible outcomes. When foresters planted oaks, they did so knowing that they would not benefit from them, and it might be generations before they were harvested. They did it anyway, inspired by the same ethic as contemporary cathedral builders.

There are modern long-term successes too. Huddled in Longyearbyen in the Svalbard archipelago, the world's most northern settlement of over one thousand people, is the Global Seed Vault, a snow-covered testament to long-term thinking. The vault protects one of the most precious things we have as a species: the world's genetic diversity in the form of seeds. As new diseases or agricultural disasters emerge, genetic diversity gives us a reservoir of nature's best ideas to help plants survive and thrive, potentially the difference between the extinction and survival of key crops and humanity itself. The vault is intended to preserve the seeds for hundreds or thousands of years, guarding against the loss of biodiversity.

Sometimes referred to as a doomsday vault, it is designed to survive a loss of power, the melting of the ice caps, the many roaming polar bears, and, with its concave tunnel head and 120 metre tunnel extending into a rock mountain, even the force of a missile or asteroid strike. Its construction is both a symbol of our ability to think long term and a tangible step forward. In an ironic twist of fate, it is also a symbol of our challenges: global warming has started melting the permafrost surrounding the vault, and it has begun to flood, endangering the seeds.

There have been other wins. The Spaceguard program's success in identifying asteroids that could hit Earth is a major victory against what could have posed an existential threat. The recent American focus on natural capital is a step forward in better counting of national wealth, not just income. The Montreal Protocol combatting ozone depletion was a significant victory and a landmark moment for countries coming together to solve a global issue. Institutions such as Finland's Committee for the Future, Norway's sovereign wealth fund, and Wales's Commissioner for Future Generations and their corresponding Well-being of Future Generations Act demonstrate that progress is possible and we can shift governments in a more long-termist direction.

RECOMMENDATIONS

We sometimes focus too much on the tension between present and future generations, when in reality many decisions do not pose this problem. Building a park or museum today can help both the present and the future. Even climate change, often taken as a defining example of the tension between present and future, does not always lead to a conflict; making our cities more climate proof may also reduce pollution and encourage walking for the current generation, for example.[2] As we have seen, though, our governments are increasingly facing short-term pressures while at the same time making decisions with more and more potential impacts on the future.

This book seeks to draw lessons from behavioural science to help fight government short-termism and establish behaviourally informed governance. These insights suggest our governments can make key changes in how they work in order to nudge long-term thinking by our leaders in the future. Those changes need not be complicated, and which are best will vary by the cultural context and history of a given government and society. Some countries may choose to embed climate change in their constitution, while others will see that as a lightning rod for controversy. Some societies may have a strong cultural tradition related to how the views of future generations should be considered, such as the Haudenosaunee seventh generation principle, and leveraging that can support a broader culture of long-termism.

In general, I recommend a few key changes:

1 **Make the impact of present decisions on the future obvious.** As the case studies of infrastructure and climate change show, good data on how we are impacting the future is often a critical first step to improving decisions and holding our governments accountable for them. This information could be included in a richer, more meaningful measure of national wealth such as gross domestic wealth rather than GDP and be regularly updated by governments.
2 **Make it easier for governments to focus on the future.** Carve out dedicated space for thinking about the future. Encouraging governments to speak regularly to the future impacts of their decisions, whether through the annual budget process, State of the Union address, or annual report on the future, can ensure long-term thinking has the saliency it deserves, and citizens and the media have a tripwire to alert them to problems. Where possible, make long-term policies the default, such as through automatic stabilizers.

Governments should strengthen long-term guardrails by including diverse viewpoints in decisions, especially groups that will eventually be impacted. Groupthink, from Kennedy's invasion of the Bay of Pigs to the UK's failure to anticipate fraud on their learning account program, can cripple governments' ability to correctly anticipate and prepare for the future. Some viewpoints are difficult to include, such as those from generations yet unborn, but increasing the diversity of views engaged in making decisions can ensure that more information is available and more alternatives considered. Red teams, scenario planning, and delivery units can all further embed long-term thinking in policy-making.

3 **Commit to long-term measures, including through the establishment of long-term institutions.** Ask governments to make both hard and soft commitments to valuing and planning for the future. In some countries, that may include constitutional requirements related to the future. In others it may mean establishing institutions that give a dedicated voice for future generations in government deliberations and commit the government to considering that voice, as with the Finnish Committee of the Future or the Welsh Future Generations Commissioner. Where appropriate, make long-term institutions independent, as with the Norwegian sovereign wealth fund.

Soft commitments, such as public announcements and platform promises, though weaker than hard commitments, can be rendered more effective by making them clear, concrete, measurable, non-partisan, and with a public constituency to support their delivery.

4 **Iterate.** Finally, governments need to experiment and iterate. We cannot predict the future, especially in our fast-changing modern world. Attempting to decide everything in advance and rushing into it as quickly as possible is a recipe for trouble. Try something, test it, then rinse and repeat. Scale up what works and cancel what doesn't. As citizens we need to give our governments the space to say they don't know all the answers and the time to test possible solutions to identify what works best, while still holding them accountable for the final outcome.

The strategies explored in this book seek to counteract the high and increasing short-term pressures on our governments and leaders, to allow them space and ability to plan and prepare for the long term.

These can be particularly effective in informing decisions that are not already highly politicized. It is important to recognize however that they are not miracle cures and may sometimes sit in tension with other values or considerations. Nudges have limits, and using them does not preclude more systemic changes.

LIMITS

A first and fundamental limitation is that even unbiased policy-making is challenging. Cognitive biases are not the whole story, and if short-termism were to vanish entirely from human nature our governments face other barriers to long-term action. We may lack the necessary technology; have insufficient resources; be unable to overcome polarization or distrust; be limited by our culture, economics, or politics; fail to solve collective action problems; or simply make mistakes. Introducing behavioural thinking into our governments will not suddenly solve the complex, systemic, long-term issues we face; they will require action across a wide range of fronts. Eliminating short-term bias is irrelevant if the government lacks the power or resources to address the issue, in the same way that a low-income household may not have enough to save for retirement regardless of which behavioural strategies it applies.

Within government, long-termist leaders can be captured by short-term interests as they seek to strike the right balance between short- and long-term needs. Governments will still have to navigate complex networks of lobbyists, industries, special interests, and other groups who oppose long-term policies due to their own material or partisan interests. Most decisions will create both winners and losers in the present and the future, and leaders will have to balance conflicts within generations as well as across them. Nudging governments may not be enough if power is allocated in society in such a way that the government is unable or unwilling to implement changes.

There is also inevitably uncertainty over the future impact of decisions, with governments genuinely unsure what options are best for the present or the future. It can be hard or impossible to identify the right answer. Legitimate choices can be made that harm the future and help today, and people can disagree about that without being present biased. There is no easy answer to this.

The strategies we have explored can help push back against the present bias we as humans and our governments tend to demonstrate, but they do not remove the need for more fundamental democratic engagement and deliberation as we struggle to make the right decisions. Changes such as improving the quality of parliamentary debate or governments' engagement with citizens, even if not directly focused on long-term thinking, can improve policy-making overall.

In my view behaviourally informed governance is part of the solution to short-termism, but it should be pursued in tandem with other strategies. Change is difficult, and questions around how power is allocated get at the heart of intergenerational trade-offs, particularly because, almost by definition, a generation that is alive today will have more power than a generation that is not. I do not want to underestimate the power of behavioural interventions, and as we see in the case of individuals, small changes in the environment can lead to large changes in behaviour. Still, though behavioural nudges can help reduce the short-term pressures on governments, broader questions of the allocation of resources and power are fundamentally political ones and will not be solved solely by nudges.

Another way to think about this limitation is the difference between nudging individuals and groups. When an individual is nudged, they then make and carry out a decision, for example, to save for retirement or not. Nudging a group is different because the group will likely not be unanimous; therefore, making and carrying out the decision requires navigating the power and disagreement within the group. Even if a majority of a group is in favour of a long-term decision, collective action problems or internal disagreement by minority groups may persist, and individuals or groups with power can block decisions they oppose. In other words, nudging may help reduce the pressure on the group to be short term, but more may be needed to build consensus and encourage action among different stakeholders. Long-term thinking in leadership is key; however, if a leader is motivated to act on a long-term problem, they still have to navigate the political and bureaucratic process to get things done.

A second and related limitation is that sometimes nudges may be insufficient to change behaviour. Some leaders or governments may be uninterested in the long-term impacts of their decisions due to their own personality or reflecting the interests of groups they represent. They may be focused on providing immediate transactional benefits for their followers, for example, even if doing so leads to unsustainable quick fixes and risks to the future; polarization may make some leaders or voters unwilling to consider evidence about long-term harms.[3]

In those cases, publishing more information about the impact on the future or introducing tripwires or guardrails of some kind will simply not be enough. Even commitments can founder without enough popular support. Fortunately, many examples of government short-termism are none of the above. Instead we see leaders who want to do a good job and leave a positive legacy, but are overwhelmed or caught in a scarcity mindset, forced to react without thinking deeply. Behaviourally informed governance may be most effective for such leaders, who already want to make positive impact but may struggle to focus on the future, much like an individual nudging themselves to save more for retirement.

That said, behavioural governance can still impact leaders uninterested in the long term. Some of the strategies affect the short-term incentives such leaders face, for example, by making national wealth more salient to voters through the use of a national balance sheet and thus changing voter patterns of support. Short-termist leaders may pay little attention to issues that do not receive political attention, leaving space for changes that inform decisions that are not particularly partisan but can still influence future generations. Commitments can impose real costs on leaders seeking to deviate from long-term policies, discouraging such decisions. The bottom line, though, is behavioural strategies leave leaders with considerable autonomy. Leaders play an important role in any society, and behaviourally informed governance does not remove that importance. Indeed, a challenge facing our governments is the need to find or nurture transformational, long-termist leaders.[4]

A final limitation is that these changes may sometimes conflict with our democratic values in at least two ways. First, a democracy that introduces an independent institution that is not bound to follow the will of future governments is limiting the democratic supremacy of those future governments, who have less ability to affect policy decisions no matter what voters want. Insofar as we value the democratic principle of having voters able to make their own decisions, this may be problematic. For many of the strategies we have discussed, in my view this concern is relatively minor. Various unconscious factors already pressure governments to be short-termist. Better measurements of our impact on the future, guardrails and tripwires in decision processes, or encouraging a more iterative and experimental approach provide a fairly small limitation on a government or voters while also counterbalancing short-term pressures. Nudges that support a leader in following through on their intentions later in their mandate are also largely unproblematic.

Commitments and defaults can present more of a challenge. How much right do present generations have to shape or limit the decisions of future ones? There is no right or wrong answer, but there is a tension there. In addition to any moral or philosophical concerns we might have with binding the hands of our descendants, by definition we do not know what circumstances the future holds. Any commitments we make today might turn out to be useless or harmful if conditions prove different than we expect. One advantage of the changes we explore here is that although they pressure future generations to make decisions in certain ways, they allow for more flexibility than a more fundamental institutional or structural change. Governments can still choose to renege or change the rules, even when it comes to constitutional requirements or independent institutions. But nudges create some level of constraint. That is the point, after all.

In the end, commitments by governments that bind future ones are well-established in democracies worldwide. Almost any decision by a government today can have an effect on future ones. Many democracies have constitutions that help steer policy well after the writers are no longer in power or independent institutions, such as central banks or sovereign wealth funds. Most democracies also accept an unelected public service or bureaucracy that implements decisions by elected officials, but this means the bureaucracy can influence how those decisions are carried out. As scholars have argued, this can be justified on democratic grounds; the key is to do it in a way that strikes a balance and maintains democratic legitimacy and supremacy. Public debate over the right balance is likely both inevitable and desirable.[5]

For me, the lesson here is not that we should avoid making commitments, but rather we should use them in moderation and ensure they are established democratically and there is some form of democratic oversight and review. Commitments and independent institutions can help make long-term policies not easily reversible by new governments; however, political decision-making is important, particularly when it comes to questions around representing the interests of those affected and navigating conflicts between groups.[6] Successful commitments should be designed to strike a balance and may well have both political and independent elements, as in the Finnish foresight system, which includes a role for both independent experts and the elected parliament.

A second tension with democratic values is that debate, discussion, and deliberation are at the core of democratic decision-making. Democracies are supposed to make decisions by engaging with voters and convincing them to vote for a given party or leader, unlike non-democracies which may use coercion, deception, or threats.[7] Nudges which seek to unconsciously influence leaders or voters to be more long-termist, though desirable, may run counter to the value democracies put on debate and deliberation. More practically, sidestepping debate may ultimately undermine the support for long-term thinking itself. Futurist institutions may be more effective if they are independent of democratic politics, but if as a result they lack legitimacy and their advice is not followed, then the effort is ultimately counterproductive. We cannot nudge our way into democratic legitimacy, nor should we try.

In behavioural terms, we might prefer voters use Kahneman's System 2 for making policy decisions, using analytical reasoning and deliberation and not the automatic and unconscious System 1. Over time, too much use of System 1 may also reduce public support for long-term thinking, if voters no longer engage with or consider the issue. Is the correct role of government to avoid public discussion of those topics in the future by making policy automatic or to encourage such discussion and debate? This is a legitimate concern. That said, when done well, introducing behaviourally informed governance can provoke more, not less, public discussion around sustainable, long-term wealth and human flourishing. Publishing measures of national wealth instead of GDP, for example, can support more debate on the topic. Requiring a review of independent institutions or automatic stabilizers at a set interval, perhaps every ten or twenty years, could encourage the kind of public debate that is otherwise avoided by default policies, although it may also make them more subject to cancellation.

It is also the case that governments are inevitably affected by their environment in some way. Some use of System 1 is unavoidable. The situation is similar to putting healthy foods instead of snacks at eye level in a cafeteria in order to encourage healthy eating: one nudge is replaced with another. Doing so does not replace the need to have a broader conversation about diets, but it makes it easier for people to stick to healthy foods. Introducing behavioural strategies to help governments fight short-term pressures does not replace the need for democratic debate on long-term issues, but it can complement it and make long-termism easier. As with the tension around limiting the decisions of future governments, navigating this tension will require judgment from governments and society. When such methods are pursued, we will need to find ways to introduce them democratically and legitimately.

Ultimately, supporting long-term thinking across generations requires some form of ongoing public support for and engagement with it. No matter how long-termist a government is, if voters have no interest in the future, it is hard to sustain long-term policies. As Michael MacKenzie points out, future generations will make their own decisions, and if the goal is to have them buy into or support projects launched today, such as nuclear non-proliferation or climate change agreements, then reason giving, justification, and persuasion are some of the only tools available to coordinate action between generations.[8] Action on this front is necessary. Cultural change is difficult, however, and convincing people to care more about the future, while valuable, will not be easy. Behavioural policies can support long-term action in parallel to the public debate and can be designed to provoke debate as well.

Given the above limitations, where the cost of failure is so high as to be unacceptable or behavioural interventions seem unlikely to succeed, we may as a society wish to consider more radical or fundamental changes. Some challenges may be so insurmountable or face such entrenched opposition from powerful interests that a broader rebalancing of power and influence may be required to ensure the future is well-represented in decisions. Some scholars have suggested the nature of capitalism itself creates incentives for short-termism, for example.[9] One interesting suggestion is the use of mini-publics as part of a broader move to deliberative democracy, where a diverse group of often randomly selected citizens is assembled to deliberate and decide on a public policy issue.[10] Such deliberative democracy initiatives align well with the approaches taken in this book, emphasizing as they do the process by which opinions and decisions are made rather than just the final choice. Though not widely used today, mini-publics could help insulate decisions from electoral pressures (since decision-makers would be randomly selected and not eligible for election), and ensure the views of groups from across society are represented. Such institutions could play a dedicated role in representing the needs of future generations, perhaps through auditing decisions made by the government or by making substantive decisions on key issues directly.

Mini-publics have a variety of virtues, but of interest for our purposes is research that suggests introducing deliberation as part of the policy process can increase support for the long-term, such as a willingness to support and pay a gas tax to fight climate change.[11] My own view is that they may not automatically be a success when it comes to long-term thinking, since, as we have seen, groups of people can also be short-termist and future generations, by definition not yet born, would not represented in the group. If done well, however, mini-publics could provide opportunities to encourage and support long-term thinking, and the requirement for deliberation could encourage consideration of the needs of future generations. There is research suggesting that mini-publics can be combined with perspective-taking exercises to encourage participants to consider the future, for example.[12] Mini-publics can also insulate decisions from special interests or lobby groups, which could further carve out space for long-term views, especially on topics where those groups are highly influential or short-term. Consideration is needed about which topics and contexts mini-publics can be most helpful.

Another example is the role of digital technology in democracy. This could involve using digital platforms to engage citizens more widely in the process of taking decisions, similar to mini-publics.[13] Like mini-publics, I suspect this could be done well or poorly when it comes to long-term thinking. However, well-designed digital platforms could have their own guardrails and tripwires about the future when it comes to decisions, such as an automatic prompt reminding people to consider the future in their deliberations or an automatically generated analysis of the future implications of a proposed decision. Any such change would require careful testing to assess the effects.

A larger, more radical change using digital technology would be to use AI to make or challenge decisions. As AI advances, it could be capable of doing an analysis or audit of each government decision and its implications for the future, much like an independent institution. At the extreme, an AI could even be given some decision-making powers when it comes to the future. At the micro level, such as identifying where infrastructure investment is needed, this may be relatively straightforward, but any powers of an AI to limit or influence decisions by government will likely be controversial and brings a host of considerations that would need to be explored, not least the cost of effectively giving away some of our democratic autonomy to a machine as well as the risk of bias or error by the AI. Given the pace of technological change today it can be tempting to rely on technology to solve our problems, but it can also create new issues and requires investment in the right institutions to lead to positive technological impacts.

IMPLEMENTATION

Regardless of exactly which strategies we pursue, what incentives do governments have to implement them at all? How do we go from our current short-term governments to a thoughtfully designed and planned system that prioritizes the long term? Assessing this requires us to think more about the dynamics of politics and power that might enable or hinder these measures. As we have seen, there is a strategic incentive for groups and politicians whose priorities are disadvantaged by the strategies we have explored to oppose them. Worse yet, groups that benefit from the status quo and are therefore more likely to oppose change are also more likely to have the power and influence to actually resist options that might limit their power or reallocate resources to long-term issues and away from their priorities. Ironically, the reasons these changes might be desirable are the same reasons they may be difficult to implement, given their benefits are largely long term and the beneficiaries are not yet around to vote. If governments cared about the future enough to implement these changes, you might worry, we wouldn't need them in the first place.

This is a fundamental challenge with any type of reform: groups who benefit from the status quo, whether businesses, individuals, or politicians, are likely to want to resist change and have the power to do so. Why support national balance sheets if your goal is to get support for a new mining project that will increase GDP? Why agree to new tripwires, default policies, or independent institutions if the decisions currently being made favour you or your group? These incentives can also apply within the bureaucracy; current departments and decision-makers have power due partly to the system they work in, and changes to that system could privilege different viewpoints or perspectives.

Of course, other parties or groups will support the reforms because they anticipate they will flatter or support their preferred policies or disadvantage their opponents. In some cases, elites with power may also be more likely than the general public to support long-term thinking. Research in Finland found politicians were more likely than voters to support long-term policy-making.[14] This may be particularly likely when elites are confident about staying in power over time. In that case, they are insulated from short-term pressures, and may also have an incentive to act to keep that power in the future by averting future crises or issues. This has been suggested as an explanation for the German introduction of old age pensions, for instance, when the government had a strong majority but was concerned support for the opposition might increase in the future unless the issue was resolved.[15]

Implementation is thus an important challenge. One core lesson is that many of the strategies discussed are probably of most interest to a government when they support what that government wanted to do in the first place. National balance sheets or new guardrails or tripwires may be of interest when the government wants to invest in infrastructure, reduce the deficit, or fight climate change, and introducing them helps the government build their case for those policies. The trade-off is that this also makes them subject to reversal or being ignored by future governments who no longer agree with the policies, unless they are done in ways that build and sustain public and institutional support and engagement.

Commitments, including the creation of independent institutions that can engage with and assess information created by other strategies, are helpful in reducing the risk of a future government ignoring or reversing measures by making it more costly to do so. However, if commitments are too strong they start to create tension with democratic principles. Experimentation is perhaps the most challenging measure to implement, requiring a shift in how we and our governments think about failure, though there is promise in reframing the political benefits of iteration. Ultimately, public and media demand for and support of long-term thinking is crucial to keeping any of the strategies in place over time. Without public support and engagement, a future government can always renege when it is convenient to do so.

Beyond the considerations for specific strategies, to my mind there are three areas of broad promise for implementation. First are some lessons of behavioural science. Benartzi and Thaler's Save More Tomorrow program, previously mentioned, encourages employee participation by having employees commit today to taking deductions from their salary tomorrow.[16] As Alan Jacobs at the University of

British Columbia points out, tweaking how policies are designed can help make the future impacts more salient, or the current costs less so.[17] To help sway voters and make long-term policies more attractive, governments can explore bringing forward benefit streams while deferring costs to tomorrow so that voters see some positives immediately, in order to leverage the human bias toward the present. Though it will not work for all policies, doing so where possible can minimize the political opposition to introducing future-oriented policies while still implementing the change over time.

A second broad lesson for implementation is the role of individual leaders. Yes, some leaders may never care about the future or are exclusively focused on what maximizes their chances of being elected. One theme arising from this book, however, is that many of the reasons governments and politicians are short-termist are frustrating for them as well. Politicians rarely go into office hoping to deal with short-term crises day after day. They too want to change the world and leave it a better place for their children. They lack the space, time, and incentives to do so, and all those are affected by how we structure our governments.

Many elected and unelected officials seem to genuinely care about climate change, for example. For those leaders, there will be moments when they have time to consider the bigger picture, few as they may be. The key is to use that time well. Instead of trying to solve a single issue or problem, governments could take the opportunity to prioritize a structural change that supports long-term decisions, perhaps drawing inspiration from the options discussed here. Imagine, for example, that each time a new government is elected, the leader prioritizes one long-term change before they are caught up in the hustle and bustle of governing. Incremental changes over time can be powerful. Even if only one or two changes are made at a time, each one can help the next leader carve out more moments to focus on the long term and make their own changes. In some cases, they may end up nudging their future selves, making it easier later in their mandate to take time to focus on long-term issues. The long term is just that, and governments can gather momentum piece by piece and change by change.

A third area of potential promise is the opposite: crises. No one should want a crisis, of course, but they frequently enable or encourage changes that are otherwise not possible. As we have seen, evolving attitudes toward climate change due to natural disasters may enable action that was previously impossible. The risk, though, is that the changes coming from a crisis make things worse, not better.[18] Adding more duct tape to a rickety system in response to an emergency is not helpful. But if as a society we can think through the kind of changes we want in advance, then it can provide an opportunity for reforms. Even if the focus is initially on the topic or issue in crisis, in the future those changes can serve as precedent and foundation for initiatives that help us deal with a wide range of long-term issues.

A likely path for implementation, it seems to me, is that behaviourally informed long-term institutions are initially set up for specific topics where there is a compelling case for forward-looking thinking. Climate change, perhaps, or AI governance. A crisis in those areas could help build the case, or it could simply reflect changing generational or cultural perspectives. If the targeted measures survive and are successful, they can serve as a precedent for more widespread use of these strategies, either on specific topics or informing governance more generally.

Ultimately, I am optimistic when it comes to the implementation of behaviourally informed governance. Many of the strategies explored here have the potential to benefit governments pursuing policies that these strategies would support. Once a measure is in place, various forms of commitment may avoid their reversal by subsequent governments. And the measures can reinforce each other, in the same way that the foresight mechanism within the office of the Finnish prime minister reinforces the parliament's Committee for the Future, and vice versa. Rather than trying for one big reform all at once, there is time for measures to happen one by one, with each one building the case for future ones. Gross domestic wealth can encourage better guardrails, tripwires, and defaults to protect national wealth, which can in turn be protected with commitments and bolstered by an iterative approach. As each new measure is introduced, they can hopefully create more space and incentives for governments to think long-term, making the case for more such measures. Long-term thinking will require long-term reform, and that is okay.

There are limitations. Institutional changes can be slow and halting, and many fail or are abandoned partway through. Even successful reforms can create new problems to solve. In some cases, behavioural science can help us find ways to avoid or limit the need for institutional change, but others, such as setting up long-term institutions, may require complex political and policy negotiation. Having those changes survive future governments means building and keeping public support for them, a challenge in any democracy.

Politicians, bureaucrats, the media, scholars, and individual voters will all play a role in changing how our system operates. Having insights from behavioural science reflected in government policy is almost certainly itself a long-term process. Governments slowly absorb information from universities, think tanks, and the air around them and implement them internally, though rarely as fast as outsiders might want. There will be failures as well as successes, but the increasing impact our societies have on the future means the case for long-termism will continue to build.

FINAL THOUGHTS

None of us will live forever. Our effects on future generations, good and bad, are the result of the decisions we have made: institutions we have built or destroyed, resources we have contributed to or exhausted. How much we prioritize the present or future reflects a fundamental decision about what we want to leave to our children and our children's children, and about the kind of country and world we want to live in.

There is no one right answer: both the present and future matter, and how much we choose to discount the future depends on our own experiences as well as our environment. Today's governments, though, suffer from too much short-termism. Whether because of the democratic system, the twenty-four-hour political news cycle, or simply human nature, government priorities have swung too far toward the present, and our future is starting to suffer. The falling levels of trust in government in many countries, combined with increased skepticism as a result of ideological polarization, risks a self-fulfilling prophecy where voters lose faith in governments' ability to act for the long term. As a result, they do not bother pressing for long-term action, and governments feel less pressure to consider the future, becoming more present biased and breeding yet more distrust. We need to take a step back and build our institutions to ensure that the future is also cared for. If we don't, our children may live worse lives than we do.

There is no silver bullet to planning for the future. Like losing weight or saving for retirement, the future is usually determined by a series of small decisions, not one big one. We need to make sure our governments are behaving well over time. As citizens we need to push them to care for the future and hold them to account for the impact their decisions have on the next generation. The quality of our leaders is also fundamental to achieving this goal, helping push for long-term decisions.

This book has recommended four strategies to strengthen the incentives and ability of governments to do just that. Measuring what matters; making it easy by using guardrails, tripwires, and defaults; creating commitments; and taking a nimble, experimental approach can help ensure our societies think beyond today. It isn't wrong to prioritize the short term, but governments should do so in full awareness of and transparency about the impact it will have on the future, so that they, and voters, can make an informed choice and be held to account for the consequences.

Not all those strategies will work everywhere, and not all the problems of government relate to cognitive biases or a pressure to be short-term. The broader point is that we need to test and try new forms of governance and organization in order to confront and overcome the challenges that face us and our governments. Behaviourally informed institutions and governance is one possible direction, but there are many others, from deliberative democracy to the use of new technologies. Regardless of the approach we adopt, an iterative method that allows for us to test, learn, and adapt as necessary can help us identify what works and what doesn't.

We can do better in fighting government short-termism. Yes, some short-term decisions will still be made and some leaders will pay no attention to the future. But it is important not to lose sight of the big picture. For each high-profile short-termist policy we may see a government or leader pursue, there are dozens of other opportunities to be long-termist in less politically controversial contexts. Democracies do have pressure to be short-termist, but there are actions we can take to reduce that pressure and help our governments think long term. As this suggests, I do not agree with those who argue that we need to abandon democratic principles in order to protect the interests of the future. In my view, dictatorships are actually worse than democracy for long-term thinking in the long run, and the lack of checks and balances, weaknesses in their ability to respond to citizen preferences, and the problem of succession mean one short-termist dictator could do tremendous harm. The diverse, contentious nature of democracies may mean that sometimes short-termism wins out, but that same nature is also a strength. Behaviourally informed governance provides us with an opportunity to improve how our democracies work without sacrificing democratic principles.

Ten thousand years ago, about one million humans roamed the earth, some of them starting to domesticate animals and cultivate crops as part of an Agricultural Revolution that would transform how humans lived and co-operated, allowing for permanent settlements. It would be two thousand years more until bread was invented, and six thousand until the first sips of beer were taken. Our world today is built on the work those humans did so long ago, on the institutions they built, and the discoveries they made. We owe it to our descendants to leave them the same: to advance the human project that gives our children the opportunities, or more, that we have had.

Notes

CHAPTER ONE

1 Davis, *River Notes*; and Nijhuis, "When the Snows Fail."
2 World Resources Institute, "Aqueduct Water Risk Atlas."
3 Parker, "What Happens to the U.S. Midwest When the Water's Gone?"
4 Kellett and Caravani, "Financing Disaster Risk Reduction."
5 Healy and Malhotra, "Myopic Voters and Natural Disaster Policy."
6 FAO, *The State of World Fisheries and Aquaculture 2020*.
7 Sumaila and Suatoni, "Fish Economics."
8 Dasgupta, *Final Report – The Economics of Biodiversity*.
9 O'Neill, "Tackling Drug-Resistant Infections Globally."
10 IPCC, *Global Warming of 1.5°C: An IPCC Special Report*.
11 Oxford Economics and Global Infrastructure Hub, "Global Infrastructure Outlook."
12 Ord, *The Precipice*.
13 Jacobs, *Governing for the Long Term*; Boston, *Governing for the Future*; MacKenzie, *Future Publics*; and G. Smith, *Can Democracy Safeguard the Future?*
14 Duranton and Turner, "The Fundamental Law of Road Congestion."
15 Randers, *2052*.
16 Sunstein and Hastie, *Wiser*.
17 Sampson and Shi, "Are U.S. Firms Becoming More Short-Term Oriented?"
18 Nijhuis, "When the Snows Fail."

CHAPTER TWO

1 O'Donoghue and Rabin, "Doing It Now or Later."
2 Ainslie, *Picoeconomics*.

3 Haselton, Nettle, and Murray, "The Evolution of Cognitive Bias."
4 Kahneman and Tversky, "Prospect Theory."
5 Krawchenko and Foster, "'Generationing' Public Policy."
6 Read, Loewenstein, and Kalyanaraman, "Mixing Virtue and Vice."
7 Read and van Leeuwen, "Predicting Hunger."
8 Mitchell et al., "Medial Prefrontal Cortex Predicts Intertemporal Choice."
9 Thaler and Shefrin, "An Economic Theory of Self-Control"; Fudenberg and Levine, "A Dual-Self Model of Impulse Control"; Jamison and Wegener, "Multiple Selves in Intertemporal Choice"; and Chesterley, "Optimal Policy and Inconsistent Preferences."
10 Schelling, "How to 'No Thyself' All Year Round, Not Just New Year's."
11 Hershfield et al., "Increasing Saving Behavior Through Age-Progressed Renderings of the Future Self."
12 Enke, Graeber, and Oprea, "Complexity and Time."
13 Keidel et al., "Individual Differences in Intertemporal Choice."
14 Kim, Sung, and McClure, "The Neural Basis of Cultural Differences in Delay Discounting."
15 H. Chen, Ng, and Rao, "Cultural Differences in Consumer Impatience."
16 Carter et al., "Religious People Discount the Future Less."
17 M. Wang, Rieger, and Hens, "How Time Preferences Differ."
18 Matsuyama et al., "Delay Discounting in Children Exposed to Disaster."
19 M.K. Chen, "The Effect of Language on Economic Behavior."
20 Chetty et al., "Active vs. Passive Decisions and Crowd-Out in Retirement Savings Accounts."
21 Choi et al., "For Better or For Worse."
22 Kahneman, *Thinking, Fast and Slow*.
23 Thaler and Sunstein, *Nudge*.
24 Carr, *The Shallows*.
25 Toffler, *Future Shock*.
26 Silver, *The Signal and the Noise*.

CHAPTER THREE

1 Ramsey, "A Mathematical Theory of Saving."
2 Pigou, *The Economics of Welfare*, 25.
3 Confucius, *Wisdom of Confucius*, 181; and Murphy, "The Constitution of the Iroquois Nations," n.p.
4 Elliot, "The Rights of Future People"; and de-Shalit, "Community and the Rights of Future Generations."

5 Grattan et al., "The First Polluted River?"
6 Sunstein, *Laws of Fear*.
7 Rawls, *A Theory of Justice*.
8 Pinker, *The Better Angels of Our Nature*.
9 MacAskill, *What We Owe the Future*.
10 Wilson, *On Human Nature*.
11 Breuer, *Sociobiology and the Human Dimension*.
12 Keynes, *A Tract on Monetary Reform*.
13 Kidd, Palmeri, and Aslin, "Rational Snacking."
14 Cowen and Parfit, "Against the Social Discount Rate."
15 Stern, *The Economics of Climate Change: The Stern Review*.
16 Nordhaus, "A Review of the *Stern Review on the Economics of Climate Change*."
17 Office of Management and Budget, "Circular No. A-94 Revised"; and Office of Management and Budget, "Draft Circular A-4."
18 Freeman, Groom, and Spackman, "Social Discount Rates for Cost-Benefit Analysis."
19 Eden, "The Cross-Sectional Implications of the Social Discount Rate."
20 Frederick, Loewenstein, and O'Donoghue, "Time Discounting and Time Preference."
21 Manning et al., "Personality Influences Temporal Discounting Preferences."
22 Warner and Pleeter, "The Personal Discount Rate"; van der Wal et al., "Do Natural Landscapes Reduce Future Discounting in Humans?"; and Galor and Özak, "The Agricultural Origins of Time Preference."
23 Dasgupta, "The Stern Review's Economics of Climate Change."
24 Arrow et al., "How Should Benefits and Costs be Discounted in an Intergenerational Context?"
25 Pearce et al., "Valuing the Future."
26 Roser, "The Future Is Vast."
27 United Nations Secretary-General, *Intergenerational Solidarity and the Needs of Future Generations*.

CHAPTER FOUR

1 Lewis, *The Fifth Risk*.
2 Sunstein and Hastie, *Wiser*.
3 Jacobs, *Governing for the Long Term*.
4 Savoie, *Governing from the Centre*; and Poguntke and Webb, *The Presidentialization of Politics*.

5 Lewis, *The Fifth Risk*.
6 Nordhaus, "The Political Business Cycle."
7 Shi and Svensson, "Political Budget Cycles."
8 Katsimi and Sarantides, "Do Elections Affect the Composition of Fiscal Policy in Developed, Established Democracies?"
9 Jacobs, *Governing for the Long Term*.
10 Ibid.
11 Norris et al., "Government Reshuffles."
12 Mitchell and Conway, "From the Deputy Shuffle to the Deputy Churn."
13 Center for Presidential Transition, "2020 Presidential Transition Guide."
14 Berman, "'The Most Important Takeover of Any Organization in History.'"
15 Lewis, *The Fifth Risk*.
16 Carreras, "Outsiders and Executive-Legislative Conflict in Latin America (1980–2007)"; and Carreras, "Outsider Presidents, Institutional Performance, and Governability in Latin America."
17 Yew, *From Third World to First*.
18 Mitter and Johnson, "What the West Gets Wrong About China."
19 Randers, *2052*, 27.
20 Warren, "Three Challenges for Long-Term Decision-Making in Democracies."
21 Wintrobe, *The Political Economy of Dictatorship*; and Deacon, "Public Good Provision under Dictatorship and Democracy."
22 MacKenzie, Setälä, and Kyllönen, *Democracy and the Future*.
23 Gibbon, *History of the Decline and Fall of the Roman Empire*, 35.
24 Rodrik, "Democracy and Economic Performance."
25 Healy and Malhotra, "Myopic Voters and Natural Disaster Policy."
26 Chesterley and Roberti, "Populism and Institutional Capture."
27 Falk et al., "Global Evidence on Economic Preferences."
28 Agan et al., "Automating Automaticity."
29 Jacobs and Matthews, "Why Do Citizens Discount the Future?"
30 Boston, *Governing for the Future*.
31 Burke, "Speech to the Electors of Bristol," n.p.
32 Matsusaka, "When Do Legislators Follow Constituent Opinion?"
33 Gilens, *Affluence and Influence*.
34 Quinlan and McAllister, "Leader or Party?"
35 D.K. Goodwin, *No Ordinary Time*, 320.
36 Savoie, *Governing from the Centre*.
37 Rhodes, "Everyday Life in a Ministry," 10.

38 Evans, "Organizing for British National Strategy," 519.
39 Rosenberg and Feldman, *No Time to Think*.
40 B.D. Jones and Baumgartner, *The Politics of Attention*.
41 Frey and Osborne, "Technology at Work."
42 "Data Never Sleeps 11.0."
43 Rhodes, "Everyday Life in a Ministry," 10.
44 Rosenberg and Feldman, *No Time to Think*.
45 Marland, Giasson, and Lawlor, *Political Elites in Canada*.
46 Hallsworth et al., "Behavioural Government."
47 Eisensee and Strömberg, "News Droughts, News Floods, and U.S. Disaster Relief."
48 Hallsworth et al., "Behavioural Government."
49 Mullainathan and Shafir, *Scarcity*.
50 Koller, Manyika, and Ramaswamy, "The Case against Corporate Short Termism."
51 Boston, *Governing for the Future*; Jacobs, *Governing for the Long Term*; and González-Ricoy and Gosseries, *Institutions for Future Generations*.
52 Jacobs, *Governing for the Long Term*.
53 Besley and Case, "Does Electoral Accountability Affect Economic Policy Choices?"
54 Carey, Niemi, and Powell, "The Effects of Term Limits on State Legislatures."
55 Burgat, "Five Reasons to Oppose Congressional Term Limits."
56 D. Smith, "The Senate of Canada," 233.
57 Docherty, "The Canadian Senate."
58 Savoie, *Court Government and the Collapse of Accountability*.
59 Poguntke and Webb, *The Presidentialization of Politics*.
60 "Dialing for Dollars"; and Ratliff, "The Congressional Fundraising Treadmill."
61 Jacobs, *Governing for the Long Term*.
62 J. Heath, *The Machinery of Government*.
63 Savoie, *Governing from the Centre*.
64 Voyer, "Policy Analysis in the Federal Government"; Evans, "Organizing for British National Strategy"; and Craft and Howlett, "Policy Capacity and the Ability to Adapt to Climate Change."
65 Craft, *Backrooms and Beyond*.
66 Ditchburn, "The Coolest Government Org You've Never Heard Of."
67 J. Heath, *The Machinery of Government*.
68 Boston, *Governing for the Future*; Jacobs, *Governing for the Long Term*.
69 Jacobs, *Governing for the Long Term*.
70 Hallsworth et al., "Behavioural Government."

CHAPTER FIVE

1 Norwich, *A History of Venice*.
2 Ariely, "You Are What You Measure."
3 Chetty, Looney, and Kroft, "Salience and Taxation."
4 Bollinger, Leslie, and Sorensen, "Calorie Posting in Chain Restaurants."
5 Gilbert and Graff Zivin, "Dynamic Salience with Intermittent Billing"; Bollinger, Leslie, and Sorensen, "Calorie Posting in Chain Restaurants"; Huebner, Fleisch, and Ilic, "Assisting Mental Accounting Using Smartphones."
6 Vanwormer et al., "The Impact of Regular Self-Weighing on Weight Management."
7 Tversky and Kahneman, "Availability."
8 G.P. Goodwin and Landy, "Valuing Different Human Lives."
9 Stiglitz, Sen, and Fitoussi, *Report by the Commission on the Measurement of Economic Performance and Social Progress*, 7.
10 Soll, "The Vanished Grandeur of Accounting."
11 Penn, *Winter King*.
12 Coyle, *GDP*.
13 Bureau of Foreign and Domestic Commerce and Kuznets, "National Income, 1929–1932," 5–6.
14 C.I. Jones and Klenow, "Beyond GDP?"
15 Oxford Economics and Global Infrastructure Hub, "Global Infrastructure Outlook.:"
16 ASCE, "ASCE's 2021 American Infrastructure Report Card."
17 Schumacher, *Small Is Beautiful*.
18 FAO, *Building on Gender, Agrobiodiversity and Local Knowledge*.
19 Dasgupta, *Final Report – The Economics of Biodiversity*.
20 Fowler, "Can We Preserve Seed Diversity for the Future?"
21 "Banks for Bean Counters."
22 UN Environment Program, *Inclusive Wealth Report 2018*.
23 Acemoglu and Robinson, *Why Nations Fail*.
24 Robinson, Acemoglu, and Johnson, "Institutions as a Fundamental Cause of Long-Run Growth."
25 Dimock and Gramlich, "How America Changed During Trump's Presidency."
26 Watts, *Mortal Republic*.
27 Ibid, 1–2.
28 UN Environment Program, *Inclusive Wealth Report 2018*.
29 Ibid.

30 Case and Deaton, "Life Expectancy in Adulthood Is Falling for Those Without a BA Degree."
31 OECD, "OECD Better Life Index."

CHAPTER SIX

1 Service et al., "EAST."
2 C. Heath and D. Heath, *Decisive*.
3 Sunstein and Hastie, *Wiser*.
4 Phillips, "How Diversity Makes Us Smarter."
5 Phillips, Northcraft, and Neale, "Surface-Level Diversity and Decision-Making in Groups."
6 Sommers, "On Racial Diversity and Group Decision Making."
7 Hallsworth et al., "Behavioural Government."
8 Phillips, Liljenquist, and Neale, "Is the Pain Worth the Gain?"
9 Johnson, *Farsighted*.
10 Bock, *Work Rules!*
11 Hallsworth et al., "Behavioural Government."
12 Gates, *How to Prevent the Next Pandemic*.
13 Tetlock and Gardner, *Superforecasting*.
14 Hallsworth et al., "Behavioural Government."
15 Ayres, *Carrots and Sticks*.
16 C. Heath and D. Heath, *Decisive*.
17 MacKenzie, *Future Publics*.
18 Congressional Budget Office, "The Budget and Economic Outlook: Fiscal Years 2012 to 2022."
19 Brewer and Tasseva, "Did the UK Policy Response to Covid-19 Protect Household Incomes?"
20 Boushey, Nunn, and Shambaugh, *Recession Ready*.
21 Boadway and Koeppl, "The 'Demand Stabilization Mechanism.'"; and Blundell, "Assessing the Temporary VAT Cut Policy in the UK."
22 MacKenzie, *Future Publics*.

CHAPTER SEVEN

1 Logsdon, "John F. Kennedy's Space Legacy and Its Lessons for Today."
2 Ibid., n.p.
3 Logsdon, *John F. Kennedy and the Race to the Moon*.
4 DellaVigna and Malmendier, "Paying Not to Go to the Gym."
5 Ariely and Wertenbroch, "Procrastination, Deadlines, and Performance."

6 Ashraf, Karlan, and Yin, "Tying Odysseus to the Mast."
7 Boadway and Koeppl, "The 'Demand Stabilization Mechanism.'"
8 Republic of Ecuador, "Ecuador: 2008 Constitution in English," n.p.
9 Mega, "Cuba Acknowledges Climate Change Threats in Its Constitution."
10 Jacobs, "Policy Making for the Long Term in Advanced Democracies."
11 González-Ricoy and Gosseries, *Institutions for Future Generations*.
12 Parliament of Finland, "Committee for the Future."
13 Koskimaa, "The Finnish National Foresight System."
14 N. Jones, O'Brien, and Ryan, "Representation of Future Generations in United Kingdom Policy-Making."
15 Ibid.
16 Nestbit and Illés, "Establishing an EU 'Guardian for Future Generations.'"
17 Robinson, *The Ministry for the Future*, 3.
18 Caney, "Political Institutions for the Future."
19 N. Jones, O'Brien, and Ryan, "Representation of Future Generations in United Kingdom Policy-Making."
20 Wells, "Votes for the Future."
21 Ekeli, "Giving a Voice to Posterity," 429.
22 MacKenzie, *Future Publics*; and G. Smith, *Can Democracy Safeguard the Future?*
23 MacKenzie, *Future Publics*.
24 Bohn and Inman, "Balanced-Budget Rules and Public Deficits."
25 Kennedy, "Address at Rice University on the Nation's Space Effort," n.p.
26 Thomson et al., "The Fulfillment of Parties' Election Pledges."
27 Jacobs and Matthews, "Policy Attitudes in Institutional Context."
28 Lord, Ross, and Lepper, "Biased Assimilation and Attitude Polarization."
29 Kahan et al., "Motivated Numeracy and Enlightened Self-Government."
30 Cohen, "Party Over Policy."
31 Butler et al., "Ideology, Learning, and Policy Diffusion."
32 Chong and Mullinix, "Information and Issue Constraints on Party Cues."
33 Hahn and Stavins, "The Effect of Allowance Allocations on Cap-and-Trade System Performance."
34 Norges Bank Investment Management, "The Fund."
35 Øvald, Tranøy, and Raknes, "The Norwegian Petroleum Fund."
36 Norges Bank Investment Management, "The Fund," n.p.
37 Øvald, Tranøy, and Raknes, "The Norwegian Petroleum Fund."

38 Clemens and Murphy, "Reforming Alberta's Heritage Fund."
39 Thaler and Sunstein, *Nudge*.
40 Chingos, Whitehurst, and Johnson, "Are Public Pensions Keeping Up with the Times?"
41 MacKenzie, *Future Publics*.
42 Haldane, "Central Bank Independence."
43 MacKenzie, Kyllönen, and Setälä, "Conclusion: Future-Regarding Governance."
44 Moore, "Reversability and Democracy."
45 G. Smith, *Can Democracy Safeguard the Future?*

CHAPTER EIGHT

1 Mazzucato, *The Entrepreneurial State*.
2 Tetlock and Gardner, *Superforecasting*.
3 Liu, Stoutenborough, and Vedlitz, "Bureaucratic Expertise, Overconfidence, and Policy Choice."
4 Sheffer and Loewen, "Electoral Confidence, Overconfidence, and Risky Behavior."
5 Malmendier and Tate, "CEO Overconfidence and Corporate Investment"; and Vivalt and Coville, "How Do Policy-Makers Update Their Beliefs?"
6 Radzevick and Moore, "Competing to Be Certain (but Wrong)."
7 Taleb, *The Black Swan*.
8 Tetlock and Gardner, *Superforecasting*.
9 Christensen, *The Innovator's Dilemma*.
10 Ries, *The Lean Startup*.
11 Yarow, "The Zappos Founder."
12 OECD, "The Innovation System of the Public Service of Canada."
13 King and Crewe, *The Blunders of Our Governments*.
14 S. Wang and Yang, "Policy Experimentation in China."
15 Zeng, "Building Engines for Growth and Competitiveness in China."
16 Yeung, Lee, and Kee, "China's Special Economic Zones at 30."
17 Heilmann and Perry, *Mao's Invisible Hand*.
18 S. Wang and Yang, "Policy Experimentation in China."
19 Lowery, Gray, and Baumgartner, "Policy Attention in State and Nation."
20 King and Crewe, *The Blunders of Our Governments*, 138.
21 Irwin and Nightingale, "Putting It All Together."
22 Halpern, *Inside the Nudge Unit*.
23 Festenstein, "Dewey's Political Philosophy."

CHAPTER NINE

1 IPCC, *Global Warming of 1.5°C: An IPCC Special Report.*
2 IPCC, *Climate Change* 2022.
3 Ibid., 20.
4 Hardin, "The Tragedy of the Commons."
5 Mann, *1493*.
6 Yuanfang, "Memorial Requesting a Ban on Shack People Reclaiming Mountains," n.p.; quoted in Mann, *1493*, 186.
7 Osborne, "Barren Mountains, Raging Rivers."
8 Committee on Homeland Security and Governmental Affairs, "Hurricane Katrina."
9 OECD, *Green Budgeting in OECD Countries.*
10 Edwards and Fry, "Life Cycle Assessment of Supermarket Carrierbags."
11 DeSombre, "The Experience of the Montreal Protocol."
12 Republic of Ecuador, "Ecuador: 2008 Constitution in English."
13 Sloggy et al., "Changing Climate, Changing Minds?"
14 Tyson and Kennedy, "Two-Thirds of Americans Think Government Should Do More on Climate."

CHAPTER TEN

1 Oxford Economics and Global Infrastructure Hub, "Global Infrastructure Outlook."
2 Flyvbjerg and Gardner, *How Big Things Get Done.*
3 ASCE, "ASCE's 2021 American Infrastructure Report Card."
4 Ibid., n.p.
5 Olson and Wessel, "The Case for Spending More on Infrastructure Maintenance."
6 Bellis et al., "Repair Priorities 2014."
7 Kornejew, Rentschler, and Hallegatte, "Well Spent."
8 Miller, *Lincoln's Virtues.*
9 Moley, "Foreword," in *Public Works*, xi; quoted in Caro, *The Power Broker*, 847.
10 Ibid.
11 MacKenzie, *Future Publics.*
12 Chambers, "Africa's Not-so-Magic Roundabout."
13 Monkkonen, "Understanding and Challenging Opposition to Housing Construction in California's Urban Areas."
14 Buell, Porter, and Norton, "Surfacing the Submerged State."

15 Galston and Davis, "Setting Priorities, Meeting Needs."
16 Flyvbjerg and Gardner, *How Big Things Get Done*, xxvii.
17 Schrank et al., *2021 Urban Mobility Report*.
18 Duranton and Turner, "The Fundamental Law of Road Congestion."
19 Caro, *The Power Broker*.
20 Duvall et al., "A New Look at Autonomous-Vehicle Infrastructure"; and Snyder, "Street Design Implications of Autonomous Vehicles."
21 Jiang, Zevenbergen, and Ma, "Urban Pluvial Flooding and Stormwater Management."
22 IPCC, *Climate Change 2022*.
23 Unruh, "Understanding Carbon Lock-In"; and Goldthau, "Rethinking the Governance of Energy Infrastructure."
24 Beck et al., "Manifesto for Agile Software Development."
25 de Weerdt et al., "Agile Delivery of Capital Projects."
26 McKinsey, "Capital Projects 5.0."
27 Standish Group, *2015 Chaos Report*.

CONCLUSION

1 Hajer, "Oxford's Oak Beams, and Other Tales."
2 MacKenzie, Setälä, and Kyllönen, *Democracy and the Future*.
3 Burns, *Leadership*.
4 MacKenzie, "Future-Regarding Democratic Leadership."
5 J. Heath, *The Machinery of Government*.
6 MacKenzie, Kyllönen, and Setälä, "Conclusion: Future-Regarding Governance."
7 MacKenzie, *Future Publics*.
8 Ibid.
9 Randers, *2052*.
10 MacKenzie, *Future Publics*.
11 MacKenzie and Caluwaerts, "Paying for the Future."
12 Herne, "Perspective-Taking, Deliberation and Future Generations."
13 MacKenzie, *Future Publics*.
14 Rapeli, "Voter Myopia Reassessed."
15 Jacobs, *Governing for the Long Term*.
16 Thaler and Benartzi, "Save More TomorrowTM."
17 Jacobs, "Policy Making for the Long Term in Advanced Democracies."
18 MacKenzie, *Future Publics*.

Bibliography

Acemoglu, Daron, and James A. Robinson. *Why Nations Fail: The Origins of Power, Prosperity, and Poverty*. Reprint edition. New York: Crown Currency, 2013.

Agan, Amanda Y., Diag Davenport, Jens Ludwig, and Sendhil Mullainathan. "Automating Automaticity: How the Context of Human Choice Affects the Extent of Algorithmic Bias." Working Paper Series. National Bureau of Economic Research, February 2023. https://doi.org/10.3386/w30981.

Ainslie, George. *Picoeconomics: The Strategic Interaction of Successive Motivational States within the Person*. Ill. ed. Cambridge: Cambridge University Press, 2010.

American Society of Civil Engineers (ASCE). "ASCE's 2021 American Infrastructure Report Card," 2021. https://infrastructurereportcard.org/.

Ariely, Dan. "You Are What You Measure." *Harvard Business Review*, 1 June 2010. https://hbr.org/2010/06/column-you-are-what-you-measure.

Ariely, Dan, and Klaus Wertenbroch. "Procrastination, Deadlines, and Performance: Self-Control by Precommitment." *Psychological Science* 13, no. 3 (May 2002): 219–24. https://doi.org/10.1111/1467-9280.00441.

Arrow, Kenneth J., Maureen Cropper, Christian Gollier, Ben Groom, Geoffrey M. Heal, Richard G. Newell, William D. Nordhaus, et al. "How Should Benefits and Costs be Discounted in an Intergenerational Context? The Views of an Expert Panel." In *Resources for the Future Discussion Paper No. 12-53*. Rochester, NY, 2013. https://doi.org/10.2139/ssrn.2199511.

Ashraf, Nava, Dean Karlan, and Wesley Yin. "Tying Odysseus to the Mast: Evidence From a Commitment Savings Product in the Philippines." *Quarterly Journal of Economics* 121, no. 2 (May 2006): 635–72. https://doi.org/10.1162/qjec.2006.121.2.635.

Ayres, Ian. *Carrots and Sticks: Unlock the Power of Incentives to Get Things Done*. New York: Bantam, 2010.

"Banks for Bean Counters." *The Economist*, 10 September 2015. https://www.economist.com/international/2015/09/10/banks-for-bean-counters.

Beck, Kent, Mike Beedle, Arie van Bennekum, Alistair Cockburn, Ward Cunningham, Martin Fowler, James Greening, et al. "Manifesto for Agile Software Development." Accessed 15 February 2022. https://agilemanifesto.org/.

Bellis, Rayla, Alex Dodds, Steve Ellis, Chelsea Hogan, Michael Maragos, and Roger Millar. "Repair Priorities 2014: Transportation Strategies to Improve Road Conditions and State Fiscal Outlooks." Smart Growth America. Accessed 13 February 2022. https://smartgrowthamerica.org/resources/repair-priorities-2014-transportation-strategies-to-improve-road-conditions-and-state-fiscal-outlooks/.

Berman, Russell. "'The Most Important Takeover of Any Organization in History.'" *The Atlantic*, 22 April 2016. https://www.theatlantic.com/politics/archive/2016/04/improving-the-presidential-transition-2016/477528/.

Besley, Timothy, and Anne Case. "Does Electoral Accountability Affect Economic Policy Choices? Evidence from Gubernatorial Term Limits." *Quarterly Journal of Economics* 110, no. 3 (August 1995): 769–98. https://doi.org/10.2307/2946699.

Blundell, Richard. "Assessing the Temporary VAT Cut Policy in the UK." *Fiscal Studies* 30, no. 1 (March 2009): 15 April 2009. https://ifs.org.uk/publications/4479.

Boadway, Robin, and Thorsten Koeppl. "The 'Demand Stabilization Mechanism': Using Temporary GST Cuts as Automatic Fiscal Policy." C.D. Howe Institute Commentary, November 2021. https://www.cdhowe.org/media-release/automatic-gst-cuts-should-be-ottawas-tool-box-fight-downturns.

Bock, Laszlo. *Work Rules! Insights from Inside Google That Will Transform How You Live and Lead*. Ill. ed. New York: Twelve, 2015.

Bohn, Henning, and Robert P. Inman. "Balanced-Budget Rules and Public Deficits: Evidence from the U.S. States." *Carnegie-Rochester Conference Series on Public Policy* 45 (December 1996): 13–76. https://doi.org/10.1016/S0167-2231(96)00017-6.

Bollinger, Bryan, Phillip Leslie, and Alan Sorensen. "Calorie Posting in Chain Restaurants." *American Economic Journal: Economic Policy* 3, no. 1 (February 2011): 91–128. https://doi.org/10.1257/pol.3.1.91.

Boston, Jonathan. *Governing for the Future: Designing Democratic Institutions for a Better Tomorrow*. Bingley, UK: Emerald Group Publishing Limited, 2016.

Boushey, Heather, Ryan Nunn, and Jay Shambaugh, eds. *Recession Ready: Fiscal Policies to Stabilize the American Economy*. Brookings Institution, 2019. https://www.brookings.edu/multi-chapter-report/recession-ready-fiscal-policies-to-stabilize-the-american-economy/.

Breuer, Georg. *Sociobiology and the Human Dimension*. CUP Archive, 1983.

Brewer, Mike, and Iva Valentinova Tasseva. "Did the UK Policy Response to Covid-19 Protect Household Incomes?" *Journal of Economic Inequality* 19, no. 3 (2021): 433–58. https://doi.org/10.1007/s10888-021-09491-w.

Buell, Ryan W., Ethan Porter, and Michael I. Norton. "Surfacing the Submerged State: Operational Transparency Increases Trust in and Engagement with Government." *Manufacturing & Service Operations Management* 23, no. 4 (September 2020). https://doi.org/10.1287/msom.2020.0877.

Bureau of Foreign and Domestic Commerce, and Simon Kuznets. "National Income, 1929–1932." Washington: US Government Printing Office, 1934.

Burgat, Casey. "Five Reasons to Oppose Congressional Term Limits." Brookings Institution Commentary, January 2018. https://www.brookings.edu/articles/five-reasons-to-oppose-congressional-term-limits/.

Burke, Edmund. "Speech to the Electors of Bristol." In *The Works of the Right Honourable Edmund Burke*, vol. 2 (of 12), 2005. https://www.gutenberg.org/ebooks/15198.

Burns, James MacGregor. *Leadership*. New York: HarperCollins, 1978.

Butler, Daniel M., Craig Volden, Adam M. Dynes, and Boris Shor. "Ideology, Learning, and Policy Diffusion: Experimental Evidence." *American Journal of Political Science* 61, no. 1 (2017): 37–49. https://doi.org/10.1111/ajps.12213.

Caney, Simon. "Political Institutions for the Future: A Fivefold Package." In *Institutions for Future Generations*, edited by Iñigo González-Ricoy and Axel Gosseries. Oxford: Oxford University Press, 2016. https://doi.org/10.1093/acprof:oso/9780198746959.003.0008.

Carey, John M., Richard G. Niemi, and Lynda W. Powell. "The Effects of Term Limits on State Legislatures." *Legislative Studies Quarterly* 23, no. 2 (1998): 271–300. https://doi.org/10.2307/440283.

Caro, Robert A. *The Power Broker: Robert Moses and the Fall of New York*. New York: Vintage, 1975.

Carr, Nicholas. *The Shallows: What the Internet Is Doing to Our Brains*. Updated edition. New York: WW Norton, 2020.

Carreras, Miguel. "Outsider Presidents, Institutional Performance, and Governability in Latin America." PhD diss., University of Pittsburgh, 2014. https://www.proquest.com/openview/097025eafda8f9da7d106e47f9d63912/1?pq-origsite=gscholar&cbl=18750.

– "Outsiders and Executive-Legislative Conflict in Latin America

(1980–2007).” *Latin American Politics and Society* 56 (September 2014). https://doi.org/10.1111/j.1548-2456.2014.00241.x.

Carter, Evan C., Michael E. McCullough, Jungmeen Kim-Spoon, Carolina Corrales, and Adam Blake. “Religious People Discount the Future Less.” *Evolution and Human Behavior* 33, no. 3 (May 2012): 224–31. https://doi.org/10.1016/j.evolhumbehav.2011.09.006.

Case, Anne, and Angus Deaton. “Life Expectancy in Adulthood Is Falling for Those Without a BA Degree, but as Educational Gaps Have Widened, Racial Gaps Have Narrowed.” *Proceedings of the National Academy of Sciences of the United States of America* 118, no. 11 (March 16, 2021): e2024777118. https://doi.org/10.1073/pnas.2024777118.

Center for Presidential Transition. “2020 Presidential Transition Guide.” Partnership for Public Service, May 2020. https://presidentialtransition.org/publications/presidential-transition-guide/.

Chambers, Andrew. “Africa's Not-So-Magic Roundabout.” *Guardian*, 24 November 2009. https://www.theguardian.com/commentisfree/2009/nov/24/africa-charity-water-pumps-roundabouts.

Chen, Haipeng (Allan), Sharon Ng, and Akshay R. Rao. “Cultural Differences in Consumer Impatience.” *Journal of Marketing Research* 42, no. 3 (August 2005): 291–301. https://doi.org/10.1509/jmkr.2005.42.3.291.

Chen, M. Keith. “The Effect of Language on Economic Behavior: Evidence from Savings Rates, Health Behaviors, and Retirement Assets.” *American Economic Review* 103, no. 2 (April 2013): 690–731. https://doi.org/10.1257/aer.103.2.690.

Chesterley, Nicholas. “Optimal Policy and Inconsistent Preferences: Behavioural Policymaking and Self-Control.” DPhil thesis, Oxford University, UK, 2015.

Chesterley, Nicholas, and Paolo Roberti. “Populism and Institutional Capture.” *European Journal of Political Economy* 53 (20 June 2017). https://doi.org/10.1016/j.ejpoleco.2017.06.004.

Chetty, Raj, John Friedman, Søren Leth-Petersen, Torben Nielsen, and Tore Olsen. “Active vs. Passive Decisions and Crowd-Out in Retirement Savings Accounts: Evidence from Denmark.” *Quarterly Journal of Economics* 129, no. 3 (September 2014): 1141–1219. https://doi.org/10.1093/qje/qju013.

Chetty, Raj, Adam Looney, and Kory Kroft. “Salience and Taxation: Theory and Evidence.” *American Economic Review* 99, no. 4 (September 2009): 1145–77. https://doi.org/10.1257/aer.99.4.1145.

Chingos, Matthew M., Grover J. “Russ” Whitehurst, and Richard W. Johnson. “Are Public Pensions Keeping Up with the Times?” Accessed 29 July

2023. https://www.brookings.edu/articles/are-public-pensions-keeping-up-with-the-times-2/.

Choi, James, David Laibson, Brigitte Madrian, and Andrew Metrick. "For Better or For Worse: Default Effects and 401(k) Savings Behavior." In *Perspectives in the Economics of Aging*, edited by David A. Wise. Chicago: University of Chicago Press, 2004. Chicago Scholarship Online, 2013. https://doi.org/10.7208/chicago/9780226903286.003.0003.

Chong, Dennis, and Kevin J. Mullinix. "Information and Issue Constraints on Party Cues." *American Politics Research* 47, no. 6 (November 2019): 1209–38. https://doi.org/10.1177/1532673X18803887.

Christensen, Clayton M. *The Innovator's Dilemma: The Revolutionary Book that Will Change the Way You Do Business*. Reprint edition. New York: HarperBusiness, 2011.

Clemens, Jason, and Robert P. Murphy. "Reforming Alberta's Heritage Fund: Lessons from Alaska and Norway." Alberta Prosperity Initiative. Fraser Institute, March 2013. https://bit.ly/3G1L3rc.

Cohen, Geoffrey L. "Party Over Policy: The Dominating Impact of Group Influence on Political Beliefs." *Journal of Personality and Social Psychology* 85 (2003): 808–22. https://doi.org/10.1037/0022-3514.85.5.808.

Committee on Homeland Security and Governmental Affairs. "Hurricane Katrina : A Nation Still Unprepared : Special Report of the Committee on Homeland Security and Governmental Affairs, United States Senate, Together with Additional Views." Washington: US GPO, 2006. https://lccn.loc.gov/2007361256.

Confucius. *Wisdom of Confucius*. Edited by Lin Yutang. New York: Modern Library, 1977.

Congressional Budget Office. "The Budget and Economic Outlook: Fiscal Years 2012 to 2022." Congress of the United States, January 2012. https://www.cbo.gov/sites/default/files/cbofiles/attachments/01-31-2012_Outlook.pdf.

Cowen, Tyler, and Derek Parfit. "Against the Social Discount Rate." In *Justice Between Age Groups and Generation*, edited by Peter Laslett and James S. Fishkin, 144–61. New Haven: Yale University Press, 1992.

Coyle, Diane. *GDP: A Brief but Affectionate History – Revised and Expanded Edition*. Princeton: Princeton University Press, 2015.

Craft, Jonathan. *Backrooms and Beyond: Partisan Advisers and the Politics of Policy Work in Canada*. Ill. ed. Toronto: University of Toronto Press, 2016.

Craft, Jonathan, and Michael Howlett. "Policy Capacity and the Ability to Adapt to Climate Change: Canadian and U.S. Case Studies." *Review of Policy Research* 30, no. 1 (2013): 1–18. https://doi.org/10.1111/ropr.12000.

Dasgupta, Partha. *Final Report – The Economics of Biodiversity: The Dasgupta Review*. GOV.UK. Accessed 5 February 2022. https://www.gov.uk/government/publications/final-report-the-economics-of-biodiversity-the-dasgupta-review.

– "The Stern Review's Economics of Climate Change." *National Institute Economic Review*, no. 199 (2007): 4–7.

"Data Never Sleeps 11.0." Domo, 2023. https://www.domo.com/learn/infographic/data-never-sleeps-11.

Davis, Wade. *River Notes: A Natural and Human History of the Colorado*. Washington: Island Press, 2013.

de Weerdt, Claire, Alistair Hamilton, Kevin Stokvis, and Pasley Weeks. "Agile Delivery of Capital Projects." *Voices on Infrastructure: The Project of the Future*. McKinsey, September 2020. https://www.mckinsey.com/business-functions/operations/our-insights/agile-delivery-of-capital-projects.

Deacon, Robert T. "Public Good Provision under Dictatorship and Democracy." *Public Choice* 139, no. 1/2 (2009): 241–62.

DellaVigna, Stefano, and Ulrike Malmendier. "Paying Not to Go to the Gym." *American Economic Review* 96, no. 3 (June 2006): 694–719. https://doi.org/10.1257/aer.96.3.694.

de-Shalit, Avner. "Community and the Rights of Future Generations: A Reply to Robert Elliot." *Journal of Applied Philosophy* 9, no. 1 (1992): 105–15. https://doi.org/10.1111/j.1468-5930.1992.tb00301.x.

DeSombre, Elizabeth R. "The Experience of the Montreal Protocol: Particularly Remarkable, and Remarkably Particular." UCLA *Journal of Environmental Law and Policy* 19 (2002 2000): 49.

"Dialing for Dollars." *60 Minutes*. CBS News, 24 April 2016. https://www.cbsnews.com/video/dialing-for-dollars/.

Dimock, Michael, and John Gramlich. "How America Changed During Trump's Presidency." *Pew Research Center* (blog), 29 January 2021. https://www.pewresearch.org/2021/01/29/how-america-changed-during-donald-trumps-presidency/.

Ditchburn, Jennifer. "The Coolest Government Org You've Never Heard Of." *Policy Options*, 28 December 2017. https://policyoptions.irpp.org/magazines/december-2017/the-coolest-government-org-youve-never-heard-of/.

Dobuzinskis, Laurent, Michael Howlett, and David Laycock. *Policy Analysis in Canada: The State of the Art*. Toronto: University of Toronto Press, 2007. https://doi.org/10.3138/9781442685529.

Docherty, David C. "The Canadian Senate: Chamber of Sober Reflection or

Loony Cousin Best Not Talked About." *The Journal of Legislative Studies* 8, no. 3 (September 2002): 27–48. https://doi.org/10.1080/714003922.

Duranton, Gilles, and Matthew A. Turner. "The Fundamental Law of Road Congestion: Evidence from US Cities." *American Economic Review* 101, no. 6 (October 2011): 2616–52. https://doi.org/10.1257/aer.101.6.2616.

Duvall, Tyler, Eric Hannon, Jared Katseff, Ben Safran, and Tyler Wallace. "A New Look at Autonomous-Vehicle Infrastructure." McKinsey, 22 May 2019. https://www.mckinsey.com/industries/travel-logistics-and-infrastructure/our-insights/a-new-look-at-autonomous-vehicle-infrastructure.

Eden, Maya. "The Cross-Sectional Implications of the Social Discount Rate." *Econometrica* 91, no. 6 (2023): 2065–88. https://doi.org/10.3982/ECTA20844.

Edwards, Chris, and Jonna Meyhoff Fry. "Life Cycle Assessment of Supermarket Carrierbags: A Review of the Bags Available in 2006." Horizon House, Deanery Road, Bristol, BS1 5AH: Environment Agency, 2011. https://www.gov.uk/government/publications/life-cycle-assessment-of-supermarket-carrierbags-a-review-of-the-bags-available-in-2006.

Eisensee, Thomas, and David Strömberg. "News Droughts, News Floods, and U.S. Disaster Relief." *The Quarterly Journal of Economics* 122, no. 2 (2007): 693–728.

Ekeli, Kristian Skagen. "Giving a Voice to Posterity – Deliberative Democracy and Representation of Future People." *Journal of Agricultural and Environmental Ethics* 18, no. 5 (September 2005): 429–50. https://doi.org/10.1007/s10806-005-7048-z.

Elliot, Robert. "The Rights of Future People." *Journal of Applied Philosophy* 6, no. 2 (1989): 159–69.

Enke, Benjamin, Thomas Graeber, and Ryan Oprea. "Complexity and Time." Working Paper Series. National Bureau of Economic Research, March 2023. https://doi.org/10.3386/w31047.

Evans, Alexander. "Organizing for British National Strategy." *International Affairs (Royal Institute of International Affairs 1944–)* 90, no. 3 (2014): 509–24.

Falk, Armin, Anke Becker, Thomas Dohmen, Benjamin Enke, David Huffman, and Uwe Sunde. "Global Evidence on Economic Preferences." *Quarterly Journal of Economics* 133, no. 4 (November 2018): 1645–92. https://doi.org/10.1093/qje/qjy013.

FAO (Food and Agriculture Organization). *Building on Gender, Agrobiodiversity and Local Knowledge*. Rome, Italy: FAO, 2006. https://www.fao.org/documents/card/en/c/79c1ae5f-c15a-567f-9467-6beca7e90797.

– *The State of World Fisheries and Aquaculture 2020: Sustainability in action*.

State of World Fisheries and Aquaculture (SOFIA) 2020. Rome, Italy: FAO, 2020. https://doi.org/10.4060/ca9229en.

Festenstein, Matthew. "Dewey's Political Philosophy." In *Stanford Encyclopedia of Philosophy*, edited by Edward N. Zalta and Uri Nodelman, spring 2023. Metaphysics Research Lab, Stanford University, 2023. https://plato.stanford.edu/archives/spr2023/entries/dewey-political/.

Flyvbjerg, Bent, and Dan Gardner. *How Big Things Get Done: The Surprising Factors That Determine the Fate of Every Project, from Home Renovations to Space Exploration and Everything in Between*. Oxford: Signal, 2023.

Fowler, Cary. "Can We Preserve Seed Diversity for the Future?" TED Radio Hour, 9 min. Accessed 5 February 2022. https://www.npr.org/2016/09/30/494774836/can-we-preserve-seed-diversity-for-the-future.

Frederick, Shane, George Loewenstein, and Ted O'Donoghue. "Time Discounting and Time Preference: A Critical Review." *Journal of Economic Literature* 40, no. 2 (2002): 351–401.

Freeman, Mark, Ben Groom, and Michael Spackman. *Social Discount Rates for Cost-Benefit Analysis: A Report for HM Treasury*, 2016. https://assets.publishing.service.gov.uk/government/uploads/system/uploads/attachment_data/file/935551/Social_Discount_Rates_for_Cost-Benefit_Analysis_A_Report_for_HM_Treasury.pdf.

Frey, Carl Benedikt, and Michael Osborne. *Technology at Work: The Future of Innovation and Employment*. Citi GPS Report. Oxford Martin School and Citi, 2015. https://www.oxfordmartin.ox.ac.uk/publications/technology-at-work-the-future-of-innovation-and-employment/.

Fudenberg, Drew, and David K. Levine. "A Dual-Self Model of Impulse Control." *American Economic Review* 96, no. 5 (December 2006): 1449–76. https://doi.org/10.1257/aer.96.5.1449.

Galor, Oded, and Ömer Özak. "The Agricultural Origins of Time Preference." *American Economic Review* 106, no. 10 (October 2016): 3064–3103. https://doi.org/10.1257/aer.20150020.

Galston, William A., and Korin Davis. "Setting Priorities, Meeting Needs: The Case for a National Infrastructure Bank." Brookings, December 13, 2012. https://www.brookings.edu/research/setting-priorities-meeting-needs-the-case-for-a-national-infrastructure-bank/.

Gates, Bill. *How to Prevent the Next Pandemic*. Knopf Canada, 2022.

Gibbon, Edward. *History of the Decline and Fall of the Roman Empire*. Vol. 1. 6 vols. J.A. James, 1840.

Gilbert, Ben, and Joshua Graff Zivin. "Dynamic Salience with Intermittent Billing: Evidence from Smart Electricity Meters." *Journal of Economic*

Behavior & Organization 107 (November 1, 2014): 176–90. https://doi.org/10.1016/j.jebo.2014.03.011.

Gilens, Martin. *Affluence and Influence: Economic Inequality and Political Power in America*. Ill. ed. Princeton, NJ, Oxford: Princeton University Press, 2014.

Goldthau, Andreas. "Rethinking the Governance of Energy Infrastructure: Scale, Decentralization and Polycentrism." *Energy Research & Social Science* 1 (March 1, 2014): 134–40. https://doi.org/10.1016/j.erss.2014.02.009.

González-Ricoy, Inigo, and Axel Gosseries, eds. *Institutions for Future Generations*. Oxford: Oxford University Press, 2017.

Goodwin, Doris Kearns. *No Ordinary Time: Franklin and Eleanor Roosevelt: The Home Front in World War II*. Ill. ed. New York: Simon & Schuster, 1995.

Goodwin, Geoffrey P., and Justin F. Landy. "Valuing Different Human Lives." *Journal of Experimental Psychology: General* 143, no. 2 (2014): 778–803. https://doi.org/10.1037/a0032796.

Grattan, J.P., R.B. Adams, H. Friedman, D.D. Gilbertson, K.I. Haylock, C.O. Hunt, and M. Kent. "The First Polluted River? Repeated Copper Contamination of Fluvial Sediments Associated with Late Neolithic Human Activity in Southern Jordan." *Science of the Total Environment* 573 (December 2016): 247–57. https://doi.org/10.1016/j.scitotenv.2016.08.106.

Hahn, Robert W., and Robert N. Stavins. "The Effect of Allowance Allocations on Cap-and-Trade System Performance." *Journal of Law & Economics* 54, no. 4 (2011): S267–94. https://doi.org/10.1086/661942.

Hajer, Charlotte. "Oxford's Oak Beams, and Other Tales of Humans and Trees in Long-Term Partnership." *Blog of the Long Now* (blog), 31 December 2014. https://blog.longnow.org/02014/12/31/humans-and-trees-in-long-term-partnership/.

Haldane, Andrew G. "Central Bank Independence – What We Know and What We Don't." Norges Bank. 16 April 2021. https://www.norges-bank.no/bankplassen/arkiv/2021/central-bank-independence-a-practitioners-perspective/.

Hallsworth, M., M. Egan, J. Rutter, and J. McCrae. *Behavioural Government*. The Behavioural Insights Team, 2018. https://www.bi.team/publications/behavioural-government/.

Halpern, David. *Inside the Nudge Unit: How Small Changes Can Make a Big Difference*. Reprint edition. London: Random House UK, 2016.

Hardin, Garrett. "The Tragedy of the Commons." *Science* 162, no. 3859 (1968): 1243–48.

Haselton, Martie G., Daniel Nettle, and Damian R. Murray. "The Evolution of Cognitive Bias." In *The Handbook of Evolutionary Psychology*, 1–20. John Wiley & Sons, 2015. https://doi.org/10.1002/9781119125563.evpsych241.

Healy, Andrew, and Neil Malhotra. "Myopic Voters and Natural Disaster Policy." *American Political Science Review* 103, no. 3 (August 2009): 387–406. https://doi.org/10.1017/S0003055409990104.

Heath, Chip, and Dan Heath. *Decisive: How to Make Better Choices in Life and Work*. Toronto: Random House Canada, 2013.

Heath, Joseph. *The Machinery of Government: Public Administration and the Liberal State*. New York: Oxford University Press, 2022.

Heilmann, Sebastian, and Elizabeth J. Perry, eds. *Mao's Invisible Hand: The Political Foundations of Adaptive Governance in China*. Vol. 17. Harvard University Asia Center, 2011. https://doi.org/10.2307/j.ctt1sq5tc6.

Herne, Kaisa. "Perspective-Taking, Deliberation and Future Generations." In MacKenzie, Setälä, and Kyllönen, *Democracy and the Future*, 99–112.

Hershfield, Hal E., Daniel G. Goldstein, William F. Sharpe, Jesse Fox, Leo Yeykelis, Laura L. Carstensen, and Jeremy N. Bailenson. "Increasing Saving Behavior Through Age-Progressed Renderings of the Future Self." *Journal of Marketing Research* 48, no. SPL (February 2011): S23–37. https://doi.org/10.1509/jmkr.48.SPL.S23.

House of Commons Public Administration Select Committee. *Governing the Future*. London: Stationery Office, 6 March 2007. https://publications.parliament.uk/pa/cm200607/cmselect/cmpubadm/123/123i.pdf.

Huebner, Johannes, Elgar Fleisch, and Alexander Ilic. "Assisting Mental Accounting Using Smartphones: Increasing the Salience of Credit Card Transactions Helps Consumer Reduce Their Spending." *Computers in Human Behavior* 113 (December 2020): 106504. https://doi.org/10.1016/j.chb.2020.106504.

IPCC (Intergovernmental Panel on Climate Change). *Climate Change 2022: Impacts, Adaptation and Vulnerability*. Working Group II Contribution to the IPCC Sixth Assessment Report. Cambridge: Cambridge University Press, 2022. https://www.ipcc.ch/report/ar6/wg2/.

– *Global Warming of 1.5°C: An IPCC Special Report on the Impacts of Global Warming of 1.5°C above Pre-Industrial Levels and Related Global Greenhouse Gas Emission Pathways, in the Context of Strengthening the Global Response to the Threat of Climate Change, Sustainable Development, and Efforts to Eradicate Poverty*, 2018.

Irwin, Molly, and Demetra Smith Nightingale. "Putting It All Together: The Case of the U.S. Department of Labor's Evidence-Building Strategy." *New*

Directions for Evaluation 2022, no. 173 (2022): 101–16.https://doi.org/10.1002/ev.20489.

Jacobs, Alan M. *Governing for the Long Term: Democracy and the Politics of Investment*. Cambridge University Press, 2011.

– "Policy Making for the Long Term in Advanced Democracies." *Annual Review of Political Science* 19, no. 1 (2016): 433–54. https://doi.org/10.1146/annurev-polisci-110813-034103.

Jacobs, Alan M., and J. Scott Matthews. "Policy Attitudes in Institutional Context: Rules, Uncertainty, and the Mass Politics of Public Investment." *American Journal of Political Science* 61, no. 1 (2017): 194–207. https://doi.org/10.1111/ajps.12209.

– "Why Do Citizens Discount the Future? Public Opinion and the Timing of Policy Consequences." *British Journal of Political Science* 42, no. 4 (October 2012): 903–35. https://doi.org/10.1017/S0007123412000117.

Jamison, Julian, and Jon Wegener. "Multiple Selves in Intertemporal Choice." *Journal of Economic Psychology*, Special Issue on Decision Neuroscience, 31, no. 5 (October 2010): 832–39. https://doi.org/10.1016/j.joep.2010.03.004.

Jiang, Yong, Chris Zevenbergen, and Yongchi Ma. "Urban Pluvial Flooding and Stormwater Management: A Contemporary Review of China's Challenges and 'Sponge Cities' Strategy." *Environmental Science & Policy* 80 (February 2018): 132–43. https://doi.org/10.1016/j.envsci.2017.11.016.

Johnson, Steven. *Farsighted: How We Make the Decisions that Matter the Most*. New York: Riverhead Books, 2018.

Jones, Bryan D., and Frank R. Baumgartner. *The Politics of Attention: How Government Prioritizes Problems*. Chicago, IL: University of Chicago Press, n.d.

Jones, Charles I., and Peter J. Klenow. "Beyond GDP? Welfare across Countries and Time." *American Economic Review* 106, no. 9 (September 2016): 2426–57. https://doi.org/10.1257/aer.20110236.

Jones, Natalie, Mark O'Brien, and Thomas Ryan. "Representation of Future Generations in United Kingdom Policy-Making." *Futures* 102 (September 2018): 153–63. https://doi.org/10.1016/j.futures.2018.01.007.

Kahan, Dan M., Ellen Peters, Erica Cantrell Dawson, and Paul Slovic. "Motivated Numeracy and Enlightened Self-Government." *Behavioural Public Policy* 1, no. 1 (May 2017): 54–86. https://doi.org/10.1017/bpp.2016.2.

Kahneman, Daniel. *Thinking, Fast and Slow*. New York: Farrar, Straus and Giroux, 2013.

Kahneman, Daniel, and Amos Tversky. "Prospect Theory: An Analysis of

Decision under Risk." *Econometrica* 47, no. 2 (1979): 263–91. https://doi.org/10.2307/1914185.

Katsimi, Margarita, and Vassilis Sarantides. "Do Elections Affect the Composition of Fiscal Policy in Developed, Established Democracies?" *Public Choice* 151, no. 1 (April 2012): 325–62. https://doi.org/10.1007/s11127-010-9749-8.

Keidel, Kristof, Qëndresa Rramani, Bernd Weber, Carsten Murawski, and Ulrich Ettinger. "Individual Differences in Intertemporal Choice." *Frontiers in Psychology* 12 (April 2021): 643670. https://doi.org/10.3389/fpsyg.2021.643670.

Kellett, Jan, and Alice Caravani. "Financing Disaster Risk Reduction: A 20 Year Story of International Aid." ODI: Think Change, 27 June 2014. https://odi.org/en/publications/financing-disaster-risk-reduction-a-20-year-story-of-international-aid/.

Kennedy, John F. "Address at Rice University on the Nation's Space Effort." Rice University, 12 September 1962. https://www.rice.edu/jfk-speech.

Kennedy, Robert F. "Remarks at the University of Kansas, March 18, 1968." Speech, University of Kansas, 18 March 1968. https://www.jfklibrary.org/learn/about-jfk/the-kennedy-family/robert-f-kennedy/robert-f-kennedy-speeches/remarks-at-the-university-of-kansas-march-18-1968.

Keynes, John Maynard. *A Tract on Monetary Reform*. London: Macmillan, 1923.

Kidd, Celeste, Holly Palmeri, and Richard N. Aslin. "Rational Snacking: Young Children's Decision-Making on the Marshmallow Task Is Moderated by Beliefs about Environmental Reliability." *Cognition* 126, no. 1 (January 2013): 109–14. https://doi.org/10.1016/j.cognition.2012.08.004.

Kim, Bokyung, Young Shin Sung, and Samuel M. McClure. "The Neural Basis of Cultural Differences in Delay Discounting." *Philosophical Transactions of the Royal Society B: Biological Sciences* 367, no. 1589 (March 2012): 650–56. https://doi.org/10.1098/rstb.2011.0292.

King, Anthony, and Ivor Crewe. *The Blunders of Our Governments*. Rev. ed. London: Oneworld Publications, 2014.

Koller, Tim, James Manyika, and Sree Ramaswamy. "The Case against Corporate Short Termism." *Milken Institute Review*, 4 August 2017. https://www.milkenreview.org/articles/the-case-against-corporate-short-termism.

Kornejew, Martin, Jun Rentschler, and Stephane Hallegatte. "Well Spent: How Governance Determines the Effectiveness of Infrastructure Investments." Working Paper. Washington, DC: World Bank, June 2019. https://doi.org/10.1596/1813-9450-8894.

Koskimaa, Vesa. "The Finnish National Foresight System." In MacKenzie, Setälä, and Kyllönen, *Democracy and the Future*, 195–214.

Krawchenko, Tamara, and Karen R. Foster. "'Generationing' Public Policy: A Multicountry Review of Intergenerational Equity Policies." *Public Policy and Governance Review* 7, no. 2 (Spring 2016): 95–119.

Lewis, Michael. *The Fifth Risk*. Ill. ed. New York: W.W. Norton, 2019.

Liu, Xinsheng, James Stoutenborough, and Arnold Vedlitz. "Bureaucratic Expertise, Overconfidence, and Policy Choice." *Governance* 30, no. 4 (2017): 705–25. https://doi.org/10.1111/gove.12257.

Logsdon, J. *John F. Kennedy and the Race to the Moon*. New York: Palgrave Macmillan, 2013.

Logsdon, John M. "John F. Kennedy's Space Legacy and Its Lessons for Today." *Issues in Science and Technology*, Spring 2011. https://issues.org/p_logsdon-3/.

Lord, Charles, Lee Ross, and Mark Lepper. "Biased Assimilation and Attitude Polarization: The Effects of Prior Theories on Subsequently Considered Evidence." *Journal of Personality and Social Psychology* 37 (November 1979): 2098–109. https://doi.org/10.1037/0022-3514.37.11.2098.

Lowery, David, Virginia Gray, and Frank R. Baumgartner. "Policy Attention in State and Nation: Is Anyone Listening to the Laboratories of Democracy?" *Publius: The Journal of Federalism* 41, no. 2 (January 2011): 286–310. https://doi.org/10.1093/publius/pjq039.

MacAskill, William. *What We Owe the Future*. New York: Basic Books, 2022.

MacKenzie, Michael K. *Future Publics: Democracy, Deliberation, and Future-Regarding Collective Action*. New York: Oxford University Press, 2021.

– "Future-Regarding Democratic Leadership." In MacKenzie, Setälä, and Kyllönen, *Democracy and the Future*, 134–54.

MacKenzie, Michael K., and Didier Caluwaerts. "Paying for the Future: Deliberation and Support for Climate Action Policies." *Journal of Environmental Policy & Planning* 23, no. 3 (May 2021): 317–31. https://doi.org/10.1080/1523908X.2021.1883424.

MacKenzie, Michael K., Simo P. Kyllönen, and Maija Setälä. "Conclusion: Future-Regarding Governance – Four Tensions and a Research Agenda." In MacKenzie, Setälä, and Kyllönen, *Democracy and the Future*, 252–75.

MacKenzie, Michael K., Maija Setälä, and Simo P. Kyllönen, eds. *Democracy and the Future: Future-Regarding Governance in Democratic Systems*. Edinburgh: Edinburgh University Press, 2023.

Malmendier, Ulrike, and Geoffrey Tate. "CEO Overconfidence and Corporate Investment." *Journal of Finance* 60, no. 6 (2005): 2661–700. https://doi.org/10.1111/j.1540-6261.2005.00813.x.

Mann, Charles C. *1493: Uncovering the New World Columbus Created*. New York: Vintage, 2011.

Manning, Joshua, Trey Hedden, Nina Wickens, Susan Whitfield-Gabrieli, Drazen Prelec, and John D.E. Gabrieli. "Personality Influences Temporal Discounting Preferences: Behavioral and Brain Evidence." *NeuroImage* 98 (September 2014): 42–9. https://doi.org/10.1016/j.neuroimage.2014.04.066.

Marland, Alex, Thierry Giasson, and Andrea Lawlor, eds. *Political Elites in Canada: Power and Influence in Instantaneous Times*. Reprint ed. Vancouver: UBC Press, 2019.

Matsusaka, John G. "When Do Legislators Follow Constituent Opinion? Evidence from Matched Roll Call and Referendum Votes." USC CLASS Research Paper No. CLASS15-18, 27 February 2021. https://doi.org/10.2139/ssrn.2612342.

Matsuyama, Yusuke, Takeo Fujiwara, Yasuyuki Sawada, Junko Yagi, Hirobumi Mashiko, and Ichiro Kawachi. "Delay Discounting in Children Exposed to Disaster." *PLOS ONE* 15, no. 12 (December 2020): e0243994. https://doi.org/10.1371/journal.pone.0243994.

Mazzucato, Mariana. *The Entrepreneurial State: Debunking Public vs. Private Sector Myths*. London: Anthem Press, 2013.

McKinsey. *Capital Projects 5.0: Reimagining Capital- Project Delivery*. McKinsey Insights, February 2021. https://www.mckinsey.com/~/media/mckinsey/business%20functions/operations/our%20insights/capital%20projects%2050%20reimagining%20capital%20project%20delivery/capital-projects-50-reimagining-capital-project-delivery.pdf.

Mega, Emiliano Rodríguez. "Cuba Acknowledges Climate Change Threats in Its Constitution." *Nature* 567, no. 7747 (March 2019): 155. https://doi.org/10.1038/d41586-019-00760-3.

Miller, William Lee. *Lincoln's Virtues: An Ethical Biography*. Repr. ed. New York: Vintage, 2003.

Mitchell, David, and Ryan Conway. "From the Deputy Shuffle to the Deputy Churn: Keeping the Best and Brightest in Ottawa." *Policy Options*, May 2011. https://policyoptions.irpp.org/fr/magazines/provincial-deficits-and-debt/from-the-deputy-shuffle-to-the-deputy-churn-keeping-the-best-and-brightest-in-ottawa/.

Mitchell, Jason P., Jessica Schirmer, Daniel L. Ames, and Daniel T. Gilbert. "Medial Prefrontal Cortex Predicts Intertemporal Choice." *Journal of Cognitive Neuroscience* 23, no. 4 (April 2011): 857–66. https://doi.org/10.1162/jocn.2010.21479.

Mitter, Rana, and Elsbeth Johnson. "What the West Gets Wrong About China." *Harvard Business Review*, May 2021. https://hbr.org/2021/05/what-the-west-gets-wrong-about-china.

Moley, Raymond. "Foreword." In *Public Works: A Dangerous Trade*, by Robert Moses, n.p. New York: McGraw-Hill, 1970.

Monkkonen, Paavo. "Understanding and Challenging Opposition to Housing Construction in California's Urban Areas." SSRN Scholarly Paper. Rochester, NY. 1 December 2016. https://doi.org/10.2139/ssrn.3459823.

Moore, Alfred. "Reversability and Democracy: The Epistemic Functions of Political Competition." In MacKenzie, Setälä, and Kyllönen, *Democracy and the Future*, 55–76.

Mullainathan, Sendhil, and Eldar Shafir. *Scarcity: Why Having Too Little Means So Much*. New York: Times Books, 2013.

Murphy, Gerald. *The Constitution of the Iroquois Nation: The Great Binding Law, Gayanashagowa*. Cybercasting Services Division of the National Public Telecomputing Network (NPTN). October 2001. https://web.pdx.edu/~caskeym/iroquois_web/html/greatlaw.html.

Nestbit, M., and A. Illés. *Establishing an EU 'Guardian for Future Generations.'* Report and Recommendations for the World Future Council. London: Institute for European Environmental Policy, 2015. https://ieep.eu/publications/establishing-an-eu-guardian-for-future-generations/.

Nijhuis, Michelle. "When the Snows Fail." *National Geographic*, 2014. http://www.nationalgeographic.com/west-snow-fail/.

Nordhaus, William D. "The Political Business Cycle." *The Review of Economic Studies* 42, no. 2 (1975): 169–90. https://doi.org/10.2307/2296528.

– "A Review of the *Stern Review on the Economics of Climate Change*." *Journal of Economic Literature* 45, no. 3 (September 2007): 686–702. https://doi.org/10.1257/jel.45.3.686.

Norges Bank Investment Management. "The Fund." Norges Bank Investment Management, 30 March 2022. https://www.nbim.no/.

Norris, Emma, Tom Sasse, Tim Durrant, and Ketaki Zodgekar. "Government Reshuffles: The Case for Keeping Ministers in Post Longer." Institute for Government, January 2020. https://www.instituteforgovernment.org.uk/publication/report/government-reshuffles-case-keeping-ministers-post-longer.

Norwich, John Julius. *A History of Venice*. London: Viking, 2013.

O'Donoghue, Ted, and Matthew Rabin. "Doing It Now or Later." *American Economic Review* 89, no. 1 (March 1999): 103–24. https://doi.org/10.1257/aer.89.1.103.

OECD (Organisation for Economic Co-operation and Development). *Green Budgeting in OECD Countries*. OECD Publishing, 2021. https://doi.org/10.1787/acf5d047-en.

– "The Innovation System of the Public Service of Canada." Paris: OECD, 2018. https://doi.org/10.1787/9789264307735-en.

– "OECD Better Life Index." Accessed 5 February 2022. https://www.oecd betterlifeindex.org/.

Office of Management and Budget. "Circular No. A-94 Revised," 19 October 1992. https://www.whitehouse.gov/wp-content/uploads/2023/04/Circular A94.pdf.

– "Draft Circular A-4," 6 April 2023. https://www.whitehouse.gov/wp-content /uploads/2023/04/DraftCircularA-4.pdf.

Olson, Peter, and David Wessel. "The Case for Spending More on Infrastructure Maintenance." *Brookings* (blog), 31 January 2017. https://www .brookings.edu/blog/up-front/2017/01/31/the-case-for-spending-more-on-infrastructure-maintenance/.

O'Neill, Jim. "Tackling Drug-Resistant Infections Globally: Final Report and Recommendations." *Review on Antimicrobial Resistance*, May 2016. https://amr-review.org/sites/default/files/160525_Final%20paper _with%20cover.pdf.

Ord, Toby. *The Precipice: Existential Risk and the Future of Humanity*. New York: Hachette Books, 2021.

Osborne, Anne Rankin. "Barren Mountains, Raging Rivers: The Ecological and Social Effects of Changing Landuse on the Lower Yangzi Periphery in Late Imperial China." PhD diss. Columbia University, 1989.

Øvald, Camilla Bakken, Bent Sofus Tranøy, and Ketil Raknes. "The Norwegian Petroleum Fund as Institutionalized Self-Restraint." In *Great Policy Successes*, edited by Paul 't Hart and Mallory Compton, 244-63. Oxford: Oxford University Press, 2019. https://doi.org/10.1093/oso /9780198843719.003.0013.

Oxford Economics, and Global Infrastructure Hub. "Global Infrastructure Outlook: Infrastructure Investment Needs 50 Countries, 7 Sectors to 2040." n.p. 2017.

Parker, Laura. "What Happens to the U.S. Midwest When the Water's Gone?" *National Geographic*, 14 July 2016. https://www.nationalgeographic.com/magazine/article/vanishing-midwest-ogallala-aquifer-drought.

Parliament of Finland. "Committee for the Future." Accessed 30 March 2022. https://www.eduskunta.fi:443/EN/valiokunnat/tulevaisuusvaliokunta /Pages/default.aspx.

Pearce, David, Ben Groom, Cameron Hepburn, and Phoebe Koundouri. "Valuing the Future: Recent Advances in Social Discounting." *World Economics* 4, no. 2 (2003): 121–41.

Penn, Thomas. *Winter King: Henry VII and the Dawn of Tudor England*. Ill. ed. New York: Simon & Schuster, 2012.

Phillips, Katherine W. "How Diversity Makes Us Smarter." *Scientific American*, October 2014. https://doi.org/10.1038/scientificamerican1014-42.

Phillips, Katherine W., Katie A. Liljenquist, and Margaret A. Neale. "Is the Pain Worth the Gain? The Advantages and Liabilities of Agreeing with Socially Distinct Newcomers." *Personality and Social Psychology Bulletin* 35, no. 3 (March 2009): 336–50. https://doi.org/10.1177/0146167208328062.

Phillips, Katherine W., Gregory B. Northcraft, and Margaret A. Neale. "Surface-Level Diversity and Decision-Making in Groups: When Does Deep-Level Similarity Help?" *Group Processes & Intergroup Relations* 9, no. 4 (October, 2006): 467–82. https://doi.org/10.1177/1368430206067557.

Pigou, Arthur. *The Economics of Welfare*. London: Routledge, 2018.

Pinker, Steven. *The Better Angels of Our Nature: Why Violence Has Declined*. Ill. ed. New York: Penguin Books, 2012.

Poguntke, Thomas, and Paul Webb, eds. *The Presidentialization of Politics: A Comparative Study of Modern Democracies*. Rev. ed. Oxford: Oxford University Press, 2007.

Quinlan, Stephen, and Ian McAllister. "Leader or Party? Quantifying and Exploring Behavioral Personalization 1996–2019." *Party Politics* 28, no. 1 (January 2022): 24–37. https://doi.org/10.1177/1354068821 1019239.

Radzevick, Joseph R., and Don A. Moore. "Competing to Be Certain (but Wrong): Market Dynamics and Excessive Confidence in Judgment." *Management Science* 57, no. 1 (2011): 93–106. https://doi.org/10.1287/mnsc .1100.1255.

Ramsey, F.P. "A Mathematical Theory of Saving." *Economic Journal* 38, no. 152 (1928): 543–59. https://doi.org/10.2307/2224098.

Randers, Jorgen. *2052: A Global Forecast for the Next Forty Years*. Ill. ed. White River Junction, VT: Chelsea Green Publishing, 2012.

Rapeli, Lauri. "Voter Myopia Reassessed." In MacKenzie, Setälä, and Kyllönen, *Democracy and the Future*, 215–32. *Future-Regarding Governance in Democratic Systems*, edited by Michael K. MacKenzie, Maija Setälä, and Simo P. Kyllönen, 1st edition. Edinburgh: Edinburgh University Press, 2023.

Ratliff, Amisa. "The Congressional Fundraising Treadmill, July–September 2021." *Issue One* (blog), 24 October 2021. https://issueone.org/articles/the-congressional-fundraising-treadmill-5-key-numbers-to-know-from-the-newest-house-and-senate-campaign-finance-filings/.

Rawls, John. *A Theory of Justice: Revised Edition*. 2nd ed. Cambridge, MA: Belknap Press, 1999.

Read, Daniel, and Barbara van Leeuwen. "Predicting Hunger: The Effects of Appetite and Delay on Choice." *Organizational Behavior and Human Deci-

sion Processes 76, no. 2 (November 1998): 189–205. https://doi.org/10.1006/obhd.1998.2803.

Read, Daniel, George Loewenstein, and Shobana Kalyanaraman. "Mixing Virtue and Vice: Combining the Immediacy Effect and the Diversification Heuristic." *Journal of Behavioral Decision Making* 12, no. 4 (1999): 257–73. https://doi.org/10.1002/(SICI)1099-0771(199912)12:4<257::AID-BDM327>3.0.CO;2-6.

Republic of Ecuador. "Ecuador: 2008 Constitution in English." Accessed 17 February 2024. https://pdba.georgetown.edu/Constitutions/Ecuador/english08.html.

Rhodes, R.A.W. "Everyday Life in a Ministry: Public Administration as Anthropology." *The American Review of Public Administration* 35, no. 1 (March 2005): 3–25. https://doi.org/10.1177/0275074004271716.

Ries, Eric. *The Lean Startup: How Today's Entrepreneurs Use Continuous Innovation to Create Radically Successful Businesses*. New York: Currency, 2011.

Robinson, James, Daron Acemoglu, and Simon Johnson. "Institutions as a Fundamental Cause of Long-Run Growth." *Handbook of Economic Growth* 1A (2005): 386–472.

Robinson, Kim Stanley. *The Ministry for the Future*. New York: Orbit, 2020.

Rodrik, Dani. "Democracy and Economic Performance," 1997. https://drodrik.scholar.harvard.edu/publications/democracy-and-economic-performance.

Roosevelt, Franklin D. "Oglethorpe University Address | The New Deal," 22 May 1932. Pepperdine School of Public Policy. https://publicpolicy.pepperdine.edu/academics/research/faculty-research/new-deal/roosevelt-speeches/fr052232.htm.

Rosenberg, Howard, and Charles S. Feldman. *No Time to Think: The Menace of Media Speed and the 24-Hour News Cycle*. New York: Continuum, 2008.

Roser, Max. "The Future Is Vast: Longtermism's Perspective on Humanity's Past, Present, and Future." *Our World in Data* (blog). 15 March 2022. Accessed 3 April 2022. https://ourworldindata.org/longtermism.

Sampson, Rachelle C., and Yuan Shi. "Are U.S. Firms Becoming More Short-Term Oriented? Evidence of Shifting Firm Time Horizons from Implied Discount Rates, 1980–2013." *Strategic Management Journal*, Special Issue (March 2020). https://doi.org/10.1002/smj.3158.

Savoie, Donald. *Court Government and the Collapse of Accountability in Canada and the United Kingdom*. Toronto: University of Toronto Press, 2008.

– *Governing from the Centre: The Concentration of Power in Canadian Politics*. Toronto: University of Toronto Press, 1999.

Schelling, Thomas C. "How to 'No Thyself' All Year Round, Not Just New Year's." *Washington Post*, 28 December 1980. https://www.washingtonpost

.com/archive/opinions/1980/12/28/how-to-no-thyself-all-year-round-not-just-new-years/b65f8243-0cf1-4213-b4f4-8e2d7174e393/.

Schrank, David, Luke Albert, Bill Eisele, and Tim Lomax. *2021 Urban Mobility Report*. Texas A&M Transportation Institute, 27 August 2020. https://mobility.tamu.edu/umr/report/.

Schumacher, E.F. *Small Is Beautiful*. Point Roberts, WA: Hartley & Marks, 1999.

Service, Owain, Michael Hallsworth, David Halpern, Felicity Algate, Rory Gallagher, Sam Nguyen, Simon Ruda, and Michael Sanders. *EAST: Four Simple Ways to Apply Behavioural Insights*. Behavioural Insights Team, 2014. https://www.bi.team/publications/east-four-simple-ways-to-apply-behavioural-insights/.

Sheffer, Lior, and Peter Loewen. "Electoral Confidence, Overconfidence, and Risky Behavior: Evidence from a Study with Elected Politicians." *Political Behavior* 41, no. 1 (March 2019): 31–51. https://doi.org/10.1007/s11109-017-9438-0.

Shi, Min, and Jakob Svensson. "Political Budget Cycles: Do They Differ across Countries and Why?" *Journal of Public Economics* 90, no. 8 (September 2006): 1367–89. https://doi.org/10.1016/j.jpubeco.2005.09.009.

Silver, Nate. *The Signal and the Noise: Why So Many Predictions Fail – but Some Don't*. New York: Penguin Press, 2012.

Sloggy, Matthew R., Jordan F. Suter, Mani Rouhi Rad, Dale T. Manning, and Chris Goemans. "Changing Climate, Changing Minds? The Effects of Natural Disasters on Public Perceptions of Climate Change." *Climatic Change* 168, no. 3 (October 2021): 25. https://doi.org/10.1007/s10584-021-03242-6.

Smith, David E. "The Senate of Canada: Renewed Life to an Original Intent." In *Reforming Senates: Upper Legislative Houses in North Atlantic Small Powers 1800-Present*, edited by Nikolaj Bijleveld, Colin Grittner, David E. Smith and Wybren Verstegen, 75–87. London: Routledge, 2019.

Smith, Graham. *Can Democracy Safeguard the Future?* Cambridge: Polity, 2021.

Snyder, Ryan. "Street Design Implications of Autonomous Vehicles." *Public Square: A CNU Journal*, 12 March 2018. https://www.cnu.org/publicsquare/2018/03/12/street-design-implications-autonomous-vehicles.

Soll, Jacob. "The Vanished Grandeur of Accounting." *Boston Globe*, 8 June 2014. https://www.bostonglobe.com/ideas/2014/06/07/the-vanished-grandeur-accounting/3zcbRBoPDNIryWyNYNMvbO/story.html.

Sommers, Samuel R. "On Racial Diversity and Group Decision Making: Identifying Multiple Effects of Racial Composition on Jury Deliberations." *Journal of Personality and Social Psychology* 90, no. 4 (2006): 597–612. https://doi.org/10.1037/0022-3514.90.4.597.

Standish Group. *2015 Chaos Report*, 2015. https://www.infoq.com/articles/standish-chaos-2015/.

Stern, Nicholas. *The Economics of Climate Change: The Stern Review*. Cambridge University Press, 2007.

Stiglitz, Joseph E, Amartya Sen, and Jean-Paul Fitoussi. *Report by the Commission on the Measurement of Economic Performance and Social Progress*. Commission on the Measurement of Economic Performance and Social Progress, 2009. https://ec.europa.eu/eurostat/documents/8131721/8131772/Stiglitz-Sen-Fitoussi-Commission-report.pdf.

Sumaila, U.R., and E. Suatoni. *Fish Economics: The Benefits of Rebuilding U.S. Ocean Fish Populations*. Fisheries Economics Research Unit, 2005. https://feru.oceans.ubc.ca/2005/10/01/benefits-rebuilding-ocean-fish-populations/.

Sunstein, Cass R. *Laws of Fear: Beyond the Precautionary Principle*. Cambridge: Cambridge University Press, 2005.

Sunstein, Cass R., and Reid Hastie. *Wiser: Getting Beyond Groupthink to Make Groups Smarter*. Boston: Harvard Business Review Press, 2014.

Taleb, Nassim Nicholas. *The Black Swan: The Impact of the Highly Improbable*. 2nd ed. New York: Random House, 2010.

Tetlock, Philip E., and Dan Gardner. *Superforecasting: The Art and Science of Prediction*. New York: Crown, 2015.

Thaler, Richard H., and Shlomo Benartzi. "Save More Tomorrow™: Using Behavioral Economics to Increase Employee Saving." *Journal of Political Economy* 112, no. S1 (2004): S164–87. https://doi.org/10.1086/380085.

Thaler, Richard H., and H.M. Shefrin. "An Economic Theory of Self-Control." *Journal of Political Economy* 89, no. 2 (April 1, 1981): 392–406. https://doi.org/10.1086/260971.

Thaler, Richard H., and Cass R. Sunstein. *Nudge: Improving Decisions About Health, Wealth, and Happiness*. New York: Penguin Books, 2009.

Thomson, Robert, Terry Royed, Elin Naurin, Joaquín Artés, Rory Costello, Laurenz Ennser-Jedenastik, Mark Ferguson, et al. "The Fulfillment of Parties' Election Pledges: A Comparative Study on the Impact of Power Sharing." *American Journal of Political Science* 61, no. 3 (2017): 527–42.

Thunberg, Greta. *No One Is Too Small to Make a Difference*. London: Penguin UK, 2020.

Toffler, Alvin. *Future Shock*. New York: Bantam, 1984. First published 1970 by Random House.

Tversky, Amos, and Daniel Kahneman. "Availability: A Heuristic for Judging Frequency and Probability." *Cognitive Psychology* 5, no. 2 (September 1973): 207–32. https://doi.org/10.1016/0010-0285(73)90033-9.

Tyson, Alec, and Brian Kennedy. "Two-Thirds of Americans Think Government Should Do More on Climate." *Pew Research Center Science & Society* (blog), 23 June 2020. https://www.pewresearch.org/science/2020/06/23/two-thirds-of-americans-think-government-should-do-more-on-climate/.

United Nations Environment Program. *Inclusive Wealth Report 2018*, 21 November 2018. http://www.unep.org/resources/inclusive-wealth-report-2018.

United Nations Secretary-General. *Intergenerational Solidarity and the Needs of Future Generations*. New York: UN, 15 August 2013. https://digitallibrary.un.org/record/756820.

Unruh, Gregory C. "Understanding Carbon Lock-In." *Energy Policy* 28, no. 12 (October 2000): 817–30. https://doi.org/10.1016/S0301-4215(00)00070-7.

van der Wal, Arianne J., Hannah M. Schade, Lydia Krabbendam, and Mark van Vugt. "Do Natural Landscapes Reduce Future Discounting in Humans?" *Proceedings of the Royal Society B: Biological Sciences* 280, no. 1773 (December 22, 2013): 20132295. https://doi.org/10.1098/rspb.2013.2295.

Vanwormer, Jeffrey J., Simone A. French, Mark A. Pereira, and Ericka M. Welsh. "The Impact of Regular Self-Weighing on Weight Management: A Systematic Literature Review." *International Journal of Behavioral Nutrition and Physical Activity* 5 (November 2008): 54. https://doi.org/10.1186/1479-5868-5-54.

Vivalt, Eva, and Aidan Coville. "How Do Policy-Makers Update Their Beliefs?" World Bank Working Paper, 2021. https://evavivalt.com/wp-content/uploads/How-Do-Policymakers-Update.pdf.

Voyer, Jean-Pierre. "Policy Analysis in the Federal Government: Building the Forward-Looking Policy Research Capacity." In *Policy Analysis in Canada: The State of the Art*, edited by Laurent Dobuzinskis, Michael Howlett, and David Laycock, 317-41. IPAC Series in Public Management and Governance. Toronto: University of Toronto Press, 2007.

Wang, Mei, Marc Rieger, and Thorsten Hens. "How Time Preferences Differ: Evidence from 45 Countries." *SSRN Electronic Journal* (January 2010). https://doi.org/10.2139/ssrn.1481443.

Wang, Shaoda, and David Y. Yang. "Policy Experimentation in China: The Political Economy of Policy Learning." NBER Working Papers, Working Paper Series, no. 29402 (October 2021). https://doi.org/10.3386/w29402.

Warner, John T., and Saul Pleeter. "The Personal Discount Rate: Evidence from Military Downsizing Programs." *American Economic Review* 91, no. 1 (2001): 33–53.

Warren, Mark E. "Three Challenges for Long-Term Decision-Making in

Democracies: Boundaries, Knowledge and Incentives." In MacKenzie, Setälä, and Kyllönen, *Democracy and the Future*, 19–37.

Watts, Edward J. *Mortal Republic: How Rome Fell into Tyranny*. Ill. ed. New York: Basic Books, 2020.

Wells, Thomas. "Votes for the Future." *Aeon*, 8 May 2014. https://aeon.co/essays/we-need-to-listen-to-our-future-citizens-here-s-how-to-tune-in.

Wilson, Edward O. *On Human Nature*. 2nd ed. Cambridge, MA: Harvard University Press, 2004.

Wintrobe, Ronald. *The Political Economy of Dictatorship*. Cambridge: Cambridge University Press, 1998. https://doi.org/10.1017/CBO9781139174916.

World Resources Institute. "Aqueduct Water Risk Atlas," 2019. https://www.wri.org/aqueduct.

Yarow, Jay. "The Zappos Founder Just Told Us All Kinds of Crazy Stories – Here's the Surprisingly Candid Interview." *Business Insider*, 28 November 2011. https://www.businessinsider.com/nick-swinmurn-zappos-rnkd-2011-11.

Yeung, Yue-man, Joanna Lee, and Gordon Kee. "China's Special Economic Zones at 30." *Eurasian Geography and Economics* 50, no. 2 (March 2009): 222–40. https://doi.org/10.2747/1539-7216.50.2.222.

Yew, Lee Kuan. *From Third World to First: Singapore and the Asian Economic Boom*. New York: Harper Business, 2011.

Yuanfang, Wang. "Memorial Requesting a Ban on Shack People Reclaiming Mountains and Blocking Waterways in Order to Prevent Future Calamities." 1850. In *Collected Writings on Qing Statecraft*, edited by K. Sheng, 32. Taipei: Wenhai,1972.

Zeng, Douglas Zhihua. "Building Engines for Growth and Competitiveness in China: Experience with Special Economic Zones and Industrial Clusters." Washington, DC: World Bank, 2010. https://doi.org/10.1596/978-0-8213-8432-9.

Index